# ECHOES FROM THE COBBLESTONES

# ECHOES FROM THE COBBLESTONES

A memoir

By

**Nicholas A. Kefalides**

iUniverse, Inc.
New York   Bloomington

# Echoes from the Cobblestones
## A Memoir

iUniverse books may be ordered through booksellers or by contacting:

iUniverse
1663 Liberty Drive
Bloomington, IN 47403
www.iuniverse.com
1-800-Authors (1-800-288-4677)

Because of the dynamic nature of the Internet, any Web addresses or links contained in this book may have changed since publication and may no longer be valid. The views expressed in this work are solely those of the author and do not necessarily reflect the views of the publisher, and the publisher hereby disclaims any responsibility for them.

ISBN: 978-1-4401-4353-3 (pbk)
ISBN: 978-1-4401-4352-6 (ebk)

Printed in the United States of America

iUniverse rev. date: 6/2/2009

Dedicated to the memory of my parents, my grandparents, uncles, aunts, and to my cousin Nikos. Also to the memory of my dearest friend Taso Oikonomou.

Special thanks go to my wife Jane who spent precious time typing the manuscript.

# CONTENTS

# INTRODUCTION

This memoir is a chronicle that covers the first thirty years of my life. It begins during the early 1930's, when Greece, the country I was born in, was enjoying a relatively tranquil life. This early period of my childhood evokes my earliest recollection, the arrival in 1932, of Uncle John, my father's brother from America. This event culminated a long period of anticipation and longing on the part of the Kefalides family in Alexandroupolis, Greece but also on the part of Uncle John who had not seen his family for 12 years while he was working and studying to become a doctor in America.

Uncle John was regarded as the role model for the younger members of the family and also as a frequent donor of funds for the various enterprises that involved his father, my paternal grandfather, whose moniker in Greek was Big Pappous, compared to my maternal grandfather, who was physically smaller and emotionally quieter and less volatile. Despite their physical and emotional differences, the two sets of grandparents treated me like a rare find. Their love and nurturing attitude had a lasting influence on my growing up as a young boy and as an adolescent. Spending hours on my grandparent's knees brought immeasurable joy as I listened to them recounting the captivating passages of numerous fairy tales.

My paternal grandfather, Nicholas, after whom I was named, took special pride in showing me how the flour mill, that he ran along with my father and his other son, Sophocles, operated. Along with his business endeavors he had other hobbies; one that he particularly enjoyed doing and was eager to show me was the grafting of a twig from one fruit tree into another, be it from a pear onto an apple tree or an apple tree onto a peach tree. My maternal grandfather, who was essentially a carpenter and a builder, took pride in showing me some of his carpentry skills, his artistry in making wooden bowls and in the shaping of wood.

The mutual respect and esteem that developed between me and my paternal grandfather was tested when, after he and my grandmother moved to Thessaloniki in 1937, they informed my parents that I should be sent to Thessaloniki to live with them and attend the best high school in all of Greece, an annex of theUniversity of Thessaloniki, called "Peiramatikon", "Experimental" in English.

As I recall the events, my parents told me that I would be going to Thessaloniki to join my grandparents and live with them for an indefinite period of time. I was eleven years old then and I was finishing the first year of an eight-year high school in Alexandroupolis. My reaction was full of excitement at the prospect of seeing my grandparents and my Aunt Helen, their daughter, who had moved to Thessaloniki a year earlier to study law at the University. The thought of moving to Thessaloniki, a city of 250,000 people with it's antiquities and multicultural history, added to my sense of excitement and curiosity. Here I was, leaving my parents, my brother Chris, my maternal grandparents, and uncles and aunts and I don't recall anytime that I broke down crying or rebelling at the idea of being separated from my family and friends. I recall that the only substantive explanation offered by my mother was to tell me that "Big-Pappous" could not live without me.

The love and nurturing attitudes of my grandparents created in me a feeling of confidence and self-reliance that was to help me live and survive the war and occupation in Greece during the Second World War.

The tranquil period of my life in Thessaloniki, which started in the summer of 1938, gave me the opportunity to experience the making of new friends in high school, to admire the dedication of my new teachers who were so much more knowledgeable than the teachers I have had before and to see them survive the years of deprivation and starvation and continue to teach almost with the same diligence and enthusiasm as in the pre-war years.

Soon after the German occupation began in the spring of 1941, we were beginning to see and feel the effects of the occupiers. The unexpected calamities of the occupation were commonplace and were manifested in several ways. Our most precious commodity, our lives, was fast becoming a precarious quantity.

The uncertainty of the outcomes of our everyday lives was looming heavily in every turn of our daily activities. I saw a mother, standing next to me on the sidewalk, losing her five year old girl after she was struck by a German army truck, that made a sharp turn at the corner we were standing. Some months later, my father was struck by a similar German truck that tore the back of his right knee as he was getting off a city bus near our home. This episode had a less painful outcome, resulting in his hospitalization and a surgical intervention to fix his torn tendons. On innumerable occasions german troops would march into a town or village and kill the entire population as a reprisal of the killing of a German officer or of the bombing of an army convoy.

The German troops marched into the city of Thessaloniki, with an army band leading the way. The sight of soldier's boots coming down with each beat of the drums, hitting the cobblestones and emitting myriads of echoes from the metal studs of their boots, became a frequent occurrence. The echoes arising from the cobble stones as the German army boots hit the pavement, were drowning the ones emanating from the studs of my own shoes.

Resistance was initially sporadic but soon became a legitimate force that unleashed a serious harassment onto the German occupiers. By the end of 1942 strong bands of guerillas formed in the countryside and were responsible for the destruction of important bridges and the bombing of supply trains. As the resistance against the forces of occupation increased, so did the arrests, imprisonments and executions. The massive arrests of more than 40,000 citizens of Jewish descent and their deportation from Thessaloniki to the concentration camps in Europe began in March 1943 and ended in July of the same year. A number of the Jewish people of Thessaloniki were fortunate enough to be taken in by Christian Greek families, or join the guerilla forces in the mountains or escape by clandestine means to Palestine.

My joining the underground movement in 1943 was a common-place occurrence among high school and university students. Six of the 17 students in my high school class were members of the youth underground movement, which was soon joined by my brother Chris at the age of 15. The arrest of my brother and myself by the Gestapo and our imprisonment in a concentration camp in Thessaloniki are paradigmatic of the activities we were engaged in and of the uncertainty of our fate during those years.

The end of the German and Italian occupations came in late October 1944, as the Allied and Russian armies were advancing in Europe and were threatening to cut off the Axis forces in the Balkans. The end of the occupation was soon followed by a civil war between the forces that battled the Germans and the Greek government army. The civil war lasted three years and saw the killing of several thousand Greeks on both sides.

I was fortunate to have my Uncle John in America arrange for my immigrating to the United States. On May 5, 1947, I left Greece on the liner "Saturnia" and on May19, I arrived in New York City.

My arrival in the United States opened the way for my academic career. The ensuing years saw me completing my undergraduate studies, receiving a M.S. in biochemistry and my M.D. in1956 from the University of Illinois School of Medicine in Chicago. In 1965 I received a Ph. D. in Biochemistry from the same school.

After completing my internship in 1957 at the University of Illinois Research and Education Hospital, I joined the National Institutes of Health where, as a Lieutenant Commander in the Public Health Service I was asked to direct a project on the prevention and treatment of shock and infections in burns, in Lima, Peru.

In 1960 I returned to the University of Illinois School of Medicine where I took my residency in Internal Medicine, a fellowship in Infectious Diseases and in 1965 my Ph.D. in Biochemistry. In the summer of the same year I wase recruited by the University of Chicago School of Medicine as Assistant Professor of Medicine and in 1969 I was promoted to Associate Professor with tenure. My research on the isolation and structural characterization of the proteins in basement membranes was going extremely well and in 1970 I was offered a position as Associate Professor of Medicine at the University of Pennsylvania School of Medicine. In 1974 I was promoted to Professor of Medicine and in 1975 to Professor of Biochemistry and Biophysics. My academic career at the University of Pennsylvania flourished as I became the principal investigator of a Program Project grant from NIH. This grant remained active for 28 years and helped support the Connective Tissue Research Institute that I had created at the University City Science Center.

*It is indeed exasperating to have a memory that begins too young and continues too long.* Pearl Buck

# The 1930s

## 1. The Arrival of Uncle John from America

My earliest childhood recollection is a vivid picture of a seaside picnic on a summer afternoon in 1932. It was a warm day with low humidity and the sea breeze ushered in not only the saltiness of the sea but also the aromas of the blood and butchered tissues from the nearby slaughterhouse. We had all gathered around the picnic baskets that my mother, Alexandra and my aunt, Zographia, my mother's sister, had prepared early that morning. My younger brother Chris, our cousin Annoula and I went to work on the tasty salad of lettuce and tomatoes, the meat balls, the jadjiki ( a mixture of diced cucumber, crushed garlic and yogurt) and freshly baked whole wheat bread.

A glow of satisfaction was soon evident on our faces at this Lucullian masterpiece and we complimented my mother and my aunt for their culinary artistry. It did not take long for tradition to prevail and the adults with Annoula were enjoying their siesta, while Chris and I decided to hunt crabs. We waded on the shallow waters by the beach and began stepping on small black rocks with smooth, slimy surfaces that made it difficult to keep from slipping off them. As a rule the crabs were hiding underneath the rocks but some of them were crawling on top. It soon became evident that the crabs were faster and smarter than the two amateur fishermen who were menacing them. They idled there with their protruding eyes, looking straight at us, ready to sidle down the rock and into the water if we got too close. Instead of us approaching them slowly by crouching near the rocks and inching our hands toward their side, we thrust our hands toward the crabs only to come up empty handed. After more frustrating failures and as I was reaching for one of them I felt something biting my right thumb. A crab had grabbed my finger with one of his claws but I reacted quickly and with a swift motion I grabbed him with my left hand. Excited I yelled " mommy I got a crab, I got a crab" and began running toward the picnic site. As I was approaching the site, I saw a young lady coming from the opposite direction and as she reached my mother she exclaimed " the uncle from America has arrived".

Suddenly the picnic site was turned into a panic scene. My mother admonished Chris and me: "Hurry up and help with the packing; we don't want to be late at the gathering". I immediately replied, " We are doing our best. We are going to run". Dirty dishes, utensils and tablecloths were thrown into baskets, blankets were folded and I was given a clay water jug to carry on my shoulder. We all started for my paternal grandfather's home, where we knew Uncle John would be staying. Nobody thought of telling me to empty the water first, to lighten the weight of the jug. Every one began to walk fast, but Chris, Annoula and I could not keep up with the adults and we began to run. The weight of the water jug was becoming unbearable and the jug began to slip away from my fingers and before I could switch hands it fell to the ground and broke into many pieces. I began to cry, thinking that display of remorse, fear and hope would save me from any spanking that was due to me. Fortunately everyone's mind was on Uncle John from America and I was completely ignored, to my great relief. In due course we reached the front of my grandfather's house where a number of relatives and friends had gathered around Uncle John, talking and laughing and enjoying the chance to see and meet the successful doctor in the family.

Grandfather's house was a two-story building across from our house. It had an outside stairway that led to a small balcony that faced the main entrance to the house. A side door next to the stairway opened into the ground floor of the house. It was in front of that stairway where all the activity of that afternoon was centered. People were hovering around uncle John, asking him questions about his life in America, his medical studies and his trip to Europe. Uncle John was a handsome, bespectacled and polite man who was gregarious and who enjoyed talking to people. One could see that he was answering their questions with distinct pleasure and would finish his answer with a broad smile. To get a closer look at Uncle John, I began to snake around all those people to reach the man whose actions in future years were to influence the lives of many of the people around him, including my own. He spotted me and as he looked down he asked me "What is your name"? I quickly replied "Nikos" a dimunitive of Nicolaos". "You have your grandfather's name" he observed and with obvious pride in my voice I replied "nai", "yes" in Greek.

Uncle John, my father's younger brother, came to the United States in 1920 at the age of 20. My father's family, grandfather, grandmother and six children lived in the town of Forty Churches (Saranta Ekklesies), situated in the European section of Turkey. My grandfather was a merchant and his business required him to travel to the various provinces of Turkey, which included besides Turkey, areas that are now Greece and Bulgaria. His business trips took him away from home for long stretches, which necessitated my grandmother's following him on those long trips, presumably along with the older children, since the first three older ones were fluent not only in Greek but also in Turkish and Bulgarian. The oldest of the children, Uncle George, left the town of Forty Churches and came to the United States right after the end of World War I. Two years later Uncle John followed. During the next 11 years Uncle John worked evenings in a variety of jobs, from bus boy to waiter in restaurants, finished college and attended the University of Cincinnati School of Medicine, receiving his MD in 1928. After a year of internship he specialized in eye, ear, nose and throat and in 1932 he visited Vienna, then the Mecca of Medicine and of medical progress. After his visit to Vienna he traveled to Greece to visit his family in Alexandroupolis. This was going to be his first visit to Greece and the first time with his family in 12 years.

My father's family was forced out of Eastern Thrace, the European section of Turkey, in 1922 following a failed war of Greece against Turkey. The refugee family settled in Alexandroupolis, a seaport on the northern shores of the Aegean Sea, near the present Greek-Turkish border. Once settled, my grandfather became involved in two business enterprises in succession. The first was the construction of a small factory that produced clay tiles for roofs and red bricks as well as mud bricks for the numerous new houses that were needed in the area. Initially, this business was successful and provided employment for my father, and his younger brother Sophocles. The number of new homes increased with the influx of refugees in Alexandroupolis and with it the brick factory business; however, as the years went on, the need for red bricks diminished as the need for new homes reached its peak and began to fall in the next few years. It wasn't long before the brick factory was sold at a significant loss and my enterprising grandfather was looking for new business ventures. It was during this period that he began asking Uncle John in America for financial support to help start his new business, this time for a flour mill.

The evening of the day of my Uncle's arrival rolled in gradually as the sun was leaning on that wet horizon at the far end of the sea. Soon the relatives began to leave and Chris and I followed my parents across the street to our home. After supper, my mother bathed us, kissed us as we were lying in our bed and whispered: " We will have a long day tomorrow. I want you to be well rested, clean and well dressed" and told us to be ready for a long visit with Uncle John the next day.

Uncle John had only one hobby that he enjoyed and pursued with unshaken devotion. He was an amateur photographer and between taking stills and movies, he preferred the latter. The next morning, members of the immediate family began to arrive again in front of grandfather's house and the festive atmosphere was easily felt and pervaded that small segment of the street surrounding the house. None of them had ever dreamed, let alone considered being in a movie.

Uncle John informed everyone the day before that he wanted to see them dressed in their Sunday best and that's exactly how everyone showed up. My father Thanasis, short for Athanasios, who at that time was 39 years old, my mother Alexandra, who was 32, Uncle Elias, my father's youngest brother, who was 26, a lawyer, and his wife Stasa, who was also 26, a dentist, were following orders issued by Uncle John. My grandfather, Nicolaos, who was then 70 years old, my grandmother Evdoxia, who was 58 and my Aunt Helen, my father's only sister and the youngest of the six siblings, who was 16, were sitting on a bench waiting for the camera to roll. Chris and I and our cousin Annoula were sticking close to my parents. Aunt Anastasia, Uncle Sophocle's wife and cousin Nikos were also there, all decked out.

The short 15 mm film that Uncle John took that morning immortalized a poignant moment of our lives. It survived all those years and eventually the scenes were transferred from the film to a video and from there onto a DVD. If I were to recount the scenes of that day, based on my memory alone, it would not be possible to describe Uncle John's directorial input, nor could I rely on my memory to recall the serenity and furtive satisfaction on my grandmother's face as Uncle John was filming her. I will attempt to describe the scenes as they appear in the film which opens with my grandmother sitting under an apple tree, making circular motions with the handle of a cylindrical, brass coffee grinder, and allowing an expression of happiness to subtly spread on her serene face. The scene changes and suddenly Aunt Helen appears in the yard of our elementary school, located only two blocks from our house. Aunt Helen, then only 16 years old, dressed in a white skirt and white blouse, walked toward the camera, smiling broadly and revealing a happy face. At one point she is seen talking, obviously to Uncle John, who is giving her directions because the next thing she does is to stop and pose with her right hand resting on her waist. The scene changes again and now my father is directed to take the same steps as Aunt Helen; he is walking towards the camera, smiling broadly and showing a beautiful set of teeth just below the remnants of a handlebar moustache that he was reluctantly trimming, year after year, millimeter by millimeter, to satisfy my mother's admonitions to remove it altogether.

The next set of scenes shift back to grandfather's house. We see Uncle Elias walking on the side of the house towards the camera. He has very curly hair with a receding frontal hair line. His face is almost round with full cheeks that produce two dimples as he smiles. It is easily evident that his right hand is in his coat pocket, something that Uncle John obviously disapproves of, because soon he takes it out of his pocket and is pointing his index finger at Uncle John. He is waving his finger and seems to be talking to him as if saying something to the effect "You can't tell me what to do, you may be a doctor but I am a lawyer", the smile never leaving his face.

Uncle John then proceeded to photograph the family in small clusters. The arena of activity became rather narrow and extended from the front of the house and up a stairway to a small balcony. Suddenly, here I am, on the balcony, at the top of the stairway, my mother holding my hand and slowly allowing me to begin descending the steps on my own. At five years of age, in my black velvet outfit of short pants, suspenders, white shirt and a wide, red bow tie, I was coming down with an air of confidence and self assurance of a seasoned actor. Once at the foot of the stairs, my eyes are focused on the camera and then at my father who is trying to herd my three year-old brother Chris to a spot next to me so that we can be photographed together with my mother who had already come down the steps. The scenes become tight as Uncle John tries to get as many shots of the people he missed seeing for so long, the people he traveled more than four thousand miles to see.

The grandparents again dominate the scene; always smiling and seemingly talking to Uncle John. They are soon joined by Aunt Helen and Uncle Elias, who suddenly takes my hand and brings me closer to my grandfather. Finally, Uncle John himself is in the picture, sitting between his mother and brother Elias. The last scene outside the house is focused on my grandmother, who is shown crocheting lace. The final scene of the movie emerges in a small square in front of the train station. The same players form a small cluster of relatives who came to wish Uncle John bon voyage and to thank him for the pleasure he gave them during his short visit. He masterfully closed this memorable movie by focusing on his mother as she was silently wiping her tears.

*Society shapes life*
*Politics shapes society*

# 2. Early Social and Political Science Education

Alexandroupolis in the 1930's was a small town of about 12,000 people. It is situated on the northeastern shore of the Aegean Sea, a few kilometers from the river Evros that forms the border between Greece and Turkey's European portion, also known as Eastern Thrace. The city was founded by the Turks in 1860 and began to grow with the marketing of the valonia oak after 1871; it further prospered with the arrival of the Istanbul-Thessaloniki railway in 1896. Long a bone of contention between Greece and Bulgaria it was finally granted to the former after World War I, following the treaties of Neuilly in 1919 and Serves in 1920. The treaty of Lausanne legitimized its incorporation into the Greek geographical borders in 1923.

Alexandroupolis was and still is a very attractive little town, with sandy beaches, one and two story houses, neatly placed in a set of streets that run horizontal and perpendicular to each other. One of its distinctive landmarks is its lighthouse, a beautiful, white, imposing tower on the waterfront that surpassed in height most of the houses and buildings in the downtown area. From the streets in the vicinity of our house I could see to the west and south the edge of town bordering the sea; to the east the eye fell to the train station and to the north unto some low level hills. The landmark closest to our house, only two blocks away, was the First Elementary School, a beautiful, neoclassical structure. Another attractive feature of our neighborhood was a park filled with pine trees and occupying two blocks square. Marathonos street, where we lived, bisected the center of the park and continued for four more blocks to the fringes of the train station.

The homes in our neighborhood were one and two story dwellings with finished sub- basements that functioned as family rooms, kitchens and at times as work-shops. Most houses were made of stucco, some of bricks, others of limestone and some of wood siding. My maternal grandfather, who was a carpenter and a mason, built our house. It was a one story structure with a finished sub-basement. My grandfather divided the house in two and gave the part that faced Marathonos Street and south to my mother and the other that faced Voulgaroctonou Street and west to her sister, Zographia. Our end of the house, where my grandparents, my parents, Chris and I and my mother's brother John lived, had two bedrooms, a living room-dining room and a bathroom on the upstairs section and the finished sub-basement below. Although a wall separated Aunt Zographia's unit from ours, the sub-basements communicated through a door and thus we all had free access to each other's home.

## a) Early Social Experiences

The days began with breakfast in the family room. Chris and I enjoyed a cup of warm milk with toast or a cup of tea with toast and cheese. School started at 8:30 and I would be all dressed up in fresh clothes, with my school bag over my shoulder. My mother would hand me a paper bag with my sandwich and send me off to school, a two-block walk from our house. Going to school gave me a great deal of pleasure and satisfaction. Part of the reason was that I liked my teachers who were very caring and tolerant. It was not unusual for one of my teachers who, after she was satisfied that I had done my homework, would ask me to run small errands for her to the nearby grocer to buy some specific item for her. This fascination of mine with school and teachers began at an early age, sometime before kindergarten and was based on a simple childhood trait, curiosity.

Every morning, before leaving home for kindergarten, which was held at a private home, I would see students walk by our house on their way to the elemntary school and I would ask myself 'what was it like to be in a classroom'? In my mind, I would construct a palatial structure with crystal light fixtures and bands of light streaming through the windows and the teachers clad in purple robes walking up and down the classrooms waving magic wands in one hand and holding gold covered books in the other.

One beautiful, sunny day, well into my fourth year of life, I decided to venture into the holy halls of the edifice I admired and looked at with awe. I went up the outside steps and entered through the main entrance into the main lobby. Classes had started some two hours ago so that there was no traffic in the hallways. It was late spring and the classroom doors were kept open. My first impression was a disappointment of how I had fantasized the interior of the school to be. The mental picture I had constructed, no doubt was influenced by the interior of the Metropolitan church of Hagios Nicolaos. I found the school hallways to be almost dark, the ceilings tall, the only illumination coming from the light that entered from the windows that faced east and from the tall window that faced west above the central stairway that wound up to the second floor. I chose one of the classrooms that had a door on either end of the room. I entered the back of the room and sat on one of the empty desks. There was plenty of light in the classroom coming in from the tall windows that faced west towards the sea. It was quiet, the students were very attentive to what the teacher was saying and I watched her as she spoke. She was an older, tall, slightly obese lady with a pleasant face and a clear soft voice, The things she was telling the students were totally incomprehensible to me. I wasn't sure whether the teacher saw me and I tried to remain as inconspicuous as possible. At the end of the period the classroom emptied and I left the classroom as unnoticed as when I came in, so I thought.

The whole experience left me quite excited and as I was walking back to our house I felt consumed by the desire to learn what the teacher was saying to the students. I decided to go again to the same classroom the next day. I sat at the end of the room and I was as attentive as on the previous day. However, this time I noticed the teacher glancing towards me periodically and I knew I was spotted. She waited until the end of the period to approach me and in a very soft and non-threatening way she introduced herself. " Eime i Kyria Aphrodite, pio eine to onoma sou?" (" I am Mrs. Aphrodite, what is your name"?) I replied "Nikos

9

Kefalides". A big smile came over her face and said, as she patted me on the back, "Go home now". Obviously she recognized the name since her daughter, Eirene, and my aunt Helen were high school classmates.

Two days later, I ventured a third visit. No sooner I sat down and Mrs. Aphrodite approached me and looking out the window into a beautiful green meadow where several sheep were grazing said " Niko, yiati then piyenis exo na pexis sto hortari?" "Niko, why don't you go outside and play in the grass?" and I quickly replied " I am not a little lamb". This was a profound statement for me and for Mrs. Aphrodite. The end result was that my visit had not accomplished its original goal, which was to learn what the teacher was telling her students, while Kyria Aphrodite convinced me to vacate the school premises and head home. That day I told my mother and aunt Helen what I was doing and they had also been informed from Mrs. Aphrodite' daughter Eirene all about the incident with the grass and the sheep. My mother asked me, in a somewhat emphatic way, to wait until I was in first grade before I ventured again into the school classrooms and I did so, but the moniker "little lamb" stuck for a while and even when I was a regular student and Kyria Aphrodite happened to see me in school corridor she would ask with a smile "Ke pos eine to arnaki mou?" "And how is my little lamb"?

On Monday mornings, before leaving for school, my mother would ask me to stop at the grocery store, which was at the corner opposite ours, and buy some small item, a lemon or a small bag of salt, and thus give the grocer's week "kalo pothariko", loosely translated "a good beginning". My visit had to be timed right, before anyone else stepped into the store. This was not just a sign of superstition; it also reflected my mother's goodhearted attitude, her appreciation for the things we could afford and her support for a fellow refugee. Mr. Pontios, the store owner, was a refugee from Turkey; he lived with his wife and daughter above the store in an elegant two story house. He apparently accepted the custom because he looked very pleased with the gesture and reciprocated by giving me a piece of candy. To me that piece of candy was a sweet reward and a welcomed supplement to my sandwich.

Mr. Pontios was of average height, with gray hair and frontal baldness and a face that seldom smiled. It was situations like the one I just described that allowed the good side of his personality to shine.

Walking into the poorly lit store I would be welcomed by a mixture of odors emanating from different parts of the store. It was easy to notice barrels filled with olives; those oval, with a smooth, purple skin from Kalamata, the dark round ones from Chalkidiki and the small, black ones, with the wrinkled skin from the plain of Thessaloniki. There were cans containing olive oil, barrels with white cheese (the name "feta", which means slice, was given to this cheese in the post-World War II era), barrels with vinegar and sacks of oregano, flour, rice and potatoes. Short, wide baskets were full of fruit and vegetables and on a wide table there were glass jars filled with candy and chocolates. Mr. Pontios was a compulsive and neat fellow. Everything in the store was arranged in an orderly fashion and a customer was not allowed to handle the groceries. You indicated what you wanted and he would put the items in a tote bag or a net bag, the latter being the preferred mode of carrying one's groceries. The floor was unusually clean for a place that saw quite a bit of traffic from morning till evening.

Mr. Pontios' concern with cleanliness and order was further exemplified by the morning ritual of antisepsis that I had witnessed on several occasions in front of the store. He would take a small bottle containing blue alcohol (the blue color indicated that it was unsuitable for drinking), pour some into the cup of his palm and splash it on his face and bald head. The ritual would end by taking a smaller amount of alcohol and sniffing it up his nostrils.

If I were to walk to school on the opposite side of the street, I would be treated with the most tantalizing aroma that permeated the air; it was coming from the small bakery, exactly opposite Mr. Pontios' store. The owner, Mrs. Aspasia, was a tall, middle-aged lady with graying frizzy hair, whose kindness was matched by her generosity. As I stood by the store's open window and closed my eyes with my head bent slightly backwards and allowed my face to assume the expression of unfulfilled ecstasy, she would break into a hearty laughter and call to me "Ela Niko, pare ena" (Come Nick, take one") and she would hand me a boureki, a kind of cheese pie. The boureki was Mrs. Aspasia's specialty. It was made of small balls of leavened dough that were flattened with a long and narrow rolling pin to a flat round disk, about 5 inches in diameter.

To one half of the rolled dough she would add crumbs of feta cheese that were mixed with a small amount of egg and water. She would then fold over the other half and seal the edges by pressing them together, forming a half-moon; with the aid of a soft brush she would then paint the top of the boureki with a dilute mixture of egg and water and put it in the oven. The last step gave the boureki a golden brown color after baking. As I bit into the boureki that Mrs. Aspasia offered me I savored an array of delightful tastes and an aroma, which made it very hard to quit after three bites. I put the remainder of the boureki into the paper napkin that Ms. Aspasia gave me and saved it for lunch.

The walk to school was full of small encounters. All the kids that lived east of us on our street passed in front of our house as they headed to their classes. Kids my age, younger or older, went by and I would stop and talk to my classmates and some that were a class or two above me. Kostas, a classmate, lived one block east of us. He was very friendly, always making plans for games that we could play together after school. He was a short little guy, with blue eyes, dark wavy hair and muscular. It was always difficult to tackle him and try to wrest the football from him during soccer. George, in a class ahead of me, lived right across from us and was the friend with whom I played most frequently, probably because he lived so close but also because we sought each other's company.

We got along together quite well. George was of slight built and he would frequently injure himself during soccer or wrestling. He enjoyed track and field and frequently he joined me and other kids from the neighborhood in running the distance from our home for two blocks down to our school. He always came in third or fourth or just last. One of the non-athletic games that he and I enjoyed playing together was matching the cities in used train tickets. George's father was a conductor on the train line that runs north along the Evros river connecting Alexandroupolis with Didimoteichon and after crossing the Greek-Turkish border continuing on to Istanbul. The tickets were rectangular, made of thin, light blue cardboard, and measuring slightly more than two inches in length and about an inch wide.

All the tickets were cancelled ones and were collected by George's father after they had been cataloged and thrown in the trash. They represented tickets from Alexandroupolis to other towns along the line or from any of the cities along the way to Alexandroupolis or any city up and down the railroad line. During the game, the tickets were shuffled and distributed face down, ten at a time. If I laid down a ticket that had the town of Soufli, let's say, as the destination and George had a similar one, he collected both tickets. When laying down the ticket it was customary to imitate the conductor's cry announcing the next stop " Soufliiii" or "Orestiaaas". If George did not have a ticket showing the town of Soufli, then he would put down another ticket showing a different destination and I would have to match it. If I matched it I would collect all the tickets or if not I would put down another ticket, let's say Orestias, and so forth. The most rare tickets were those with destinations to the most remote towns, like Orestias or Didimoteichon. At the end of the game we counted our tickets and the one with the most was the winner.

Most of the games we played had two components to them. One was the sheer joy of the game itself. The satisfaction of being able to master the game and the sense that, after several tries, one was now proficient in it and would be able to match his skill with that of the other boys, bolstered one's self esteem and pride. The other was the competitiveness of the game that rewarded the winner with the spoils.

A good example of this was the game of spinning the top, a pear shaped structure, made of wood, like an inverted teardrop, that had a metal tip at the pointed end, usually a small nail with a stubby end. To make the top spin we would loop the end of a piece of string to the top end and bring it down and loop it around the metal end and keep winding it till it reached the upper one third of the top. With the free end of the string wrapped around the middle finger and with a snap of the wrist we would throw the top forward and watch it spin. We used several sizes of tops. The standard size top was about two inches long and an inch and three quarters at its widest point. The largest top measured about three inches in length and two and a half inches at its widest point.

One's skill was measured by the length of time that a top would spin or by one's ability to bring one's open palm down to the ground and ease the top between the third and fourth fingers into the center of the palm while it was still spinning. The competitive aspect of the game was played with determination and zeal. The object was to knock one or more of several tops, usually four or five, that were lying in a chalk-marked circle on the ground, with your own top and making sure that your top was still spinning after knocking a top outside of the circle. The person who knocked one or more tops kept them as his own and the person who knocked out the largest number was the winner.

Zaphiris, a second cousin of mine and three years older than I, was the most successful person with the game of top on our street. He used to give me tips on how to spin the top and I remember him saying, "Niko, the best way to get a fast spin is to throw the top with a scoop of the arm and a snap of the wrist". Despite the use of rules of the game, they rarely applied to the size of the top one used. It was, therefore, not surprising that the fellow using a big fat top would end up knocking out the largest number of tops, provided of course that the top remained spinning after knocking a top out of the circle. The big fat tops were not always as stable as the small and slim ones.

Another game that was popular among young kids not only in Greece but also throughout the Middle-East, going back to Iran and Afganistan, was what we called in Greek *Chilik- Chomak*, although the word was apparently borrowed from Persian or Arabic. The game was played with two pieces of wood; the one we called *Chilik*, was solid, short, about five inches long and cylindrical, whose two ends came to a point, and the other, called *Chomak*, was also also cylindrical and measured about a foot long. A third element in the game was a shallow hole in the ground, about three to three and a half inches in diameter where the *Chilik* would be placed leaving one end outside the hole, pointing upwards. Usually two teams of two to three players participated in the game. The object of the game was to hit the *Chilik* at its free end with the *Chomak* in a way that it will fly up in the air. The player had two choices, either to hit the *Chilik* with the *Chomak* hard enough so that it would fly as far away as possible and drop on the ground before it was caught by the other side or, after the *Chilic* was out of the hole, to bob it in the air with gentle hits of the *Chomak* and finally send it away with a strong whack. The latter option gave ten points automatically to the hitter with every bobbing of the *Chilic* and an additional 50 points if the *Chilik* landed on the ground before it was caught in the air by the opposing team. If the *Chilic* was caught in the air by the opposing team the player was called out. The first team that managed to amass 200 points was the winner. The number of points awarded was totally arbitrary and was determined at the beginning of each game.

Of course, when it came to competitiveness and skill no game matched the shooting of marbles. Here we had to aim at a specific marble from a distance of almost five feet, knock it out of a line-up and shoot it out of a circle. Each of us developed special ways of snapping the thumb or the middle finger in controlling the speed and the aim of the shooting marble. The stance one took was equally important and somewhat idiosyncratic with each player. At times we would bend down with one knee touching the ground and the other knee simply bent or the opposite leg extended laterally; at others we would be down on both knees and rarely, we would be totally on the ground, in the prone position. If you were not careful "you could really lose all your marbles"

The desire to participate in active sports was very strong and it was matched by an equally ardent desire to participate in creative projects. There were two students, brothers Vassilis and Evangelos Iatropoulos, two and three years ahead of me in school, respectively, who lived two houses down from Mrs. Aspasia's house, on Voulgaroctonou street, in a nice two story house with a plane tree in front of it. I spent many a day trying to scale that tree, something I finally accomplished as I became taller, stronger and more agile. Evangelos exemplified the sportive spirit in us, whereas Vassilis was the tinkering kind. Evangelos organized all kinds of track and field events with the zeal of an Olympic team manager. He would have us run 50 meter dashes, 100 meter sprints, longer races around a block and jumping events in hastily prepared sand piles. He was so consumed with these activities that at night during his sleep he would be dreaming a race and shout " On your marks, get set, go". Vassilis, the older brother, was smart, a bookworm and good with his hands.

He enjoyed making things and one time we spent about three hours in my maternal grandfather's carpentry shop making a small sail boat out of a 3x8 inch piece of wood. The shop was replete with all the necessary carpentry tools -saws, chisels, planes, files, adzes, drills, nails, string, you name it. We first took the piece of wood and drew with a carpenter's hard pencil a broad outline of the outer shape of the boat. Slowly, by cutting with a small saw and then using an adze we fashioned a rough shape of the boat. We then used the plane to even out the areas that were extending outward and finally we smoothed out the sides and the bottom of the boat with a file. It began to look like a small *varca,* a row boat, in Greek. We then secured the boat on a wooden vise and with chisels we hollowed the inside and drilled a hole in the center where we inserted a narrow reed to serve as the mast. To complete the rigging, we took an old white napkin, cut a triangular piece out and fit it on the mast. The boat now had a sail! We then had to test the sea worthiness of our little creation.

With the aid of a bucket we filled a tub with water and gingerly we lowered it just below the surface and, low and behold it floated. To me, my friend Vassilis was a master artisan. The next day, Vassilis suggested that we rig a small propeller to see whether the boat could move forward. He found a small, tin propeller, from a discarded toy and attached it to the rear of the boat by running a small nail through a hole in its center. Through the hole in the propeller he attached a rubber band and wound it around the nail. When he released the propeller, the rubber band unwound rapidly causing the propeller to spin. The boat moved for about a foot, but that was enough to excite our little hearts. We felt like the Wright brothers at Kitty Hawk.

The most unforgettable character among the kids in my immediate neighborhood was Yioryis. He was the son of a fisherman, a refugee from Turkey. His house was located between that of Mrs. Aspasia's and that of Mr. Iatropoulos'. By comparison with the rest of the families in the neighborhood, his family was poor. Yioryis was tall, thin with a perennially unwashed face and hair. He had bright brown eyes and was clad in short pants and a dark blue or at times brown shirt. He was well known not only in our neighborhood but also in most other parts of the city. His notoriety grew out of his social activities that were not the most acceptable forms of behavior for a pre-teenager. He was older than me by at least three years and, although he sometimes attended classes, he seldom was seen carrying a school bag or books with him. I remember catching up with him in the third grade and leaving him behind as I moved on to the next grade. His truancy was legendary and complemented this trait by his petty thievery and his notorious lying. He would climb over a walled fence, go up a tree and steal fruit with which he would treat the kids in the neighborhood, knowing full well that I knew he had stolen them from our yard or from one of the other kids' yards. He would go to the fish market and would return with two or three fish tucked under his shirt. Stealing fish was one of his favorite pastimes. This contributed on many occasions to the fishy smell emanating from his cloths as one approached him.

Although he was friendly and pleasant with the kids in the neighborhood and on many occasions would engage them in discussions, his many unsavory escapades made us reluctant to form strong bonds. He was always on the alert, eyes darting right and left. He was polite and yet cunning with a simplistic view of everyday life. Although he seemed to know the difference between right and wrong, he instinctively chose what was expedient for the moment and he did it with flair. One time, two of my friends and I were standing in the middle of where Marathonos and Voulgaroctonou Streets crossed, right across from our house and Mr. Pontios' grocery store. One of us had bought a chocolate that was wrapped in a yellow tin foil and had the shape of a banana, split lengthwise. As the chocolate holder began biting small pieces of it, he asked, "I wonder where cacao comes from"? One of us said "from the seeds of a tropical tree", another suggested "from the bark of a rare tree" and the chocolate eater said "from the fine shavings of the chocolate".

As the argument was going back and forth, Yioryis had approached the group unnoticed and listened intently for a few seconds. Suddenly and without hesitation he said, "this is how cacao is made", then grabbed the chocolate from the kid's hand and quickly shoved it into his mouth. He then made an about face and disappeared into the next street. The three of us stood there aghast, unable to say or do anything. Admittedly, Yioryis' rebelliousness aroused a flicker of reserved admiration in some of us, a rebelliousness that some years later, during the German and Bulgarian occupation, cost him his life.

Yioryis' legend and freedom of action were about to be tested and in a sense curbed by another person, Mr. Theodorikos, a newly arrived truant officer. Mr. Theodorikos became the terror of all school kids in the city, whether truant or not. His position was created in 1936 by fiat of the municipal government and the sanction of the new government of Greece. King George II, who came to power the year before, appointed

John Metaxas, an army general, as new prime minister who, on August 4th 1936, dissolved the parliament and established a dictatorship. Why Alexandroupolis was selected for this unique pedagogic experiment is still unclear to me. To my knowledge no other town in the counties of Evros or the adjacent Rothope were honored with a similar municipal job.

Mr. Theodorikos was born for the job and the job was vested by the terror generating appearance of a sadistic truant officer. He carried out, what he thought were his duties, with the eagerness, perseverance and sadism of a prison warden. He was tall, with squinty eyes, high cheeks and thick hands that terminated in rounded tips taking the appearance of a collection of ten clubs. A slap in the face with one of his hands would land any kid on the ground. He was always dressed in a three-piece suit with pants in the style favored by horse riders. Two more adjuncts complemented his attire. He wore knee-high, laced, high-heeled brown boots and carried a horsewhip. He carried out his duties with zeal. The moment he saw a school-age child walk alone in the street, he would ask for his name, write it down in his little notebook and then whack him on the legs a couple of times and take him to his home. There he would lecture to the kid's mother on the perils of truancy, on the consequences of inadequate education and on the need to properly educate children so that they could serve the goals of the national youth organization. It was obligatory for all students 12 to 18 years old to join the youth organization, created by Mr. John Metaxas.

On many occasions Mr. Theodorikos' eagerness and zealous attitude extended to the after school hours when most families took their siesta, usually between 3 to 5 p.m. If by any chance a student were found walking on the street during this time, he would stop him, whack him on his legs with his whip, ask him for his name and without waiting for an answer he would turn around and leave.

On one occasion late in the afternoon, when my mother sent me on an errand to a store in the center of town, as I had reached the entrance of the store, Theodorikos came from behind and without a word whacked me on the legs with his whip and walked away. I felt a severe pain going up my legs and into my spine. I was terrified with fear. I didn't know whether I should turn back and run home or go ahead and buy the groceries my mother wanted. The grocer who witnessed the incident waved me to go inside the store and said "sorry my child, no one is safe any more". After I got home and related the event to my parents, my mother put her arm around my head, brought me close to her side and with a soft voice she said in Greek " me stenachoriese, ki'afto to kako tha perasi", which means " don't worry, this bad thing will also go away" in English.

Soon, however, a nemesis was lurking for Mr. Thedorikos, one that was already made to order for him. Yioryis, the mischievous student, who skipped classes with impunity, stole fruit from the trees in the neighborhood yards or went to the fish market and absconded with one or two fish, became the truant officer's target. He caught him on several occasions and as he was bringing him to the police station, Yioryis would manage to escape and run away.

During one of his excursions to the fish market, one beautiful, sunny afternoon, Theodorikos was making his usual rounds in the fish market and around the seaport. The area was bustling with fishmongers who were advertising their various fresh catches and with customers who moved from stand to stand looking for their favorite fish. The variety was wide; you could find tuna, salmon, smelts, red mullet, sea bass, flounder, red snapper, sardines, shrimp and eel. Fishing boats were moored side by side and there were also caiques (sailing transport boats) lined up along the breakwater, with stevedores unloading fruit, melons and watermelons, lemons, and sacks of potatoes, wheat and rice.

Suddenly, Theodorikos, who spotted Yioryis loitering around the fish stores, quickened his pace and tried to get to him before Yioryis could see him. Yioryis, however, with an eye always for potential trouble, spotted the truant officer and began to run toward the line of boats with Theodorikos now in hot pursuit.

The chase began in earnest as Yiorgis, barefoot, was running and jumping from boat to boat with the gracefulness of a gazelle while his pursuer jumped clumsily from plank to plank in his high boots until he stepped on a melon rind, lost his balance and fell between two boats, making an audible and bubbly splash in the water. A crowd of onlookers had already gathered along the waterfront and the moment they saw Theodorikos fall in the water they broke into loud laughter and thunderous applause.

Yioryis took off like a flash and was nowhere to be seen. A couple of fishermen helped Theodorikos out of the water as one threw a gray blanket over his wet clothes. The only remaining visible evidence of the chase was a small notebook and a pencil that floated on the water, Theodorikos file. The crowds began to thin out rapidly as Theodorikos made his way towards a taxi. The city buzzed for days with the unfortunate outcome of the chase and Theodorikos' fate; through all this Yioryis was secretly hailed by children and parents as a silent hero. I don't know Theodorikos' ultimate fate during the ensuing years of the war and the occupation of Alexandroupolis by German and Bulgarian troops but I learned in 1945 that Yioryis, who remained in Alexandroupolis during the years of occupation, was killed by a Bulgarian patrol while dealing in contraband merchandise near the border with Turkey.

## b. Early political experiences

In the first half of the 1930's Greece was experiencing a great deal of political turmoil. Political fighting erupted between the royalists and the liberals that had its beginnings in the early 1920's. In October 1923 a royalist revolt was suppressed and King George II was forced to leave the country in December. The two parties were battling for political control of the country. In 1935 the liberal party under its leader Eleftherios Venizelos, the greatest statesman of modern Greece, attempted a coup against the government of former General George Kondylis. The coup failed and Kondylis recalled King George II from exile. During the short period of this insurrection, Alexandroupolis became the target of an air raid by the royalists who controlled the army, whereas Venizelos and his Liberal party controlled the navy. Although miniscule in scale, it was nonetheless a frightening experience for most of the inhabitants who had not lived before through a similar experience.

One sunny morning, in March 1935, a single biplane flew over the city and dropped one or more bombs on a single neighborhood, called "tsimemtenia" because they used cement to build the small houses for some of the poorer refugees who came from Turkey. Not only was the air raid a totally unexpected occurrence, the sight of a plane flying over the city was an equally rare phenomenon in those days. The initial reaction on the part of both the adults and children was to run out in the streets and gaze at the sky. The children as expected erupted in applause with the same degree of enthusiasm as when they greeted a taxi that ventured out of the center of town to the neighborhoods. As soon as my friends and I heard the explosions, we rushed to take cover in our homes at the same time as our mothers were calling us from the open windows to come inside. The air raid was short lived and the plane returned to its base, wherever that was.

Our mother waited a couple of hours before she allowed my brother and me to venture out on the street. The neighbors had gathered in small groups outside some homes discussing the air raid and pointing in the direction of a neighborhood north of us where apparently the bombs had fallen. Several adults and children began to walk in the direction of the bombed area. When we got there, we immediately noticed the effects of the explosions. Two craters were visible on the street, glass fragments from the shattered windows were strewn all over and most impressive for us kids were the pock-marks made by the bomb shrapnel on the walls of the houses. There was no evidence of massive destruction of homes or any casualties on the sidewalks or streets, although we subsequently learned that one or two people were killed during the raid. This experience, although minor in terms of damage and fatalities, upset the people who lived in the proximity of the target area. Actually, it could not be called a "target area" since there was no obvious military significance to the affected area and it was concluded that it was a scare tactic, one that could have had more serious consequences. This air raid, however, was a preamble of what was to come five years later, in 1940, when Italy attacked Greece and the real air bombing by the Italian air force began in earnest. Nor could it be considered a harbinger of what happened on a beautiful sunny day a year later.

In the early summer of 1936 there was some evidence that the economy seemed to be doing better. The major chocolate manufacturing company in Greece then was Pavlidis. It produced chocolates in all shapes and forms, from bonbons to bars of various sizes. Aggressive commercial advertising was still in its infancy, except when it came to political parties. However, the Pavlidis company came up with a very innovative idea. They decided to surprise the people of Alexandroupolis and especially the children with an unexpected type of visit. On that beautiful summer day in 1936, a plane appeared over the city, circling and banking right and left. Suddenly, out of a clear blue sky, little specs began to fall toward the ground that were hard to discern at first but soon they became very familiar; they were small chocolate bars from the Pavlidis company. Chris and I who were out playing on the street rushed and gathered as many bars as we could and began to munch on them eagerly. By contrast to the previous year's air raid this was a totally paradoxical phenomenon. I am not sure which other cities the Pavlidis plane visited but I am certain that the people in Alexandroupolis were hooked on Pavlidis chocolates.

In 1936, the year after the failed Venizelos coup, King George II appointed general John Metaxas as Prime Minister who, on August 4th, established a dictatorship and soon after suspended the parliament. The political unrest was evident throughout the country and was manifested in several ways, most notably by worker's strikes that were met with brutal force by the government. In addition to the royalist and liberal parties, several other political parties were in existence during the 30's, some with leftist ideologies and others with far right ones.

Graffiti was not unknown in those days and one morning, after I opened our front door to see my father off to work, I noticed on the wall of the house across from ours a hammer and sickle painted in red and right below it the letters "KKE". I asked my father what the letters "KKE" and the hammer and sickle meant and he quickly explained, "This is the symbol of the Greek Communist Party. The sickle symbolizes the farmers and the hammer the industrial workers". That explanation, however, did not answer the question, "Why did they have to dirty up that beautiful white wall of my grandfather's house"?

The next morning as I opened the front door I was greeted with another graffiti on the same wall that spelled in blue letters "EEE". Again I asked my father and he explained, "It stands for ' National Union of Greece'. It is a right wing party with fascist ideology". Two days later a new graffiti made its appearance between the two previous ones. It was in black and I did not need my father to explain it to me.

It was stenciled and read "Permanent Ston Argyraki", "Permanent at Argyrakis". Mr. Argyrakis was a well-known hairdresser in town who went to individual homes to give women customers a permanent. I knew him because he came to our home on those occasions when my mother felt she needed one. I had also seen his wall advertisements on previous occasions on other houses in different parts of town. The political graffiti on the otherwise clean wall stood like a harbinger of the internecine fights that would develop between the extreme elements of the Greek political arena with the innocent elements, like Mr. Argyrakis, caught in the middle.

Both of my parents' families were politically concerned but not politically active. They did not belong to any of the parties. From discussions I had heard between my father and other members of the family I was sure he was favoring Venizelos' policies. I distinctly remember one day in the spring of 1935 when my father asked me to accompany him to a political rally in the center of the city in which Venizelos was to speak. We walked from our house to the place in the center of town, outside the hotel from which he was to address the crowds. The balcony from which he was expected to speak was decorated in blue and white ribbons and with a Greek flag draped over it.

As the crowds began to arrive, my view of the hotel and the balcony was suddenly erased and I stood there looking at the backs of blue, black or brown jackets and fedora hats. Suddenly there was thunderous applause and I surmised that Mr. Venizelos must have appeared on the balcony. I pulled on my father's sleeve and told him that I could not see. Without hesitation he picked me up and before I knew I was sitting on his broad shoulders. Although only eight years old and on the chubby side, heaving me over did not present a problem for my father who was quite strong and muscular. Now I could see Mr. Venizelos, an older man with a distinctive white beard wearing a black two-pointed hat, akin to a soldier's cap, His oration was interrupted with frequent applause and when he finished the crowd erupted into another round of applause mixed with the shouts, " Zeto o Venizelos", "Long live Venizelos". That same year Venizelos attempted a coup d'etat but failed and he left on a self-imposed exile to Paris where he died the following year.

With Venizelos out of the way, King George II returned to Greece and in 1936 he made a visit to Alexandroupolis. He arrived aboard a

Greek warship that was decorated with what looked like myriads of small Greek flags. There were Greek flags everywhere in town, especially on the buildings lining the streets in the commercial center. That day there was a military parade in the main downtown avenue that was lined up by soldiers on both its sides. Many people were there to view the parade and get a glimpse of the King. I too went to the center of town, but this time without my father's accompaniment. I was a year older, a little taller and I could push my way around. There were people holding or waving small Greek flags and I found myself standing at the edge of the sidewalk with a clear view of the parading army and navy units and military vehicles. In an open car sat the king who waved to the crowds. One could hear applause coming from small groups of people that was sparse since, my guess is, most people had gone to the parade mainly out of curiosity's sake, to see the king. One thing that appeared odd to me at the time was that the soldiers were facing the crowd and not the parade or the king. One explanation could be that the authorities were afraid of an assassination attempt, another that the soldiers looked away out of deference to the monarch.

At the end of the parade we learned that the king was treated to an exceptional lunch and the rumor had it that he was served lobster. In later years, when on some occasions I was treated to lobster and I had to crack the lobster shell, I was given a protective bib to wear to prevent me from splashing the lobster contents on my shirt or tie. Ever since, I often wondered whether King George II also availed himself of a bib.

Metaxas made sweeping changes in the political and social life of Greece. One major change affected all students who in 1937 had finished fourth grade and were planning to move on to the fifth. The latter did not happen! The new educational plan called for a four-year elementary school followed by an eight-year high school. So in 1937 I began my first year of high school at the Gymnasium of Alexandroupolis. Without any prior preparation we began classes in classical Greek, Latin, Algebra and Art among others. Normally, these classes were offered in the first year of the six-year high school. I still remember the mixed feelings I had experienced during the first weeks of classes. In my naivete, I felt proud that I would be recognized as a high school student and as such I would be considered as a person who had achieved a higher level of intellectual maturity. This fantasy quickly dissipated when I began to peruse my new textbooks of Greek and Latin grammar and my elementary algebra syllabus. It was truly "all Greek" to me. The first year of Gymnasium was a totally new experience for me. We were learning new concepts from composition writing to grammar, to classical Greek that despite its designation "Greek", felt as if it were a foreign language. Latin was equally as foreign as classical Greek since we had made a quantum leap from the fourth year elementary school to the first year high school level curriculum without a transitional period. I still remember the beginning phrase of the Latin text- "*Amo, amas, amat. Agricola silvam et umbram silvarum amat*".

I survived the first year and before classes ended my family informed me that I was going to move to Thessaloniki, a city of 260,000 people, and live with my paternal grandparents. The plan was that I was to continue my Gymnasium studies at the Peiramatikon Scholeion, an experimental school of the University of Thessaloniki.

"Του παιδιου μου το παιδι το
εχω δυο φορεs παιδι".
*"My child's child is twice my child"*.
Greek saying.

## 3. Living with My Grandparents

To experience from an early age the love and affection and the nurturing devotion of both my paternal and maternal grandparents was a blessing that had a unique influence on my life. My paternal grandfather, Nicolaos, and my grandmother, Evdoxia, as well as my maternal grandfather, Hadji-Parthenis, and grandmother, Hadji-Maria, were two sets of the most loving and caring individuals that any little child could wish. These sentiments began early in my childhood and persisted into adulthood.

Both grandparents' families came to Greece as refugees from Turkey in 1922 following a failed war between Greece and Turkey the year before. At the Conference of Lausanne in 1922, Greece and Turkey agreed on a compulsory mutual transfer of their national minorities, of approximately one million people, from each country. After leaving Turkey, the two families were transported to Greece and settled in Alexandroupolis. The majority of the refugees who settled there found housing in temporary quarters for about a year to two years before moving into more permanent ones. Both my grandparents built their own houses on opposite street corners of each other.

My paternal grandfather's house was a two story stucco dwelling, which unlike most other homes in the area, had a cement staircase leading from the street in front of the house to a small fenced balcony that led to the main entrance and into the second floor of the house. The second floor had a living room, dining room, three bedrooms and a bathroom. A door at the foot of the outside staircase opened into the ground floor; it had an entry hall, a large kitchen and a den, with a good size fireplace. A large stable was attached to the side of the house on the ground floor where my paternal grandfather kept his beautiful black horse. He rode the handsome black horse to work and back three to four times a week. The remainder of the lot had a small orchard and flower bushes. A huge grape vine was climbing up along four posts on the side of the house and spread over a trellis that covered one fourth of the yard. In this house lived my grandparents and their daughter, my Aunt Helen. Occupying the opposite corner of the street was my maternal grandparents' home.

## Early Experiences with my Maternal Grandparents
**Events with rewarding experiences**

As I have mentioned earlier, my maternal grandfather was a carpenter and a mason and with some help from friends he was able to build the family's home, which he divided into two sections. One went to his older daughter, my mother Alexandra, and the other to my Aunt Zographia. My parents, my younger brother Chris and I lived with my grandparents on the first half of the house that faced Marathonos and Voulgaroctonou streets. My mother's younger brother John also lived with us.

One feature that was distinctive about my mother's house was the presence of a gray plaque above and to the left of the main entrance. The inscription said " *X-Parthenis Aimatides, 1924*", commemorating the name of the builder and the year the house was built. The letter X with a pound sign over it is an abbreviation of the word "Hadji" in Greek. Some time shortly after the turn of the 20th century my maternal grandparents went to Jerusalem on a pilgrimage where they were re-baptized in the Jordan river, a practice followed by many Christians at that time. When a person managed to go on that pilgrimage and was baptized in the Jordan river, he or she acquired the title Hadji. My maternal grandfather became Hadji-Parthenis and my grandmother Hadji- Maria. We called them Hadji-Pappou and Hadji-

Yiayia, Pappou and Yiayia being the pet names for grandfather and grandmother, respectively.

The proximity of the two houses allowed the two families to know each other better and by 1926, my future parents, Athanasios and Alexandra were married. A year later I was the first addition to the family. My birth signaled the arrival of the first grandchild in both families and the first boy at that! My cousin Nicolaos, the son of Uncle Sophocles, arrived eight months later. My cousin Annoula, daughter of my aunt Zographia came one year later. My mother's older brother, Kyriakos, had a boy named Parthenis and a girl Maria who came one and two years later, respectively. My father's three other brothers were yet without children. Needless to say that my Aunt Helen, who was only 11 years old when I arrived, was the happiest one of all because she saw me as a young baby brother. Her love and care for me remained ineffaceable until her death some 72 years later.

My two grandfathers were different in their physical appearance and their personalities. Hadji-Pappous was a lean man, about 5 feet 9 inches tall, with graying hair and a well groomed conservative mustache. His face had the countenance of serenity, his deep-set eyes conveying a sense of warmth and confidence. His voice was soft and he never showed anger or dissatisfaction by raising it.

He was caring and loving, embracing his grandchildren and kissing them on the forehead. Many a time he would put me on his knee and gently bob me up and down while he murmured a tune. Occasionally he would bring some kind of candy or sweet biscuits whenever he would visit the city center. I don't remember him sitting down with my brother Chris and me and telling us children's stories or relating experiences from his life in the city of Biga in Asia Minor, before they were forced out of Turkey. These activities were left to my Hadji-yiayia Maria and to my mother. The stories from their experiences in Turkey were a mixture of nostalgia for the beautiful life they had left behind and the painful memories of the persecutions in the months before departing for Greece. Relating the dreadful period of the weeks before their expulsion would bring tears to their eyes as they described how the bands of Turkish army irregulars would force themselves into the Greek homes, demand money and jewelry and, if they were not satisfied with the quantities of either, they would kill the adults in front of the young children before going out. We frequently heard the stories of how they managed to pay off the demands of the goons and how on occasion they had managed to hide in special crypts that Hadji-pappous had constructed in their house. Their family was among the more fortunate ones for there were reports of hundreds of violent incidents where whole families were snuffed out.

When Hadji-Pappous became older he slowed down his carpentry and house building activities. He went into business and opened a small coffee house that served Greek-style coffee, meatballs, shish-kebab and ouzo. On a few occasions I remember going to the store where I would help with insignificant tasks, such as bringing a glass of water to a customer or wiping a table. It was customary then, as it is now, to deliver coffee to the store owners and their patrons in the immediate vicinity by carrying it on a special tray. On one of these occasions I was asked to carry a glass of water right across the street holding it in my hands. The inexperience, the trepidation and my fear of dropping the glass accomplished just that. The glass fell on the ground and broke. I began to cry, as any seven year old would do, and at the top of my lungs I lamented "Hadji-Pappou to potiri espace" ("Hadji-Pappou the glass has broken") (Here I use the accusative form of the noun Pappous). My crying and my invoking my Hadji-pappous' name brought a number of people from the various stores out to see what caused the disturbance. Needless to say my grandfather quickly came to me, told me not to cry and assured me that they were many more glasses in the store. His calming words and his taking me by my hand assuaged my concerns of what in my mind then was a serious and costly accident.

In the aftermath of the failed political coup of 1935, some of the military officers of the opposition were demoted and jailed or sent into internal exile. The news made headlines and for the first time we saw pictures of men in their uniforms with stars on their epaulets described as the enemies of the monarchy. To an eight or nine year old boy the flashy uniforms, with the leather belts and the shining stars became a symbol of recognition and importance. It wasn't, therefore, surprising that groups of young boys in the various neighborhoods began to form "omathes apo stratiotakia" ("units of little soldiers"). We began to consider on how we would go about looking and behaving like little soldiers or for that matter like little officers. It was not difficult to fashion simple uniforms. Hats were made out of newspapers, epaulets were cut out from the boxes of cigarettes and stars painted on top of them. The belts were usually borrowed from older family members and if there was an abundance of them, a second belt was used as the strap that came over the shoulder and was joined with the belt at the waist. Wooden guns were very rare unless some family had the means to buy them at an expensive toy store.

Hadji-Pappous' skills as a carpenter came handy when I needed something that required the shaping of a piece of wood or helping with the making of a kite. The exception was the availability of an artisan like Hadji-pappous who could shape one from a flat piece of wood. I did not ask my grandfather to make me a wooden gun but I asked him to cut out a sword and garnish it with a hilt. Within a day he found time to fashion a nice wooden sword, about two feet long, with a hilt. I was extremely pleased and in my eagerness to express my elation I grabbed his hand and kissed it. This gesture was not uncommon between young children and older members of the family such as grandparents. It expressed respect and humility. My grandfather was equally pleased with my elation and responded by running his hand across the top of my head and saying "Na to herese", ("You should enjoy it").

The day after my grandfather's accomplishment, I paraded my military outfit in the neighborhood only to find out I wasn't the only captain and not the only one with a weapon. One of the boys, who lived across the street from us, was displaying unusual gear. He happened to be the son of an army captain who had old, used things that he was able to give to his son. He was wearing a set of old genuine epaulets with two silver stars, old medal ribbons and a wooden gun. However, his hat, like mine, was made out of newspaper, and sat on his head like a big triangle. He had no sword, although, he confided to me that his father would not allow him to wear one of his old ones.

Soon, the neighborhood was teeming with "stratiotakia". There were six of us. We allowed one of the Iatropoulos brothers, Evangelos, to be our "archigos" (our commander). There were no foot soldiers. Every one had the rank of lieutenant and above. There were chiefs but no Indians. We practiced saluting, parading and presenting arms, whether with toy guns or swords. The enthusiasm of playing make-believe soldiers spread in most neighborhoods and before we realized groups would prevent boys from another neighborhood from crossing into their area. We defended our territory by throwing stones at the "invading forces". The "invaders" also came armed with stones but except for a few cuts on the scalps of a few unfortunate boys, the casualties were minimal.

Fortunately, these neighborhood wars remained at their embryonic stage and with time fizzled out. Part of the reason was that in 1937, the government of Metaxas established the EON, the "National Organization of Youths". Every high school student was required to join and the family was expected to provide a navy blue uniform with a blue soldier's cap, and white tie. My Hadji-Pappous did not have to put himself behind the saw and plane to fashion wooden guns and swords for us because the government issued real rifles during quasi-military training and exercises of EON. During my visit to Alexandroupolis in July 1940, the Iatropoulos brothers asked me whether I wanted to go on camping trip to the Island of Thasos, organized by the local office of EON. My mother, who learned about the excursion from Mrs. Iatropoulos, said "It would be a good change for you. You should be careful, polite and should not take any chances". I replied, "I am always careful. In fact, Vassilis and Evangelos will be looking after me.

On July 23rd we took the train to Xanthi and from there we were bussed to the port of Kavala. We reached Thasos, which lies about one half hour by boat across from Kavala, in the afternoon of that day. The two week excursion to Thasos was quite pleasant with the wonderful climate and the lush wooded area, except that once a day we were submitted to quasi military exercises, We went on marches and were instructed on how to use gas masks, how to throw grenades (empty) from ditches, how to use a rifle and finally on one occasion I had to stay guard with a rifle all night long at the entrance of the camp. On August 4th, we celebrated the anniversary of Metaxas coming to power. Every one had to put on his EON uniform and salute with our arm raised and extended outward, ala Mussolini and Hitler. The obligatory participation of school children in the activities of EON was allowed to die with the invasion of Greece by Italy in October 1940.

There were two religious festivals that were most frequently attended by the people of Alexandroupolis. One was at Hagia Paraskevi and the other at Hagia Marina and both were held in July. Agia Marina's church was near the eastern outskirts of the city and easily reached by horse carriage or on foot. The year that our family decided to go to the fete of Agia Marina I was 11 years old. The night before, my mother, Hadji Yiayia and Hadji Pappous began to prepare the various foods that we were to take with us the following day. In the morning, my parents, grandparents, my brother Chris and I began to walk to the village of Maistro, where the church was located. Hadji Pappous' fame as a builder spread throughout the region; he was frequently called to assist in important construction projects.

The church of Hagia Marina was recently rebuilt with his able assistance. This gave us all a special sense of pride and my Hadji-pappous a special feeling of accomplishment. When a couple of my friends approached the church and commented how beautiful it looked, I did not hesitate to add with a whisper, "My Hadji Pappous helped build it", a bit of news that left them in awe. Soon after we arrived on the church grounds we spread our blankets under an old platanos (a plane tree). Its trunk was broad and knotty and its branches spread like a myriad of tentacles all decked in broad, green leaves. Its majestic size provided us with the necessary cool shade that mellowed the noon summer heat.

We spread a couple of blankets perpendicular to the tree trunk and soon we were joined by three more families who claimed their spots under the massive tree ; all four families were arranged like spokes in a wheel with the trunk forming the axle. Some of the older plane trees had trunks with gapping holes near the ground thus providing spaces where one could build cooking fires. Some families had arrived the night before and found their way under the many other plane trees that adorned the church environs. In the minds of the faithful, Hagia Marina was a miracle saint. A number of families brought young and old children and adults who were suffering from a variety of physical or mental ailments, in the hope that the Saint would cure them or ameliorate their suffering. The belief was so strong among some of the faithful that they would house their mentally ill relatives in specially constructed cabins with iron bars in their windows for forty days, a sort of quarantine, that would strengthen their vows to the miracle saint.

The day of the feast, the panegyric atmosphere was permeating animate and inanimate objects. Along with the faithful came an assortment of other people, musicians, vendors of pasatempo (roasted pumpkin seeds), of stragalia (roasted chick peas), ice cream, vendors of red cotton candy, gypsies with trinkets, karagiozi players (shadow theater), and the scam artists, the card sharks daring you to point to the one card among three that had the King. After the liturgy, the throng of the faithful indulged in the second most important thing of this feast, they began to eat and drink. Those who did not succumb to the stupor of excess ouzo and retsina began to dance to the tune of clarinets, drums and bagpipes. It was an opportunity for young men and women to show their talent and agility in group and solo dancing.

In the late afternoon, young and old gathered to watch an event that had no relationship to the Christian festival tradition but was a remnant of the centuries old Turkish occupation and probably went farther back a few millennia and that was the match between two bechlivanides (Turkish word for wrestlers). The wrestlers were either gypsies or of some other nationality that followed the Mohammedan religion. This wrestling had its prescribed rules that were followed with ritualistic fervor. The wrestlers stood in the middle of a ring that was dry and covered with dust. Their heads were shaved, their chests were bare and their dark skin was covered with oil from head to toe, except from their waist to the groin where leather shorts hugged tightly to the skin.

The preamble to the match was marked by a series of warm-up gestures that were repeated almost with a liturgical pattern. The two men faced each other and took a bow holding their hand over the heart. They then backed off toward the edge of the ring and began to challenge each other by crying "come on, come on" while they slapped their palms on their knees. While these challenging cries and gestures went on, the wrestlers approached each other and in the opportune moment tried to embrace their opponent only to find out that he was slippery like an eel. They grabbed each other again with groans and grunts and again the man who was under the opponents hold managed to slip away. With each embrace and fall to the ground, the oil and dust formed a brown, grimy layer on their bodies.

All this time the crowd was alternating between cries of approval and applause for their ephemeral favorite wrestler and moments of silence, as one wrestler was almost ready to pin his opponent to the ground. All you heard was the heavy breathing of the wrestlers, as their exhaling wheezed through the air. By now they were beginning to feel the effects of the summer heat and fatigue. The match suddenly would reach its climax when one of the wrestlers managed to grab his opponent, lift him up and throw him to the ground and then toss his heavy, oily body on the fallen man, making sure his back was flat on the ground. The match was over, the crowd roared and applauded as the winner raised his arms above his head and took bows of thanks. The defeated fellow walked away with his head bowed down and his torso showing the emblem of defeat, the soil that was stuck on his oiled back and shoulders.

The winner passed around a metal plate where the crowd threw in coins and at times paper money. I was fascinated with the whole affair and was hoping to have other opportunities to watch such a wrestling match. As time went on, I had the chance to witness similar matches on two other occasions but my fascination with this kind of wrestling soon dissipated when I was taken to a movie theater to watch a picture showing the famous wrestler Jim Londos, champion of the world, wrestling an opponent without the benefit of oil. Londos managed to pick the other fellow up, raise him above his head and spin him around in his famous "airplane" hold. Jim Londos was a Greek-American and the pride of all Greeks.

The evening rolled in rapidly and after we packed our blankets and eating utensils we hired two horse driven carriages and returned home, content and satisfied. It was a memorable and rewarding experience.

## Hadji-Pappous helps me make new friends

Hadji-Pappous ran a small coffee house for a while in the center of town. The nature of his business made it possible for him to meet many of the various shop owners on the street where his shop was located. One of them was Mr. Naoum, a Jewish haberdasher, who lived in a house near the center of town. In 1937, I began my high school studies in the eight-year Gymnasium that was located across from the Metropolitan church of Hagios Nicolaos. The walk from our house to the Gymnasium took about 20 minutes and the path brought me very near Mr. Naoum's house. At times I would notice two young boys coming out of the house and walking in the general direction that led to the Gymnasium. Hadji-Pappous was known for his fairness and compassionate attitude towards his fellow men and on occasions he would admonish us not to fight with our friends and that we try to love each other.

One morning before leaving for school he took me aside and asked me to stop by Mr. Naoum's house and accompany his twin sons to the Gymnasium. He explained to me that on two occasions the boys were harassed by a group of students. It wasn't clear to me why these students targeted the twin brothers. Both twins had a milky-white complexion, light blue eyes and flaming red hair. Their appearance immediately drew attention as they walked down the street. I discounted the fact that they were Jewish as the cause of their being taunted since the Jewish community was very small and there were no Jewish neighborhoods. On that day my accompanying the brothers to the Gymnasium was uneventful. We never had any students give us sneering looks. At the end of classes I waited till the twins came out of their classroom and we walked back to their home together. The topic of our conversation was the teachers we had for ancient Greek, for art and for mathematics. At the boys' father's request my grandfather asked me to accompany them on two more occasions, which I did gladly.

I found the twins very pleasant, with a good sense of humor and very bright. In the subsequent weeks there were no incidents and my duty as a guardian was allowed to lapse as unceremoniously as it started. However, we continued our friendship during the school year.

The events which took place in several Greek towns and cities six years later, when thousands of Jewish people were forcibly sent to the concentration camps by the German occupying forces, evoked anew questions in my mind about the motives for the twin boys harassment by that group of students. Statistics after the war indicated that 137 Jewish people from Alexanroupolis were sent to the concentration camps in Europe.

## Culinary talents of the women folk

My Hadji-Yiayia Maria was of average height, about 5' 3" tall, with a round face, a beautiful milky-white skin, and very expressive brown eyes. She was always busy with something. I don't remember her nodding off and falling asleep on an easy chair during the day except at siesta time. She either was knitting or crocheting something, a scarf, an undershirt or a doily. She loved to hold us close to her and murmur songs from her old but not forgotten country town of Biga in Asia Minor. Frequently, my mother and my Aunt Zographia would join her and all three would sing in perfect harmony, with their melodious, haunting voices, Greek songs or Turkish amane. An amane is a sort of a lament song. The Turkish word "aman" would be equivalent to "ah me" in English. They were love songs and dealt mainly with a broken hearted lass who was left waiting in a rendezvous place where her lover never showed up.

My mother and my Aunt Zographia became the leading chefs of both households, the one living in the Aimatides house and the other in the Kefalides house, across from each other. They owed their culinary talents to my Hadji Yiayia who brought with her the recipes she learned as a young wife from her mother when they lived in Biga. Our meals during the week were usually simple, composed of salads, made of cucumber, tomatoes and lettuce, and at times bean soup or garbanzo soup, yogurt, pasta, chicken and not infrequently meat balls, tyropita or spanakopita. On weekends, however, the meals assumed a special place of importance in our lives. Hadji-yiayia began to gather the food ingredients by mid-week, which would include eggplants, zucchini, okra, celery, leeks, tomatoes, potatoes, eggs, spices and cooking wine. Items that had to be used fresh were bought on Saturday.

The vegetable store owned by Mr. Minas was only one block away from our house. Mr. Minas had a donkey-driven cart that he would take around the neighborhoods selling a variety of fruits and vegetables. He had a loud and melodious voice and one could hear him approaching from a block away. His chanting at times was accompanied by the donkey's braying and the unintended duet made his impending visit unmistakable. On many occasions my mother would step out and wait in front of the house until the donkey-driven cart approached and would enumerate the items she wanted that Mr. Minas promptly filled. She would then pay the amount he requested in drachmas but before the transaction was over he would shout again "Mr. Minas is here! Get your vegetables". In an instant several of the neighbor ladies who were already outside their doors would approach the vegetable cart and before you knew it, Kyria Aspasia, the Papadia, the priest's wife, Kyria

Katina, Kyria Charikleia and my mother would begin to socialize. The gathering turned into a gossiping session, the whispers alternating by bursts of laughter and the session continuing long after Mr. Minas and his donkey had moved on to a different neighborhood.

The meals my brother Chris and I enjoyed the most were the pasta, the spanakopita and the tyropita. My mother prepared fresh dough for all three meals. At first she would prepare the starting dough from flour that was kneaded with water, salt and eggs and then she would roll out a lump of dough into a thin disk about two feet in diameter. This beginning phyllo would get larger and thinner as my mother twirled it at the tip of her fingers and put it aside. The first phyllo was placed aside and was followed by several additional discs that were placed one on top of the other. When several discs were stacked up she would cut the discs into long strips, a little over two inches in width. She would then cut the stacked strips into segments, about one centimeter in width, and spread them out on a wide piece of cloth to dry.

I can still picture my mother bending over the table with the knife in one hand and the other over the stack of strips cutting methodically and rhythmically the strips of noodles. This pasta was known to us as youfkades but in other parts of Greece was known as "hilopites", a flat noodle and when cooked and garnished with hot butter and grated Greek cheese it became our most delicious and favorite meal. The spanakopita and tyropita were prepared from the same kind of sheets of dough that were layered into a round cooking pan about two feet in diameter, whose bottom was greased with olive oil. After the sheets were placed on the pan, a mixture of spinach, scallions, eggs, feta and dill was layered and spread evenly followed by an equal number of phyllo sheets placed on top of the spinach mixture. The tyropita was prepared in a similar manner only that the filling was made of a mixture of Greek white cheese (feta), eggs and melted butter. Before baking, the pitas were cut in squares and the top layer of phyllo was brushed with a mixture of egg and water. Such meals were of incomparable taste and created a lasting gustatory impression in our mouths and our minds. Sunday dinner was a climactic experience that took at least two days to prepare.

Aunt Zographia's specialty was making moussaka and papoutsakia; they both were eggplant and ground meat delicacies. Her culinary technique was passed along to her daughter Annoula who even today in her late seventies makes the best papoutsakia I have ever tasted anywhere. When invited to her home for dinner, even though at the start of the meal I would try not to appear a glutton, and would put only one papoutsaki on my plate, by the time I finished my first portion, I would lose all control and become an insatiable eater. On many occasions I would compete with Maroula, Annoula's younger sister, who also loved her sister's meals.

My mother was the master of meat dishes. Hadji Yiayia insisted on buying not only fresh meats and fish but also the best quality ingredients. The success of my mother's cooking was measured by the degree of postprandial satisfaction and the amount of leftovers. Satisfaction was universal, from adults to children and the amount of leftovers was almost non-existent. The meals that made an impact on our palate included roast lamb with potatoes, lamb fricassee (a meat dish with artichokes in an avgolemono sauce), stifatho, a classic veal or beef stew seasoned with bay leaves, and lamb with okra. A dish that was always popular with the children was yuvarlakia, ground meat and rice balls in avgolemono sauce. Depending on how much and how thick the avgolemono was, the dish could fall between a soup and a stew.

At the end of each Sunday meal Uncle John, my mother's brother, would take out his mandolin and play a few tunes accompanied by my mother's singing, her voice flowing softly, rhythmically as the afternoon siesta was overtaking everyone, young and old.

All this cornucopia and food abundance was the result of economic prosperity that flowed from the steady work that Hadji Pappous and my father enjoyed during the second half of the decade of the thirties. By the end of the year 1940, however, Greece would be attacked by Italy and would enter the whirlwind of the warring nations of Europe. The war brought with it the German, Italian and Bulgarian occupations that wiped out the tranquility, peaceful existence and economic stability of the earlier years only to be replaced by hunger, despair and want of the most essential things of life. The years of occupation saw the destruction of whole villages and the killings of thousands of people.

# Early Experiences with my Paternal Grandparents
## Savoring the joys and excitement emanating from a grandfather

My paternal grandfather, Nicolaos, was the "Megalos pappous" the "Big pappous" and my grandmother, Evdoxia, was known as "Megale Yiayia" despite her diminutive size.

Big-Pappous was physically the opposite of Hadji Pappous. He was over six feet tall, with a large head, bald at the top, and a pair of blue eyes set below a pair of bushy, graying eyebrows. A thick, gray moustache spread across the upper lip and made a short dip at the corners of his mouth. His walk was distinctive and, despite his dimensions, he was nimble as his determined steps announced his arrival. His gigantic size was made more imposing by his stentorian voice. His presence was readily discernible whether he was at the mill during work giving orders, arriving at the house on horseback or visiting a coffee shop. Behind all this impressive countenance one could find a gentle man, a loving father and grandfather and a shrewd businessman. He was sincere in his dealings and made his sentiments known without equivocation.

Big Pappous made it no secret that my being the firstborn grandson in the family and carrying his name, Nicolaos, made him the undisputed guardian and mentor of the young grandson My earliest recollection of visiting my pappous' house puts me around the age of four when as I entered through the front door I would bring out all the joy and excitement that a young boy could evoke in a happy 72 year old grandfather. It was not surprising then that he soon proclaimed me to his buddies at the coffee houses as his child and as time went on I began to fall under the spell of this attractive relationship and when asked "Whose child are you?" I would answer " Tou Pappou mou", ("My grandfather's"). Visiting my grandfather's house became a daily routine; I would spend time following my Big Yiayia around as she did her chores and I would help with small tasks such as fetching a broom or taking the trash to the bin. At times I would walk around the garden among the trees and I would help myself to an apple, a quince or some grapes, whichever was in season.

The one task I did not look forward to carrying out was the various steps in the preparation of wool yarn. It was not unusual for women in those days to knit undershirts, sweaters, scarves, gloves and caps. Big Yiayia would start with large wads of wool that had to be thinned out teasing it through a pair of carding panels. The carding tool was made up of two square panels of wood 1x1 foot wide and about one half inch thick. Their surfaces were lined with rows of short, thin, strong wires all tilted in one direction. One panel was fixed on to a wooden box and the other was free, with a handle on the opposite side of the wires. The free panel would be brought down on the fixed one and moved across with the wool in between. The process of carding disentangled and mixed the fibers giving finally a sliver of wool. Following this step the wool would be spun by hand into yarn using a spindle and then wrapped around a forked cane and washed. After drying, this big loop of yarn would be kept outstretched between a person's two hands and rolled into a ball. It was this last step that my grandmother wanted me to carry out, something I did not mind doing but because of its monotony and the proximity of the nearby window facing the street where my friends were playing, I quickly would get bored and look forward to the end of the task.

Not infrequently I would find myself in front of the main entrance waiting for my grandfather's arrival on his beautiful black horse. He used to leave for work at the mill early in the morning on horse back and return late in the afternoon. Many a time, after arriving, he would not get off his horse but wait in front of the house and shout "Evdoxia", loud enough for Big Yiayia to hear from inside. This was enough of a signal for the dutiful, sweet Yiayia to scurry into the kitchen and bring out a tray with ouzo, a glass of water, sliced cucumber and tomato and a chair. After pappou alit from the horse and settled in his chair, Big yiayia would hold on to the horse, beckon me to approach and as she handed me the reigns we would lead the horse to the stable. The horse was accustomed to the routine with my grandmother and did not seem to mind being led by me at her side. Pappous would then call me over and ask me " pos einai to paidi mou?" (How is my child?), to which I would reply "Poli kala Pappou, kai pos perases tin imera sou?" ("Very well grandfather, and how did you spend your day"?). He enjoyed recounting the events of the day at the mill and would begin enumerating and describing the various customers who came with their horse-driven wagons carrying either grain, pine tree bark or acorns from oak trees.

The mill, which was located on the eastern outskirts of the city, was surrounded mainly by wheat fields and by a few buildings in a radius of a quarter of a mile. Across from the mill on the other side of the road that ran in front of it was the railroad depot, a tall, three story yellow building with green shutters, surrounded by tall maple trees. Immediately next to the mill was a house that pappous owned and on the opposite side was a house with a vineyard belonging to the railroad depot manager. Behind the mill was another house with a vineyard and in between this house and the mill was the vineyard and orchard that belonged to our family. About 200 yards away from the road was a tavern where the mill customers would frequently pass the hours until their products were ground. A set of railroad tracks ran parallel to the side of the mill about 30 yards away, crossing the main road. There was no gate, or light or even a warning bell at the crossing. The rationale behind the lack of these safety measures was no doubt the fact that the crossing was used not frequently enough to justify their installation.

At the mill Big Pappous employed two of his sons, my father and Uncle Sophocles. The two managed not only the daily function of the mill but were also responsible for its maintenance as well. On an occasional Saturday, when the mill was at rest, I would go with my father and watch him work on the massive grinding stones. With a special hammer and chisel he would sharpen the ridges that came out radially from the center of the stone in a way that the ridges of one stone would dovetail with those of its mate in order to grind the grain. He had no special eye protection except the regular eyeglasses he was wearing. Goggles were not used in those days and their need became acutely felt when a few years later Hadji Pappous lost the vision in his right eye from a chip that flew into it from a stone he was shaping in a home construction. Once the chipping of the millstones was complete, my father would move the top stone and place it on top of the fixed stone with aid of a simple pulley.

In the mornings, in preparation for the firing of the engine, my father would step on one of the spokes of an enormous steel wheel and turn it around in order to give the first spark. After a few tries the engine would start running and the stones in turn would begin to spin in a regular, rhythmic fashion, crushing away what ever was fed into them, be it the grain, the bark or the acorns. After a few minutes when enough flour was accumulated between the stones, it would begin to fall into the sacks that were attached below the stones.

My father and Uncle Sophocles left for work early in the morning. My father biked to work using an old army bicycle, World War I vintage. It was made of steel, still sporting the slots that must have held a rifle, and felt as if it weighed a ton. I discovered how unwieldy it was when I tried to learn how to ride it at age seven. My dream of having my own bicycle had to be repressed back to the stage of fantasy since our economic status did not allow for such a luxury. Learning to master my father's bicycle required an effort approaching a heroic feat, for two reasons. To begin with I was too short to be able to reach the pedals and make a complete circle from the level of the saddle and then I had trouble maneuvering it because of its weight and its old age. To overcome the first obstacle I had to reach the opposite pedal through the space below the long bar. This, however, allowed me to move the pedals only halfway, up and down and propel the bicycle forward. With time my dexterity improved and I would be able to cover several blocks half-pedaling. In a few months, as I approached my eighth year of age and having gained a couple of inches in height, I now was able to ride it like everyone else, sitting on the saddle. The use of the bicycle became almost exclusively mine in the evenings, after my father returned from work, and on weekends.

My dream of riding a modern style bicycle was partially fulfilled some three years later. A family that lived about three blocks from our house was raising a goat in their back yard and in the summer they wanted to feed it young vine shoots. The father of the family, who was also the owner of a fancy pastry shop in the center of town that many in our family frequented, knew my father and asked him whether I could bring a bundle of vine shoots from our vineyard from behind the mill, using their son's bicycle. When my father asked me to help I jumped at the opportunity. The bicycle, to my eyes, was a dream, a fancy piece of work. It had a bell, a reflector on the back fender, and a nightlight that was powered by a dynamo charged by touching the front wheel. Behind the saddle was a rectangular grid that could serve as an extra passenger seat or to carry a box or even a bundle of vine shoots. The trip to the mill by bicycle took around 20 minutes but I took the long way around and extended it to 40 minutes. The bicycle was performing like a charm and responded to my commands as I zigzagged through the downtown streets where I was sure people would notice the bicycle and in turn me. After my arrival at the vineyard I used a pair of pruning scissors to cut the shoots and make a good size bundle. The return trip took a few minutes longer because it was mostly uphill. The elation I had experienced each time I was asked to bring a bundle of vine shoots was incomparable and every time I returned the bicycle I was left with the deep sense of an unforgettable but unrequited love.

The primary function of the mill was to make flour from a variety of grains. A secondary function was to grind the bark from pine trees, the powder to be used in leather tanning because of its high content of tannic acid, and a tertiary function fulfilled another need, to produce animal feed from ground acorns.

Big Pappous took me with him to the mill on several occasions, usually on foot but at times by a horse-driven buggy. My baptism into the workings of the mill was an awesome experience. It was summer and school was out already for several weeks. We arrived in mid-morning when the grinding was in full swing. The whole place looked like a trading center of business with men in horse-driven wagons unloading sacks of wheat, corn or rye, or picking up sacks of flour and carting them away. The noise from the massive grinding stones and the rhythmic clanking of the steam engine was deafening making it necessary to shout out loudly in order to be heard. The byproduct of the steam engine was water that was funneled into the vineyard providing the necessary hydration for the vines and the many fruit trees.

On several occasions I noticed that in addition to the horse driven wagons, the mules and the donkeys, there were camels that were used by some customers to transport their sacks of grain or anything else that needed to be ground. The sight of the camels was a rare phenomenon for the children and even for some of the young adults. The camels were owned by one family that lived in a small neighborhood beyond the northern outskirts of the city that was separated by a small stream. When the camel driver left his home early in the morning to go to the seaport and make deliveries, he passed in front of our school and therefore very near our home. Chris and I and some of the other school children knew when the camels were taken to the seaport because on frequent occasions we would notice camel droppings on the road in front of the school. We knew they were camel's droppings because of their distinctive shape that was different from that of horse or donkey droppings; they looked like large size chestnuts. This told us that around 5 or 5:30 in the evening they would be coming back through the same street.

Our fascination with the camels was their enormous size, their spindly legs, their enormous flat feet and to us the great distance between their bellies and the ground. The latter feature goaded us to dare a feat, to run under a camel's belly while it was walking. The camel driver was either riding on the first camel or more often walking ahead of it holding a tether. The rest of the camels, usually five or six, were tethered to each other with long ropes and walked slowly but steadily. Initially we practiced running under the ropes between the camels, something that we had mastered very easily. Then we began the running under the camels' bellies. We had to run fast, in a crouched position and at an angle towards the front legs so that we wouldn't bump into their hind legs. Usually one time under the belly was enough to satisfy our desire; however, not infrequently we would go under twice or three times and then quit. We were elated with our success and with a degree of victorious satisfaction we would abandon our miniature circus for another day. We were all rather short and the feat was accomplished without serious mishaps.

The grinding of grain and of the acorns left considerable amounts of seeds and partially ground acorns on the floor of the mill which were properly collected and served as the feed for the dozens of chickens and a half dozen pigs that were kept in a chicken coop and a sty, respectively. The chickens gave us plenty of fresh eggs and meat, and the pigs supplied us with pork chops, pork loins and pork sausages that my grandfather prepared.

Big Pappous was considered a master of meat specialties. He would single-handedly kill a sheep or goat, blow air under the animal's skin with a hollow reed and then remove the skin with great ease. He would then remove the internal organs, which he washed extensively with water, in preparation of one or another of the varieties of soups, that we called magiritsa. The meat was cut into loin slices, chops and steaks, which would be heavily seasoned with salt, black pepper and oregano and allowed to dry in the cool atmosphere of the house cellar.

An event remains quite vivid in my mind from those early years of my childhood. One afternoon, while we were all gathered in the kitchen on the ground floor of Big Pappous' house, we felt a small shaking of the ground. We could not be sure whether it was an earthquake or an explosion somewhere. The answer came quickly when we noticed that the pork chops and steaks hanging from the ceiling began to swing rhythmically for several seconds until the shaking had stopped. An after shock caused the chops and steaks to swing again telling us with certainty that the shaking was produced by a small earthquake.

Another hobby that Big Pappous enjoyed pursuing with the fervor of an amateur botanist was grafting young shoots from one tree, say apple, into a branch of another, say a pear tree. I would watch him with admiration and awe as he made a deep slit on the branch of the recipient tree, using his ivory inlaid pen-knife, and then with the dexterity and gentleness of a surgeon, insert the young shoot from the donor tree and tie it securely with a dried grass ribbon. When I asked my grandfather how soon it would be before new fruit grows out of the graft he replied "about two to three years".

As time went on I would increase the frequency of my visits to the mill, especially in the summertime when the grapes were ripe and the many fruits were succulent and inviting. One of my curiosities was to find out what the fruit that grew out of the transplanted branch tasted like. One day I plucked a plum from a pear tree and I found it very delicious. The transplanted branch was loaded with plums and I decided to take a dozen with me home. We all heard the expression "The grass is always greener on the other side", and despite the fact that I was surrounded by vines full of ripe, sweet grapes, I could not resist the temptation of reaching across to the neighbor's vineyard and cutting off a couple of bunches of grapes. For some unexplained reason I did find them more tasty, and maybe they truly were.

Although the grains and the acorns were thrown into the center of the grinding stones unprocessed, the bark from the pine trees had to be chopped down to a small size, about three by three inches, so that they could be drawn into the space between the grinding stones.

One day, around noon, I found myself in front of a big pile of large pieces of pine bark and I noticed that the axe used to chop them down was left on the side of the pile. On several occasions, I had watched my father and Uncle Sophocles chop the bark down to size and convinced myself without hesitation that I would contribute to the general welfare of the family. I began chopping down the bark pieces as well as I could but I couldn't take them down to the size of those lying around. The smaller pieces were not stabilized well in my small hand and soon the inevitable happened. I brought down the axe on a piece I wanted to chop down to a smaller size, the bark slipped out and the axe ended on the side of my left forefinger. All of a sudden there was oozing of blood and I began to scream and cry out loud "baba" ("daddy"), Pappou, "Theio Sophocle" but there was no reply. I ran outside and I could not see anyone. Obviously, my father, Uncle Sophocles and pappous had gone to a store a couple of miles towards town to get some supplies, not suspecting that I would dare get into any trouble.

As I came out of the mill, I noticed the tavern on the other side of the road and ran towards it holding my handkerchief around my finger. When I arrived inside the tavern the owner took one look at me and said "Ti epathes?" ("What happened to you?") and without waiting for an answer asked me to approach him. He noticed the deep cut on my finger, stood for a few seconds with a contemplative look and without hesitation quickly reached into his tobacco pouch and with his thumb and index finger lifted a pinch of tobacco, placed it gingerly over the wound with the reverence of a priest anointing a new born baby and wrapped my finger with a strip of cloth that he tore off his white apron. I soon stopped crying as he took me by the hand and walked me to the mill where my father, Uncle Sophocles and pappous were frantically looking for me. My father thanked the tavern owner profusely and I managed to describe in halting sentences the near tragic event. I could have lost a finger. The therapeutic effect of tobacco still escapes me but it could have a haemostatic effect because of the vaso-constrictive effect of nicotine. Although I was permitted to visit the mill in the future, I was warned not to handle anything that wasn't mine.

One of the peculiar advantages that the proximity of the mill to the railroad tracks offered my brother and me was in helping us with the preparation of the figures which represented the characters in the shadow puppet show of Karagiozis that we played at home. In Turkish "Karagioz" means "black eyes" or "gypsy". The puppet show originated in Turkey in the 17th century and its popularity spread to Greece, Egypt and Algeria. The figures we used for the show came printed in color on sheets of paper that we traced on thin cardboard. The outline of the figure was cut out and in addition we cut out longitudinal holes of varying sizes in prescribed areas of the body using a small chisel, fashioned out of a long nail. To make the end of the nail flat and sharp we would put it across the rail with the tip near the center of the rail and wait for the passenger train to pass over it. To assure that we had at least one functional chisel we placed three or four nails at a time and usually we ended up with two or three good ones. As the train approached, Chris and I would crouch down about four to five feet away from the rails and watch as the massive train wheels went over the nails. What always fascinated us was the rhythmic up and down bobbing of the rail as each wheel came over it. This, we were told, was the result of construction by the mechanical engineers that permitted the flexibility of the railroad ties. Chris and I looked at the beveled nails and marveled at the ability of a one ounce nail to dare a 50 ton locomotive and come out only altered but not destroyed.

Our Karagiozis shows were quite successful and when we advertised them among our neighborhood friends we had a full house. Karagiozis was a very popular pastime among youngsters because it was comical, it did not require adult supervision and was easy to set up. All one needed was a white sheet, the cardboard characters that were attached to a rectangular piece of wood, a light source some distance behind the white sheet and at least two people to hold the figures onto the white sheet and carry on with the dialogue. Karagiozis, the main character, represented a Greek hero who got into repartee with Hadzavatis, his friend, whom he ridiculed and occasionally slapped around. Karagiozis was assisted by Kolitiri, his child and other characters, including Ali Pasha, the Turkish ruler and Yehudi, the Jewish character. Although movies were a year round form of recreation in our town, they were attended primarily by men and women of all ages. For the young pre-teen children the puppet show of Karagiozis was an easy and inexpensive form of entertainment.

Big Pappous enjoyed taking me with him to the center of town where he visited the main coffee houses and spent a few hours discussing business and politics with his friends. Not infrequently he would brag about his grandson and he would ask me to climb on top of a table and recite one of the poems I had recently learned in school. Needless to say, each performance was followed by the usual amount of applause. Whenever I would show signs of boredom, he would take me to the movie theater, irrespective of the nature of the picture and we would watch it together. As it often happened I would fall asleep and he would wake me up at the end of the feature. Going to the movies with my grandfather introduced me to this highly coveted form of entertainment that I gradually enjoyed deeply and pursued it as a child and in later years with inexhaustible passion.

## Enjoying religious holidays

Sundays and church holidays were special days for the children and adults as well. These were the days that our faces shone with glee and anticipation because we would put on our new clothes, our new shoes and our new hats. On some Sundays my mother would dress Chris and me in our Sunday best and we would all go to the church of Hagios Nicolaos (Saint Nicholas). After church services, if the weather was nice, the temperature around 70 degrees Fahreheit (21 degrees Celsius) and the town was bathed in sunshine, we would walk to the seashore where we would join people promenading up and down the coastal road.

After a few round trips on the promenade we would end up in the beautiful municipal gardens by the sea. There we would sit on a bench and enjoy the sea breeze and the sea-view with the many sail boats crisscrossing the waves. There was a restaurant that was serving coffee, sweet soda water and fruit juices. For those hungry enough, they also offered simple appetizers such as salads, and cheese or salami sandwiches. For Chris and me, however, the delicacy we coveted most was the "Ipovrihio" ("submarine"), a heaping teaspoonful of a gummy mixture of vanilla and sugar immersed in a glass of cold water. The quantity was not enormous and its consistency was very thick and we enjoyed it by licking it rather than biting into it. The gardens remained open all day and in the evenings they served dinner. Many people would come not so much for the dinner but mainly to hear the Orchestra and to dance to the tunes of Greek and imported popular songs.

Certain Sundays and national holidays, when the municipal and military bands participated in parades, were of special interest to us because our father played the tuba and Uncle Sophocles the trombone in the municipal band. We clapped especially hard when they marched in front of the spot where we happened to be standing. I still remember the little music books that the band musicians had affixed onto their brass or reed instruments with special holders in the shape of a lyre. Despite my father's frequent participation in a number of municipal events, I don't remember him practicing his tuba at home. I have to admit, however, that on some occasions when he was not around, I would bring the tuba and its mouthpiece to my lips and blow hard, generating the deep bass whooping sound of the instrument. My musical education remained in its infancy and did not progress to any form of maturity even though in time I came to enjoy and love popular and classical music.

On some name days honoring a saint, like Hagios Nicolaos on December 6, my grandfather, my cousin Nicolaos and I, would be celebrating the Saint's day. If the name day fell on a weekend, the house that was blessed with a celebrant would be open to visitors who would enter and wish the person with the saint's name "chronia polla", " may you live many years". On such days our home was an "open house" and we could not refuse the visit by anyone, known or unknown to us. This custom was so prevalent in Greece that to avoid receiving any visitors we would have had to make a special announcement in the daily papers informing the public that such and such a person is not accepting visits.

The customary treat to a visitor was an offering of chocolate candy or a teaspoon of fruit preserves of cherry, orange, quince or of rose petals, always accompanied by a glass of cold water. The visitors were not obligated to bring presents and usually did not except when he or she was a close relative and even then it was rare. The festive atmosphere readily was felt by everyone in the house as the constant influx of well wishers with their hugging and kissing, created a sense of instant well being in everyone and particularly in the saint's namesake. The name day of Hagios Nicolaos was the feast of the patron saint of

Alexandroupolis who was honored with the Metropolitan Church of the same name. On that particular day, Sunday, December 6, 1936, I was approaching the age of ten, and I was presented with my first sailor suit. It was made to order and I still remember the interminable visits to the tailor shop for fittings. After a number of boring sessions, with straight pins sticking all around my navy blue shirt and pants, I was told that by the time December 6 arrived I would have my new suit. The tailor kept his word and on the morning of my name day I walked out of our house proudly wearing my new suit.

I went straight to my Big Pappous' house, to show off my new suit and give him my wishes for his name day. He and my Big Yiayia and Aunt Helen received me warmly, with hugs and kisses and wished me "Chronia Polla", ("May you live many years"). I reciprocated by wishing my Pappou "Na ta ekatostisis", ("May you live to be one hundred" ). My Big Pappous smiling, took me by my hand and led me to the living room where he reached over to a table, picked up a thick book and said "Afto eine yia sena" (This is for you). It was a collection of Jules Verne's stories. This was my first book by a non-Greek author. I read it with eagerness and soon I discovered I was reading it very slowly because I did not want the stories to end too soon.

Later that morning my mother, Chris and I went to the church of Hagios Nicolaos to attend the services and take communion. It was mandatory that before taking communion the faithful had to be fasting. Except for some water we had not eaten anything that morning. When we arrived, the church was almost full and everyone was standing since it was not customary to use chairs or benches in the main hall of the church. There was a row of pews attached to the walls on either side of the church but they were already occupied. On that morning the Bishop, Gervasios of Alexandroupolis, was presiding over the services. He was a tall, imposing person with a clear and sonorous voice. He demanded discipline by the members of the congregation and was intolerant of students talking and giggling during the liturgy, especially when designated classes from the Gymnasium attended the Sunday services as a group.

An event which exemplifies the situation occurred when Aunt Helen was in her last year of Gymnasium. Her class was attending church services and before long she and two or three of her classmates began to whisper and giggle and move from side to side. The Bishop requested quiet by saying "sshhhs". The silence that ensued was temporary and the students began to whisper again, whereupon the Bishop picked up his five foot long staff, raised it and brought it down on Aunt Helen's shoulder. Countless eyes fell upon the group of girl students who stood there red faced with embarrassment. The incident for Aunt Helen ended there but with it ended any future visits to Hagios Nicolaos church by her.

As the services for Saint Nicolaos were coming to an end, Chris and I were getting progressively more bored because on such occasions, when a Saint's day is celebrated, the priests prolong the readings and incantations. We had gone to church often enough to recognize the standard hymns and the special ones that were sung in honor of the saint of the day but most of all the one near the end of the service which began "Eidomen to Fos to Alithinon, Elavomen Pneuma Epouranion" ("We saw the true light, we received the heavenly spirit"). On hearing it we suddenly felt a relief from the anxiety of tolerating the inevitable boredom. At last the services on that day of Agios Nicolaos ended, we took our communion, kissed the Bishop's hand and made our way to the church-yard where several people in small groups were socializing and greeting one another. Chris and I were patiently waiting for my mother to finish talking to another lady and one of the priests. When they finished, they both kissed the priest's hand and departed.

The respect and reverence that the people had for older relatives and especially priests at all levels of authority was genuine although, at times, it appeared to be a routine, mechanical gesture. The expression of this pious feeling was manifested not only on the animate subjects but also on the painted icons that adorned the churches. When one kissed the priest's or the Bishop's hand, the expression of reverence was reciprocated with a blessing. The love and affection the people felt for the Bishop became manifest when during that year the Bishop suffered a cerebral accident and died. The news spread rapidly throughout town and when the church authorities deemed it appropriate, they opened the church gates so that the public could come, view the body and pay their respects.

The Bishop was well respected by the general public not only because he was an intelligent person but also because of his humility. When the Patriarch of the Orthodox Church in Konstantinopole (Istanbul) died and the Patricarchate offered the position to him, he declined so that Meletios of Alexandria in Egypt could assume the highest position in the Greek Orthodox Church. The faithful came to church in large numbers as the church bells began to toll single, slow, somber tones. The Bishop, to the surprise of many, was not placed in a coffin but was placed instead in the sitting position on an elegant chair, in his formal attire and wearing his golden, jewel encrusted miter. When the people encountered the silent, lifeless body with the closed eyes, they broke into an audible keening and as they bent their heads in silence, many proceeded to kiss the kind man's cold hand.

The funeral procession was majestic but dignified. Large crowds followed the army band, which played Schubert's funeral march, the diplomatic corps and the mourners carrying numerous wreaths. I remember vividly the funeral procession because my grandfather took me with him to the center of town in a place where I could have an unobstructed view. The thing which impressed me then, as it did many onlookers, was that the Bishop was sitting on a chair, in all his regalia, carried on the shoulder's of four able soldiers and sailors above the heads of all who were there. He was buried in the yard of Hagios Eleftherios, a small church a few hundred yards behind Hagios Nicolaos. Some seventy years later, the atmosphere of mourning and the sentiments of loss that the people felt during those few days still linger in my mind.

## The benefits of sports

It was spring of 1938 and the first year of Gymnasium was winding down. I was doing well in my classes. Among the classes I particularly enjoyed were the art class, physical education and Greek literature. I began to know my teachers better and had made some new friends. Alexandroupolis had a good soccer team and some of my school friends and I began to go to the matches with some regularity. What made soccer very popular for us was not only the effectiveness of the town's team but also the accessibility of the soccer field. The southern wall of the field was non-existent; in its place was the graveled beach and beyond it the clear waters of the Aegean Sea. It was, therefore, easy for us to sneak into the field from the unguarded edges of the north and south walls and the beach. There were matches every week during the regular season between Alexandroupolis and the teams of other towns from the counties of Evros and Rodhopi.

The match that attracted the greatest interest was the one with the team from Komotini, a town of about 30,000 people and the capital of county Rodhopi. On such occasions the railroad line would set up special excursion trains and offer the people of Komotini and environs reduced round trip fares on the day of the match, which always fell on Sundays. One big fan of these matches was Uncle Triantafillos, the son of one of my father's cousins, who lived in Komotini. Uncle Triantafillos was a tall, lean, handsome man, with blond hair and blue eyes, who was always welcomed in Big pappous' house. He and his brothers were tailors and it was no surprise that he always looked dapper in his handsome, hand-made, white suit. Every time he visited Alexandroupolis he would bring a variety of things to munch on during the soccer game, such as roasted chickpeas, roasted pumpkin seeds and raisins.

During one of those Sundays he said to my folks " Tonight I want to take Nicos with me to Komotini". I immediately jumped with excitement at the prospect of visiting Komotini and before I knew it my parents agreed. Since the special train originated in Komotini it would have been impossible for me to get round trip tickets for this train. Uncle Triantafillos assured my parents that it would be no problem for me to ride as a child, which meant free. What it meant, however, was that I was going to travel as a stowaway. There were many factors that made such a venture possible. The special trains were overcrowded and many passengers had to remain standing, the return trip was at night and the lights in the train cars were dim. When the conductor came to check the tickets, Uncle Triantafillos and his buddies put me under one of the compartment seats where I remained unnoticed during the conductor's visit. Every compartment was so crowded that the conductor had to stand in the hallway and ask for the tickets, which were shown by the passengers. I was so well hidden that I doubt that he would have seen me even if he could enter the compartment.

The trip to Komotini took a little over two hours and after leaving the station Uncle Triantafillos took me by hansom buggy to his family home. There I met his mother, his brother Kostas and his sister Maria. His father had died a few years before. After a nice supper I began to feel the effects of the long day and the tiresome trip and I asked to be shown to my bed where I fell into a deep, uninterrupted sleep.

The next morning Uncle Triantafillos took me for a long tour of the town center. Komotini was the first large city I ever visited up to that time. All I knew before that time were the small villages around Alexandroupolis. The first thing to impress me, as we walked around the town center, was the number of minarets. Unlike Alexandroupolis, Komotini continued to have a sizeable Turkish community that remained after the exchange of populations between the two countries in 1922. I heard for the first time the voice of the muezzine calling the muslims to prayer. The minarets were tall, needle-like structures that ended up in a small, circular balcony before being tapered off into a point. Their height was about 120 to 125 feet from the ground and at a distance I could see the head of the muezzine, wearing his turbaned fez, as he was walking around the tiny balcony to make his call from different directions. Each minaret was attached to a mosque where the faithful would enter, shoeless, and kneel on the floor to pray.

We went around the commercial center where I saw numerous shops that appeared like miniature factories. There were shoe stores with myriads of shoes of all sizes and shapes, hanging on poles or arranged on display tables. The owners who were also the makers of the merchandise were either Greeks or Turks and it was not unusual to find Turkish shopkeepers conversing in perfect Greek. If the shopper happened to be a Greek refugee from Turkey he would readily converse in Turkish.

There were clothing stores that catered not only to the Greek population but also to the Turkish community, a number of whose members still were clad in the traditional Turkish attire. There were women dressed in dark robes with dark kerchiefs covering their heads and part of their faces, and some men sitting in front of coffee houses, smoking a nargile (hookah) and wearing a fez and baggy pantaloons.

Another unique experience with the city of Komotini was the visit to the bazaar in the center of town. It was a one day affair and took place weekly; it was a type of an open market, teeming with people, and horse or donkey driven carts. The majority of the vendors came from the neighboring villages and the rest from Komotini itself. The spaces between the displays were small, making it difficult to wind with ease around the carts and tables. Next to the enormous crowds the most impressive thing to me was the great variety of products one could find there. Fresh fruits and vegetables, nuts and raisins combined with condiments and herbs were the predominant elements in these displays. Plucked chickens, skinned rabbits, whole skinned lambs and goats or special cuts of meat from them were prominently displayed. A large number of dry goods were easily seen, hanging from small racks or lying on inclined tables. The hats and shoes, slippers and tsarouchia (a rustic sandal), fez and turbans, colorful scarves and feretzes (the veils worn by Muslim women) and a variety of suits and vests added to the kaleidoscopic aspect of the market.

Not surprisingly, since many of the goods brought to the bazaar were transported on animal driven carts, in isolated corners of the large square one could find saddle vendors. The presence of horses and donkeys brought with it the inevitable unpleasant aroma of their droppings, which people took in stride. Mixed among the throng of all these objects were the food vendors selling a variety of delicacies from sishkebab to meat balls, to feta and Greek coffee, to roasted chick peas and pumpkin seeds, to pink cotton candy. Most of the people at the bazaar were buyers but several came to look around and pass the time or maybe have a demitasse of Greek coffee or munch on some roasted chickpeas or pumpkin seeds. Uncle Triantafilos bought me a wad of cotton candy, which I thoroughly enjoyed. In all this sea of people and their products it was impossible not to notice the hard haggling that was taking place between the vendors and the buyers. Incidentally, the Greek word " to haggle over" is "pazarevo" from the word bazaar (marketplace).

The week in Komotini went by quickly and on the Sunday following my arrival my mother traveled to Komotini and we both returned to Alexandroupolis.

*Mid pleasures and palaces though we may roam,*
*Be it ever so humble, there's no place like home.*

J. H. Payne

# 4. Moving to Thessaloniki

A series of related events that involved my parental grandparents and Aunt Helen had a profound and lasting effect on my life. They played a determinant role on my subsequent social and intellectual development and I believe they marked the beginning of an inexorable procession of events that made me what I am.

## Developing a closer bond with Aunt Helen.

In the summer of 1935 Aunt Helen traveled to Athens to take the entrance exam for the dental school at the University of Athens. She passed but before she could make plans to move to Athens, her brother Elias, my father's youngest brother, a lawyer practicing in Thessaloniki, asked her to take the entrance exam for Law School at the University of Thessaloniki. She did and she passed again but this time Uncle Elias, who wielded a lot of power in family decisions, suggested that she pursue law studies. It was a very calculating move on his part because, as events showed, he was going to have an able assistant at the office during her studies and after having received her law degree. She spent the first year of law school living in the same apartment with Uncle Elias, his wife Stasa, who had a dental office in the same apartment, and Aunt Stasa's parents and an Aunt. In lieu of rent, the Elias-Stasa plan was that Aunt Helen would perform household chores that normally were left to a house-maid. Uncle Elias and Aunt Stasa took advantage of Aunt

Helen's respectful and deferential attitude towards two older members of the family, who were practicing professionals. By the end of the school year the situation became intolerable for Aunt Helen and she began to press Big pappous and Big yiayia to move to Thessaloniki.

After finishing the first year of studies at the University, Aunt Helen came to Alexandroupolis for a visit. My grandparents, my mother, father, Chris and I went to the train station to meet her. We were all excited at the prospect of seeing her and the anxiety was easily discernible as we turned our heads and stood on our toes in the direction of the arriving train. Although it was still daylight, it was easy to make out the strong, powerful light on the front of the approaching steam engine as the train came around a bend about a mile away. As soon as the train stopped we all began looking at the windows and at the doors to see if we could spot Aunt Helen. Suddenly, a handsome, well-groomed figure of a woman began to come down from one of the train cars and my first impulse was to shout "Thia Eleni, Thia Eleni" (Aunt Helen, Aunt Helen). And then, a shocking disappointment hit me as she said in a scolding way "Siope, mi fonazis etsi" ("Quiet, don't shout like that"). I couldn't explain the sudden reprimand from the person whom I adored and who also adored me. In my inexperienced nine year-old mind I could not rationalize her behavior. She hugged and kissed Chris and me and soon she was in the circle of parents and all the other relatives, talking and laughing while sending furtive looks at the direction of the crowd that was still milling around in the small station square.

There was something mysteriously subtle about Aunt Helen's attitude and two episodes that took place in the course of the next few days, threw some light on the puzzle. A few days after Aunt Helen's arrival, my mother gave me some money to go to a pastry shop in the center of town to buy a pastry for myself. As I entered the shop I noticed Aunt Helen sitting at a table in the company of a tall, handsome man, a few years older than her. We spotted each other simultaneously and, as I approached her, she asked me how I was and broke into a smile and a light, nervous laughter that betrayed a sense of embarrassment. She introduced me to her friend and asked me to sit and have a French pastry with them. I refused politely and went out.

The subsequent days passed away without either of us saying

anything about our encounter at the bakery shop to each other or to my parents. However, as I was soon to discover, there was trouble brewing between Aunt Helen and my grandparents who, after having been told by Aunt Helen about the affair, they immediately objected and the strongest argument they had offered was that the man was too old for her.

As a result of our encounter in the pastry shop, the innocent Aunt – nephew relationship that existed all these years took on an added element, a conspiratorial side, which, although not discussed, it was well understood. I became, as time will tell, her confidant. In the meantime I had to pretend as if I did not know anything and this is how the family treated me. My "innocence" served my grandparents who decided to use me as a secret messenger. One night my Big yiayia gave me a rolled piece of paper, not longer than an inch and a half and no thicker than a cigarette, and asked me to take it to an address and place it under the main entrance door where apparently Aunt Helen's friend was staying. I never knew what the written message was but I am quite sure, judging from the size of the paper, that it was rather laconic, asking Aunt Helen's friend to discontinue the relationship.

Nothing more was said about the affair to me by Aunt Helen or by anyone else. Aunt Helen's visit was over in three weeks and she left for Thessaloniki; a few months later Big pappous and Big yiayia moved also to Thessaloniki, to take her away from Uncle Elias' house and keep a close watch on her social activities. The departure of my grandparents to Thessaloniki, although not abrupt, created some consternation and sadness to all of us who remained in Alexandroupolis. Gone were the daily visits to Pappous' house, gone was the waiting for Pappous' arrival on his black horse, the telling of stories while we were sitting on his knee, his giving orders to Yiayia, to Aunt Helen and anyone around, gone were the stories of the daily encounters at the flour mill. Equally missed were the opportunities to follow Big Yiayia around and help her with her little chores or watching her dye Easter eggs and then having her run the first red egg around my face while she whispered a blessing. The warmth that the red egg left on my face is a sensation that is still evoked around Easter time. They were no longer there, they were no longer felt and as time went on we were left at the mercy of nostalgic yearnings.

It was late spring of 1938. I was 11 years old and I was thinking about the classes in the upcoming second year of Gymnasium in the fall. In two weeks we were going to receive our grades and I was anxious to find out how well I did. As I entered home in the afternoon of Friday, May 27th, my mother greeted me at the door with her beautiful smile and her soft voice, put her arm around my shoulder and said, "We received a letter from Big Pappous. He misses you very much and wants you to go and stay with them in Thessaloniki. You will be able to continue your studies in a very good school". The news came as a surprise; I was at a loss, not knowing how to respond. I felt numb and perplexed. My immediate thoughts were those of excited anticipation at the prospect of seeing my grandparents and Aunt Helen, all of whom I did miss a great deal. Soon, I was overtaken by a myriad of questions for which I could not find ready answers. What prompted this decision on the part of Big Pappous? What was my parents' initial reaction? Did they accept my grandfather's decision, without an argument, without questions? One answer my mother gave me that still lingers in my mind was "Big pappous misses you a lot and cannot not do without you".

My grades at the end of he first year of Gymnasium were either excellent or very good. Within two weeks after classes were over my grandfather came to Alexandroupolis to accompany me to Thessaloniki. Two days following his arrival, after visiting my neighborhood friends and saying my goodbye's, I was ready to leave the home where I had lived the first eleven years of my life. I was hugged and kissed repeatedly by my mother and father, Hadji Pappous and Hadji Yiayia and Uncle John. I remember saying to them reassuringly "I will write you often". My brother Chris and I kept looking at each other silently as if saying "How will I play without you?" Thoughts of my mother's ever present warm and comforting embrace, the reassuring smile and words of my father whenever an argument with a neighborhood kid would arise, surfaced in my mind. Both my parents would always admonish Chris and me not to get into fights and to back off. On the morning of departure the whole family walked the half-mile distance to the train station. At the station square, the tearful goodbyes were interspersed with my mother telling me to be careful, to listen to my grandparents and Aunt Helen and not to get into trouble with kids.

The trip to Thessaloniki lasted all day. The train made several stops and I was able to see numerous towns and villages I had seen before only as round dots on the map. I recognized Komotini with its many minarets and the memories of my visit with Uncle Triantafillos appeared rapidly as we were waiting for the passengers to get on board. I remembered the beautiful park, the city square with its bazaar bustling with vendors and their endless variety of goods. We left Komotini and the train soon entered its fertile plain passing through fields of wheat and corn, tobacco and watermelons. Xanthi was the next big town on our way. Like Komotini, it had several minarets. The buildings in the center of town were two and three stories high. The region around Xanthi represented the largest tobacco growing area in Greece and the view from the train was unmistakable as we were moving westward away from the town. Endless fields of tobacco were full of working farmhands, bending over to reach the low plants and pluck off the tobacco leaves. I could make out the women workers from the white kerchiefs covering their heads to protect them from the scorching sun. As the train sped westward passing near some of the farming villages I could see the front yards of many homes where there were series of racks with rows of tobacco leaves were strung along to dry in the summer sun and turn into a yellow, blond color.

Two years later during a visit to the plain of Komotini that also produced a considerable amount of tobacco, my parents rented two rooms in a farmhouse. The owners were tobacco growers and every morning they would leave for the fields to pick tobacco leaves. It was a hard and backbreaking job and our curiosity about the actual process of picking, stacking and stringing of the leaves was answered one morning when the farmer's wife invited us to accompany the family to the field. Chris and I immediately accepted and within 20 minutes we were in the middle of rows and rows of tobacco plants. The farmer's wife showed us in her very expert way how to pick the leaves. The easiest and most efficient way was to begin from the upper portion of the plant and pick the leaves moving the hand from side to side and going downward while stacking them in the palm of the hand. We were told not to pick the young small leaves from the top of the plant since they were not mature yet.

None of us was aware then of the potential danger that was lurking in these beautiful, deep green aromatic leaves. About 15 to 20 minutes into the process of picking I noticed that the fingers and palms of my hands became covered with a black, gummy tar. As I had found later, this substance, which covered the underside of the leaves, remained with each batch, from picking, to drying, to shredding and the eventual packaging into cigarettes. When we returned to the farmhouse, the farmer's wife helped us scrape the tar off our fingers and palms and wash our hands with strong soap and water. In many parts of the world, growing tobacco is the main source of livelihood of these farmers and although everyone is now cognizant of the health hazards of smoking tobacco, the farming still goes on.

After the train left Xanthi my grandfather suggested that we have lunch. It didn't take long to empty a small basket of its contents, which included whole wheat bread, white cheese, meatballs and a cucumber. An old wine bottle that was full of water helped with the chewing and swallowing of the rather dry repast. "The next big town will be Drama, a town of 30,000 people, also known for tobacco and rice production" my grandfather commented. From the train station Drama did not look much different than Xanthi. Drama had the same kind of two and three-story buildings that characterized the city center of Xanthi. It wasn't long before we reached Serrai, the largest of the towns before we reached Thessaloniki.

It was evening when the train pulled into Thessaloniki. Aunt Helen was at the station to greet us and without much delay we took a taxi to the suburb called Saranta Ekklesies, (Forty Churches), after the name of the town they left in Turkey, where my grandparents now lived. My Big yiayia was excited and happy to see me and quickly rushed over to hug and kiss me. She began asking me questions about my folks, Chris and all the relatives and I proceeded to give news from everyone. The house they had rented was a newly constructed building made of brick with a cement stairway leading from the street to a balcony and the main entrance. It was a spacious home, with three bedrooms, a large living room-dining room area and a good size bathroom. The ground floor was equally large but the grandparents did not furnish it with anything but the bare essentials. The suburb was on the northeastern edge of Thessaloniki and was surrounded by rocky crags, bushes and a few pine trees. Pappous and I were very tired from the long trip and we soon retired to our beds. I fell into a deep, dreamless sleep and I did not wake up until midmorning the next day.

*It is difficult for a young boy's mind to suddenly comprehend the social and emotional implications of being transplanted from a small town to a metropolis of a quarter million people.*

## 5. Beginning Life in Thessaloniki

Thessaloniki, formerly called Salonica, was and still is the second largest city and seaport of Greece and the seat of the Governor General of northern Greece. In the late 1930's, it had a population of about 260,000. Thessaloniki was founded in 315 BC and named for a sister of Alexander the Great. The city prospered and flourished in the Byzantine Empire. In 732 AD the Byzantine Emperor Leo III separated the city from papal jurisdiction and attached it to the patriarchate of Constantinople. During the iconoclastic period of Leo and his successors, Thessaloniki insisted on the use of icons in worship and thus saved many of these art treasures. The Ottoman Empire repeatedly tried to capture the city but without success. The desperate inhabitants eventually ceded the city to Venice in 1423. However, the Turkish forces finally prevailed and Sultan Murad II captured it in 1430. It remained part of the Ottoman Empire until 1912 when Greek forces liberated it.

### Awe struck by the magnifiscence of a historic city

Thessaloniki is an important industrial and commercial center. The city exports metals, ores and numerous processed agricultural products. It is the seat of the Metropolitan Bishop of the Greek Orthodox Church and a divisional headquarters of the Greek Army. The city's university was founded in 1925 and in time it has grown both in its physical layout and in the number of schools.

My first day in Thessaloniki was an eye-opener. Practically everything I saw was a first. From the square in front of Pappous' house we boarded a city bus that took us to the center of the city. This was my first bus ride. The bus had a sign indicating its destination, Venizelou, meaning that Venizelou Street was the last stop. This bus made only the trip between Venizelou Street and the suburb of Saranta Ekklesies where we were staying. A conductor, another first, soon appeared and began to dispense tickets, pink, purple and yellow, depending on whether one was going to the end of the line or planned to get off at an intermediate stop. The suburb was built on a steep hill and going down was a breeze for the bus and those people who preferred to walk. At the bottom of the hill we came upon a crossroads with a big hospital on the left and the entrance to the Christian cemetery on the right. Behind us and on the left was a sprawling area full of marble plaques; it was the city's Jewish cemetery. Ahead of us began Hagiou Dimitriou Street (Saint Dimitrios Street). It was paved with cobblestones and separated the modern part of the city to the south from the old part to the north. Next to the Christian cemetery and across from it began the remnants of the old defense walls that ran up to the northern segment of the walls, known as the Eptapyrgion. The northern part of the city was built on a hilly terrain. The majority of the houses were one story dwellings with a small yard but many of them were one room dwellings with a small kitchen, houses that were built to accommodate the large number of refugees from Turkey.

The bus turned left and continued southward and suddenly on my left I saw a new beautiful building in the style of neoclassical architecture. Above the main entrance was the inscription "Aristoteleion Panepistemion Thessalonikis", ("The Aristotleian University of Thessaloniki"). It would be seven years before the graduating class of 1945 from our Gymnasium would enter its halls. Shortly after we passed the university region, the bus stopped in front of a small square in the middle of which was a marble fountain built during the Ottoman era. The buildings in front of the square were modern, tall, five or six stories high. The street that ran in front of the bus was Egnatia Street, a wide street constructed on the remnants of the ancient Roman Via Egnatia that ran all the way to Constantinople. The traffic was heavy with buses, taxis, private cars, bicycles and trams (the electric street cars that were chuck-full of people). A number of passengers were hanging from the handles of the entrance or riding on the heavy metal extension in the back of the tram that was used for hooking onto a second car.

My first impression was that of awe at the variety of vehicles and the large number of people walking up and down the sidewalks of this wide street. After making a right turn into Egnatia Street the bus continued westward. This street that was covered with cobblestones, extended on the left eastward to the city limits and on the right westward to Vardar Square. Within a few hundred feet we came upon the ancient arch of Galerius, whose central opening was wide enough to allow two tram lines to go through. The bus, however, took the path on the left side of the street bypassing the arch. From the point where we entered Egnatia Street all the way to Hagia Sofias Street, the pavement was covered with cobblestones but after crossing that street and beyond it was covered with asphalt. Tall buildings, six and seven stories high, rose on either side. The middle of Egnatia Street was elevated about a foot to allow the running of the double streetcar lines.

After crossing Hagias Sofia's Street we came upon a huge square on the right, known as "Plateia Dikasterion", ("Square of the Courthouses"). That name was given because of a municipal plan to build the new courthouses on that enormous lot. This plan never materialized and when the new courthouses were built in the 1970's, they occupied a sprawling place in the southwestern end of the city near the old train station. The old square is still called "Plateia Dikasterion" and in the place of what might have been a conglomerate of buildings, the visitor today is treated to a treasure of excavated ancient structures that attest to the Greco-Roman consumerism, a vast forum with a double colonnade, shops, a square paved in marble, a library and other amenities. On the left of Egnatia Street, opposite Plateia Dikasterion, begins Aristotelous Street, which is lined up with a series of beautiful six story buildings with red marble columns and archways over wide sidewalks, reminiscent of the sidewalk archways of Italian buildings, This architectural gem ends in Plateia Aristotelous (Aristotle Sqare) by the sea shore.

Gradually we reached "Leoforos Venizelou" ("Avenue Venizelou") and we turned left toward the end of the line at another large square, "Plateia Eleftherias" ("Liberty Square"). All this time my eyes were feasting on the endless array of beautiful tall buildings, with shops on the street level and offices on the floors above. At the corner of Avenue Venizelou and Ermou Street, we got off the bus and crossed the street to the opposite corner to visit Uncle Elias at his law office. It was not uncommon to see tiny shops occupying the small lobbies in the entrances of these office buildings. I noticed, in the lobby of the main entrance of the building we entered, a long table and behind it rolls of clothing material. On the opposite side was a shoeshine stand with two chairs and in the back of the hall a small coffee shop, small enough to accommodate the shop keeper and the tiny stove.

To order coffee one had to ring a bell by pulling a cord that ran from the railing on the third floor down to the ground floor where the coffee shop was located and then shout out the order and the office where it was to be delivered. We found Uncle Elias sitting behind his desk writing feverishly while his secretary was typing with amazing rapidity the pages that he handed her. I had not been in a law office before, nor had I ever seen a woman hit those typewriter keys with the precision and staccato rhythm of a machine gun. Her eyes were fixed on the paper and her face was expressionless. Uncle Elias, in an obvious excited state, stood up and rushed to hug and kiss me, throwing out rapid questions about our train trip, the wellbeing of my parents and Chris, my impression of the bus ride into town and ended by asking Big Pappous if he wanted some coffee and me some lemonade or orange juice.

Big Pappous ordered coffee and I settled for a glass of cold, thirst quenching lemonade. When the secretary finished typing what Uncle Elias had given her, he introduced me to her. She was very pleasant and asked about my first impressions of the city, which were easy for me to describe. Everything I had seen during the first hour of my visit was a new experience. I couldn't help but make comparisons between the sights I was seeing in this enormous city and anything comparable that I had seen in Alexandroupolis. I quickly came to the conclusion that there was little that I could compare them with those in my hometown. If I thought smallness was an asset, then Alexandroupolis had it. With its smallness came the lack of traffic congestion, the few taxis and the nonexistent buses. Yes, the seaport was smaller but it had a lighthouse, something Thessaloniki did not. My hometown had two train lines and two stations; one line going to Thessaloniki and the other starting from the seaport and continuing on along the river Evros and ending up in Istanbul Turkey; Thessaloniki had only one; some consolation!

It was time to leave Uncle Elias office and go to a covered market a block away to buy groceries for Yiayia's kitchen. The market was called Modianou and was enormous. It had a width that ran the length of the block between Ermou and Vasileous Erakleiou Streets. The sight of the many varieties of vegetables, fruit, meats, poultry and fish was overwhelming. Different shops were specializing in only one thing. Butcher shops with skinned sheep and goats hanging from hooks were lined up one after the other. An assistant would stand outside each store chasing the flies away with a horsehair duster. Rows of fish stores displaying cases full of a variety of fish buried in crushed ice ran for several yards. The poultry shops kept live chickens in coops and when a customer approached, he would point at a specific chicken which the shop owner would remove, kill, pluck the feathers and then would singe the remnants of the feathers on the skin. This last step generated a pungent smell, which permeated the whole area.

The market was teeming with customers buying foodstuff for their homes. Big Pappous bought some fish, a few lamb chops and a watermelon before we moved on to take the bus back to Saranta Ekklesies. As we were walking to the bus stop we came upon an ice cream vendor who was selling chocolate covered ice cream bars and cassata, a slab of ice cream held together between two square wafers. Again my eyes lit up at the amount of ice cream I was going to feast on. I must mention that in Alexandroupolis the ice cream man sold shavings, rather than scoops, of ice cream, gently and carefully placed on top of a very small cone, a little over two inches long with an opening of about one inch. This tiny amount of ice cream we used to savor by licking it slowly but with tremendous satisfaction. The ice cream experience in Thessaloniki fulfilled a longstanding yen to bite into that delicious treat and let it cool my throat.

The bus trip back to my grandfather's house was full of eye pleasing sights. The bus went west on Ermou Street until we reached Plateia

(Square) Hagias Sofias, where a large beautiful, domed, church of the same name with an impressive steeple, occupied its eastern end. Architecturally beautiful, high-rise apartment buildings adorned the square. We swung on to Hagias Sofias Street and turned into Egnatia Street. We reached the beginning of the Saranta Ekkleisies road which went uphill until we reached the little square in front of Big pappous' house. Big yiayia and Aunt Helen were waiting for us and wanted to know my impressions of the sights I had seen. I gave them a detailed description of the structures that I felt were unique and unusual and emphasized the large crowds on the streets, the beautiful tall buildings, the numerous shops that occupied the street level of the apartment buildings, the quaint streetcars and the massive Arch of Galerius, which was referred to by everyone as the "Kamara".

For a week my grandfather and I took daily excursions to the center of town to visit Uncle Elias' office and take strolls down by the "paraleia", the promenade by the seashore.

Walking along the seashore evoked an unusual combination of feelings. At the edge of the promenade several caiques, sailboats and fishing boats were moored, their heavy ropes tied on iron rings along the asphalt covered road. The gently rocking of the boats made a slapping sound as the water hit their sides. The sea breeze had a cooling effect on my face and transported me back to the walks on the shore of Alexandroupolis that my mother, my brother Chris and I took. It was in moments like this that I felt I missed my family and my hometown more.

The spectrum of the multistory buildings that lined the opposite side of the seashore road and the reflections of the large ships on the massive windows of the coffee houses and restaurants created evanescent, mural-like images. At times, as the evening sun would reach the top of mount Olympus, the interlacing of the sun's rays and the thin wisps of clouds would form a fiery tableau, which would quickly dissipate as the sun hid behind the mountain. Again, I would be reminded of my hometown and its quiet, peaceful life.

At the end of this promenade stood the "White Tower", a round structure made of stone with battlements at its upper rim. The Greek flag flew from its center. The White Tower is an important landmark in Thessaloniki for it is a remnant of the wall that surrounded the north, east and west sides of the city during the Ottoman rule.

## Taking my first vacation.

As the week was coming to an end, my grandfather told me that we were going on vacation to Litohoro, a village southwest of Thessaloniki on the foothills of Mount Olympus. The train took us to Ekaterini and from there we traveled to Litohoro, which we reached by horse driven carriage. We rented a two bedroom apartment in a typical village house that was made of stone. It had a large yard that was surrounded by a tall stone wall. The family that owned the house had a boy, Vassilis, about 10 years old and two daughters, Vassiliki and Katerina, about 17 and 22 years old, respectively. They were very pleasant and always willing to help us with any of our needs. The house amenities were there but scattered. Behind the house was an outhouse, in the front yard was a water well with a clean bucket on the side, and a water pump near the edge of the garden. The well water was potable but the water coming out of the pump was used only for washing clothes, hands and faces and for taking sponge baths. In one corner of the yard was a brick oven with a whitewashed dome for baking bread and cooking meals.

I immediately became aware of the change in the atmosphere as I walked around the village streets. The air felt clean, refreshing and every breath was invigorating.

Vassilis, the young boy, took me around the village and to the main square where all the stores were located. I could easily make out the coffee shop, a butcher shop, the post office and a "pantopoleion", a grocery store that sold almost everything, from vegetables, grains, fruit, olive oil, vinegar, olives and candy, to rope, nails, hammers, faucets and parts for plows.

For some subconscious reason, I made a mental picture of the location of the post office. As it turned out, within a few days after our arrival to the village, Aunt Helen revived our dormant conspiratorial relationship. She asked me to go to the post office at the village center and ask for the section of "poste-restante", mail waiting to be picked up. The man behind the counter asked for the name and after I gave it to him he, without hesitation, reached over and retrieved an envelope from a cubicle. It was addressed to Aunt Helen and the sender was her friend who lived in Athens. As was customarily understood I handed the letter over to her, she thanked me and the matter was closed. I did not ask any questions and she did not offer any information. In the four to five weeks of our stay in the village there were several other pick-ups, but this time I discovered that I was not alone; Aunt Helen managed to recruit the aid of Katerina, the older of the girls in the house. After a while the three of us, Aunt Helen, Katerina and I formed our secret cabal that managed to keep my grandparents in the dark.

Litohoro, because of its geographic location at the foothills of Mount Olympus, was the starting point of several climbing excursions and expeditions. On frequent occasions we would see groups of climbers walking past the house, loaded with their gear of special boots, heavy socks, a cane, rope and a backpack. Short trips into the nearby dense forest of fir trees were very popular with tourists who did not care to climb the mountain sides. We, Pappous, Yiayia, Aunt Helen and I, ventured into the forest on horseback. The horses came with a guide who helped us climb onto the wide saddles. The horses must have taken the trip several times before because they did not need much guiding to move ahead on the specified paths.

The moment we entered the tree-laden area we noted three things – the daylight diminished suddenly, the air felt cooler and became scented by the fragrant aroma of the foliage of the fir trees. This excursion and two others that followed were the highlight of an exhilarating experience of my first vacation in the summer of 1938.

When we returned to Thessaloniki I wrote a long letter to my folks and Chris and described the experiences of living at the foothills of the sacred Mount Olympus. I often wondered how many, if any, of the Greeks who lived in the first millennium B.C. ventured to climb the slopes of the mountain or tried to reach the sacred peak that rose almost 10,000 feet above sea level. My guess is that such an attempt would have been an invasion of the realm of Zeus and his helper gods and therefore a sacrilege. Who heard of Mountain Climbing Clubs in 500 B.C.?

The summer went by quickly and fall arrived with its chilly temperatures and its strong winds. The cold, strong winds came from a region west of the city where the river Vardaris was running into the

Thermaikos Gulf and for this reason one heard the expression "Fysai o Vardarris" (Vardaris is blowing).

## Starting classes and making new friends in a new high school.

Preparations for the new school year, my second of the eight-year Gymnasium, were under way. Aunt Helen informed me that the school I was to attend was the best in the city and possibly in the country. It was an experimental school and an annex of the University of Thessaloniki, akin to the Experimental School of the University of Chicago, although the genesis of the former had its origins in the progressive ideas of Greek pedagogue, Mr. Delmouzos. I soon found out that, unlike the custom in regular public high schools, I was required to take an entrance examination and that I would have to pay tuition. I was very relieved when I found out that I had passed the exam.

Classes started in early October. The Peiramatikon Scholeion was an all-boys school. All the public Gymnasiums were either all-boys or all-girls schools. What also distinguished our Gymnasium was that an Elementary School was attached to it and was co-educational. Each class was allowed no more than 30 students and no new students were matriculated unless a position became vacant either because a student left voluntarily or was forced to go to a regular Gymnasium because of inability to maintain a certain required grade average.

My first day in school was truly a learning experience. None of the classmates seemed to care who I was and where I came from. I met my individual teachers only at the time they were giving a particular class, classical Greek, mathematics, biology or religion and they met us by taking roll-call. If a student was a newcomer, the teacher invariably asked a few questions about the previous school he attended or which town he lived in before coming to Thessaloniki. When I reported that I came from Alexandroupolis many heads turned towards me, some with obvious curiosity, others showing a subtle air of condescension. Although Alexandroupolis was a well-known town, it was looked upon as a provincial place and the same characterization was accorded to those coming from any place other than Thessaloniki or Athens. As the days went on I began to be approached by some of the classmates who showed interest in the neighborhood where I lived, the sports I enjoyed playing and the movies I most frequently watched.

That fall my grandparents rented a house in town, much closer to the Gymnasium. The walk to school took only 15 minutes but at times I took a little longer which gave me an opportunity to explore different ways of getting there, to examine the houses and office buildings that were of a mixture of architectural design and age. Some of the houses appeared recent, that is post-Ottoman rule, others were not only built during the Ottoman era but also maintained the design characteristic of that epoch. The latter were usually two stories high with an enclosed balcony jutting out from the second floor. The streets were paved with cobblestones, but as one approached the school, which was near the center of town, the streets on its west side and beyond were paved with asphalt.

The school itself was rather new, with two wings finished and an additional two wings to be added later, thus forming a Greek letter Π (pi). It had a red tiled roof, and all the classrooms had large windows facing east, thus giving each room an abundance of sunlight. An open corridor ran on the outside of the classrooms. The desks were all new, composed of tables for two students with an open, wide slot, underneath the top. The top was polished with an orange-yellow stain and covered with a thick, waxy surface. Each table came with two new and comfortable chairs.

The only impractical aspect of the décor was the waxed surface of the tabletops. Despite warnings that we should not write on a piece of paper without a notebook underneath to protect the surface of the top, invariably some student would forget, and would leave an imprint of his writing on the tabletop. In the majority of cases the student would catch himself or be reminded by his nearby classmate and he would quickly put a notebook under the sheet of paper. One of the teachers, Mr. Dimitrios Karasotos, who joined the faculty in 1939, was very strict about that ruling. At one time, while an unsuspecting student was busy writing without the protection of a notebook, he approached his desk very quietly and then slapped him with an open hand hard enough on the face to make his head move all the way to one side. All of us witnessed the event. The episode startled many of the students and left me full of anger.

The first school year at Peiramatikon progressed without major upheavals, either for me or for the majority of my classmates. I managed to adapt to the requirements of the courses, which in general were determined by the teachers themselves. Some of them were routine, homework assignments, such as algebra problems, compositions, translations of classical Greek and Latin into modern Greek, artwork, physics and chemistry. The classical Greek and Latin studies were demanding, especially when we had to learn the complicated grammatical rules and the declensions of nouns and conjugations of verbs.

Making new friends was finally becoming a reality. The first classmate to ask me to join him and his group was Alekos Marketos. Marketos was short with broad shoulders and muscular. He had short thick hair and a prominent square jaw. He always appeared serious but was very pleasant and when he smiled he erased any reticence on anyone's part. We hit it off right from the start and we began to get together for walks, go to the movies and study. The group of friends that Alekos had formed included George Kostopoulos, Yiannis Asimis, Thanasis Mihalopoulos, George Moustakas and Ippokratis Sokotis.

Kostopoulos was short with golden blond curly hair and brown eyes. He was pleasant, open and always participating in games and school activities. He and I became close friends. Asimis was a pleasant fellow, rather short with a thin nose, which supported a pair of glasses in front of a set of brown eyes. He was very bright and very unassuming. Mihalopoulos was tall, wore glasses, had a thick set of brown wavy hair and sky-blue eyes. He had a tendency to keep his head slightly tilted to the left. Mihalopoulos was forthright and always willing to help with math problems. Moustakas and Sokotis were two inseparable buddies. Moustakas was of average height, with somewhat dark complexion, dark straight hair, brown protruding eyes and a pronounced thin nose. He was pleasant and the clown of the group. He had a "gift" of breaking out into a high-pitched laughter, which he frequently displayed in the movie theaters during the most dramatic scenes. His laughter was infectious and invariably most of the people in the theater would break into laughter. Sokotis complemented Moustakas. He was short with straw blond hair, brown eyes and a face that formed two pursed lips under a small well sculptured nose. Both George and Ippocratis were very pleasant. The whole group treated me as if I were in that school forever. I, nevertheless, was quite defensive of my provenance and I would frequently retort, when someone made a snide remark about Alexandroupolis, by telling them that it was so beautiful that it was considered a "miniature Paris", a true exaggeration but an amazing remark that quieted the teasers down.

The geographic separation or proximity of the students' homes to the Peiramatikon School became a determinant factor that influenced the formation of groups among our classmates. Marketos and I and the rest of our group were living very close to the school. Alexis Maniatis, Alekos Andreadis, Nikos Triantafilou, Tasos Oikonomou and Sotiris Tjiridis, who formed a second group, all lived in the center of the city within two or three blocks of each other. However, the geographic factor did not always apply. Vasilis Dimitradis, who lived in an apartment builing only a block from the Peiramatikon, did not belong to the Marketos group and I don't think he particularly sought the company of any group. A number of students did not belong to any particular group although Ioulios Iosifidis interacted with Jo Saporta and George Gratsianis. Kostas Melissaratos and Dimitrios Kajakidis were unattached although Kajakidis joined the Marketos group when the latter became part of the youth resistance group of EPON (Helenic Patriotic Organization of Youths). Two students, Angelos Kalogeropoulos and George Karavas, who did not live too far from our school, also joined EPON and became very active members of the resistance group.

The third year of the eight-year Gymnasium and for me the second year at Peiramatikon began in the fall of 1939. The Second World War had already begun on September 1st. The second year at Peiramatikon was also marked by the arrival of new students, notable among them, Tasos Oikonomou, a bright fellow with a quiet demeanor and a distinctive Peloponnesian accent. Although Tasos and I were not very close in the early years before the war, with time, he and I became close friends and have remained so until the present time.

Another new arrival was that of a teacher of philology, Dimitrios Karasotos. He was one of the most effective teachers we had. In addition to classical studies he also taught ancient history. Mr. Karasotos was a trim man with sparse hair on the top of his head. He had a narrow, long nose that looked as if it was added to his face after the head was completed. He had a penetrating look jutting out of a pair of brown eyes and with his voice carefully modulated he would utter his words with a precise, staccato diction that reflected his rigid, compulsive, obsessive personality. He was very demanding of our performance and enjoyed in making minor grammatical corrections with the air of a dramatic actor. A typical example that all the classmates remember even today was the use of the accusative form of the word "metera" ("mother"). He would place his right index finger at the corner of his mouth and blurt out "Ohi tin metaran ala tin metera", ("Not meteran but metera"), that is metera without the "n". Another example of his rigid personality was his emotional struggle with limitations of conduct, manifested in not allowing even a letter in a composition book to escape outside the margins of a page. Such a transgression resulted in having the student's notebook torn in half.

My friendship with Marketos flourished and in September, when the annual Industrial Exposition of Thessaloniki opened, Alekos' father, Mr. Spyros, asked me to accompany him and Alekos to the Exposition where several European countries were represented. We arrived in the afternoon of a Saturday. The first thing that impressed me was the large number of people that walked around visiting the various exhibits. Machinery of all sorts and equipment for a variety of functions were on display in the foreign pavilions. In addition to the exhibits there were small restaurants scattered around that served German beer and sausages. Alekos' father suggested that we rest for a while and spent the next hour talking while sipping beer and munching on the bun and sausage. This was my first taste of beer which I found quite satisfying and unforgettable.

Two of our best friends, George Moustakas and Ippokratis Sokotis were not allowed to return to Peiramatikon for their third year and had to register in one of the "regular" Gymnasiums. This event, however, did not prevent our group from remaining intact and continue our activities after school hours. Our friendship became stronger and continued to blossom as the years went on and even later when Greece was drawn into the war with Italy in 1940 and during the occupation by German, Italian and Bulgarian troops from1941 to late 1944.

The summer of 1939 was even more memorable because I had the opportunity to visit my parents and Chris in Alexandroupolis for the first time since I moved to Thessaloniki the year before. During the school year my mind was so preoccupied with my classes that I did not have time to dwell on my yearnings to visit my parents. In fact, I don't even recall my grandparents and Aunt Helen discussing the possibility of a trip to Alexandroupolis in the months of late spring. However, as the end of the school year approached, hints of a trip to Alexandroupolis were dropped casually and one day my grandfather told me with obvious delight that in July we would be going together to Alexandroupolis. July arrived quickly and he and I embarked on a passenger steamship bound for Alexandroupolis. This was going to be my first trip on a steamship. I became quite excited at the prospect of visiting my folks after being separated for a year and I began to fantasize the scenes of encountering my mother, my father and Chris in front of the house and of me telling them my countless impressions of the big city Thessaloniki. I was equally eager to see again my maternal grandparents and my mother's brother, Uncle John. Aunt Zographia, Uncle Stavros, Annoula and her sister Maroula, now six years old, had already moved to Thessaloniki where the railroad office had relocated Uncle Stavros the year before.

Because it was summer, daylight persisted beyond 9 P.M. My grandfather and I were lounging on two easy chairs on the deck of the steamboat with our bodies covered with blankets. We enjoyed the cool breeze making its way across the deck and marveled at the magnificent sunset as the sun made its way down beyond the horizon and behind snow capped Mount Olympus. We arrived in Alexandroupolis in the early morning hours and took a horse driven carriage to the house. Seeing the old sights and old neighborhoods evoked feelings of excitement and questions arose as to how would my folks look, how I would react seeing Chris and the other neighborhood friends.

Our arrival to the house was greeted with excitement and joy. My mother hugged me and held me close to her chest as she kissed me while at the same time trying to dry her tears. My father was equally joyous and constantly smiled and laughed as he hugged me. Chris was all smiles and asked me what I liked best about Thessaloniki. Hadji pappous and Hadji yiayia could not control their excitement either. Big pappous sat in a chair at the corner of the living room and appeared to enjoy the outpouring of love and affection. My mother served hot tea, toast and cheese for breakfast to the hungry group. When we finished breakfast and all the excitement waned, my mother beckoned me to come to her, put me on her lap, wrapped her arms around my waist and held me there quietly. I felt the comfort of her lap and bosom, closed my eyes and relaxed. The feelings of calmness and serenity were not unlike the times in the evenings when, as a younger boy, after running around the neighborhood playing with my friends to the point of exhaustion, I would walk over to her as she was sitting in front of the house and plop myself on her lap. Ten minutes of relaxation time would recharge my energy and off I would go back into the street. This time there was no need to recharge my energy. I simply wanted to feel the embrace.

The days and weeks went by quickly. Big Pappous went back to Thessaloniki after one week and I spent time visiting with my old neighborhood friends. We played games and did many athletic activities. Chris and I and my parents went on a couple of picnics by the sea, events that I missed in Thessaloniki. On frequent occasions, Chris and I would go swimming at the nearby beach where we managed to get a welcomed tan. My mother was doting on both of us with her special meals and desserts and by giving small parties for our close friends and us.

One of our close neighborhood friends was Louis, the son of an army captain,who lived on our street. Louis was a bright, friendly boy who enjoyed playing with gadgets, but above all he tinkered with his father's hunting guns. One time he loaded a double barrel gun with two empty cartridges, pushed it through the open window and discharged it. I, not knowing that the cartridges were empty, froze with fear, thinking that some unsuspecting passerby was going to be hit with myriads of buckshot. He quickly assuaged my concern and we both had a good laugh.

During one of my visits to their home, Louis' father happened to be there and he asked me if I would care to visit a submarine of the Greek navy. I did not hesitate too long before I had accepted the invitation. On the upcoming weekend Louis' father, older sister, Louis and I walked to the port and took a launch into the open sea where the submarine was anchored. The excitement and anticipation of visiting a submarine were indescribable and these two feelings were mounting as we were approaching this black, slick, naval structure. The first thing to catch my attention was the periscope which I had recognized from war movies I had seen. Then came a small cannon on the prow of the ship. There were sailors on deck to help us board the ship and lead us down a narrow chute into the insides of the submarine. Everything looked polished and shiny, freshly painted and crowded with sailors who manned their posts. The officer who was assigned to us explained the workings of the various gauges, the radio station, the torpedo tubes and the small, tight, sleeping quarters of the sailors.

The "piece de resistance" was the opportunity the captain of the ship had offered us to look through the periscope. We scanned the surface of the sea and the horizon and then we zeroed in on a warship that had accompanied the submarine in its visit. We were all at awe at the new technologies that were available to carry out warfare. We finished our visit by going through the mess hall and again we were impressed by the smallness of elbow space. We thanked the captain and those of the crew who were near us and made our way back on the deck and on to the waiting launch that took us ashore.

The visit to Alexandroupolis came to a close and I got ready to travel back to Thessaloniki. My mother prepared my suitcase with fresh new clothes, underwear and socks. She did not forget to supply me with a small bag full of fruit, cheese, meatballs and bread. At the train station I said my goodbyes and my mother visibly sad to see me go again could not stop from wiping the tears from her eyes. A similar scene would be repeated many years later and every time I would leave Greece to return to the U.S.A. where I had immigrated in 1947.

The third year of my eight-year Gymnasium began with a great deal of anticipation. We learned that new teachers were added to the faculty and the anxiety was evident as we began our classes. There was a new teacher in philology and one in mathematics. Not only new teachers but new students as well made their appearance. The new curriculum was demanding and left us with very little leisure time. Weekends were always reserved for the movies and for attending soccer matches. Thessaloniki had several movie theaters that showed American, French and British movies. Marketos and I frequented the movie theaters that were showing American westerns, with Tom Mix and Tim Tyler. We also enjoyed watching Shirley Temple and Laurel and Hardy movies that were among the most popular with kids our age. Although not the most popular, serialized movies attracted many kids since the next episodes were always shown on weekends when school was out.

The Second World War in Europe began on September 1, 1939 when Germany invaded Poland. The quick collapse of Poland created a great deal of concern and some degree of panic among the adults and even among children of our age, 11 and 12 years old. Many of my classmates began to develop an interest in the various battles and the war's progress. One of them, Sotiris Tziridis, was quite talented and whenever he became bored during a class he would begin to draw sketches of soldiers fighting in the trenches or having airplanes attacking the soldiers on the ground or depicting dogfights between German and British fighter planes. He told us that he collected his images from war movies showing battles of the First World War. As the Greek newspapers gave us detailed descriptions of the battles between the French and British forces and the German army, Tziridis adjusted his sketches to be truer to the current war conflict and he showed us battles with tanks and attacks with Stuka dive bombers.

We quickly became aware of the existance of the Maginot and Ziegfried defense lines along the French and German borders. In the minds of most people the defenses were thought to be impenetrable not only to attacks by infantry but by tanks as well. As the war progressed, our lives began to take on new concerns. Part of the daily discussions at home, at school or in gatherings at the coffee houses and restaurants revolved around the battles fought by these massive armies. Before long people began to take sides, not so much as to whom they wished to win the war but who they thought would win it. The initial successes of the German army seemed to support those who thought Germany would win it.

My classmates and I developed special attachments to one country leader or another based mainly on the information we had gathered from newspaper stories about them. Our decisions were also influenced by what our foreign country attachment was before the war. Many Greek people had an attachment to France and England, a sentiment that had been fostered by the fact that Greece was an ally of France and

Great Britain during the First World War. I found that many of my classmates were on the side of the French and the British. As the war in Europe went on, the French leaders and especially General Charles de Gaulle became prominent. I seemed to have grown fond of de Gaulle. I copied a sketch of de Gaulle that I found in a newspaper article and I pasted it on the wall of my room. For some unexplained reason I remember copying a sketch of the French economist Jean Monnet, which I promptly placed next to that of de Gaulle. Both men had faces that were ideal for caricatures, since both had big balding heads and great noses.

The war in Europe was not going well for the French and the British and by May 1940 the German army advanced through Belgium and into France overcoming the resistance of the French and Belgian forces. On June 14th Paris fell undefended. The redundant fortifications of the Maginot Line were taken in the rear and on June 22nd France signed an armistice. The British with French and Belgian assistance were able to extricate themselves from the French western shores. Between May 27trh and June 4th they evacuated more than 330,000 troops through the port of Dunkirk. All these events helped deepen the concerns and fears of the people of Greece. It was not uncommon to hear comments like " Will we be attacked?" and "How soon before they march down the Balkans?"

The summer of 1940 was still full of hopeful yearnings and the people continued to carry out their daily routines. In July I started my vacation by visiting my parents in Alexandroupolis. About one week after my arrival, my mother, Chris and I traveled to Komotini to visit Uncle Triantafillos' family. That summer my father was working with a harvesting company in a small town near Komotini, called Yenisea. The town was near a marshy, mosquito infested area. We visited my father for only two days and then returned to Komotini. The mosquitoes made it unbearable to stay any longer.

Within a week after we returned to Komotini I came down with chills and fever, sweating and generalized weakness. A doctor was called and he quickly made the diagnosis of malaria. He prescribed oral quinine and before any effects became noticeable, I developed delirium. This prompted the doctor to switch to intramuscular injections, which had a dramatic effect. The fever and chills subsided markedly as did the delirium but in the process I lost my hearing. I still remember carrying out a one sided conversation with the doctor who was conversing with me but I could not hear anything he was saying. As soon as the quinine was stopped my hearing was gradually restored but I continued to feel weak and unsteady on my feet.

After a few days of rest we returned to Alexandrouplis and soon after I traveled to Thessaloniki. My Big pappous decided that I needed a period of recuperation and in a few days, my grandparents, Aunt Helen and I we were on our way to a village, called Vavdos, which sits on the highest peak of Mount Holomontas in Chalkidiki. From the edge of the village one could see the big valley below, extending all the way to the Thermaikos Gulf of Thessaloniki. From the same vantage point we could see the general area of the military airport of Micra but we were too far away to see any military planes taking off or landing.

Vavdos was then and still is today accessible only by car or bus. Its isolation, tranquility and excellent climate made it a favorite spot for vacations. We spent a month, from the middle of August to the middle of September 1940, in peaceful tranquility, isolated from the outside world. Two of the daily newspapers that were published in Thessaloniki, Makedonia and Fos, were irregularly delivered to the one and only kafeneion (coffee house). There was only one functioning radio, which operated by car battery and was kept at the Koinotita (Village Hall) office. Every noon the older men sitting in the kafeneion, drinking the traditional Greek coffee and either playing cards or backgammon, would ask me and a friend of mine, that I had met in Vavdos, to go to the Township office and listen to the news from radio Athens. Whenever we would ask for the key to the office, the Village Hall officer would say "go ahead, it's open". The officer never stayed in the office but could be found every day at the kafeneion playing cards while he flipped his worry beads. The kafeneion denizens expected us to listen to the news, retain as many details as possible and then return to their cozy spot and recount the current events. Both my friend and I were becoming very well informed on the war's progress, the specific sites of battles fought and any attempts at negotiations or suggestions of forming new alliances among the warring nations.

The vacation in Vavdos ended in the middle of September, 1940 and after we returned to Thessaloniki we moved to a new house, on

Apostolou Pavlou Street, near the Arch of Galetrius and just south of the Rotonda, an old, Roman, cylindrical edifice that at one time served as a church, then as a mosque and now as a museum. Next to it stands a minaret, nearly 120 feet tall. Our new house was a two-story building, with a finished basement, owned by Uncle Elias and was rent-free.

The fourth year of our eight-year Gymnasium began at Peiramatikon Scholeion on Tuesday October 1, 1940. We were all happy to be back and see our friends who had spent their vacations in diverse parts of Greece. I got together with Alekos Marketos, George Kostopoulos, Thanasis Michalopoulos and Yiannis Asimis. Asimis was interested in many extracurricular activities, from art to singing and music. His father had an excellent collection of classical 75-records and when I asked whether I could borrow some he was more than happy to loan me a half a dozen discs. Thus I was introduced to classical music and its magical moods. The records I had borrowed contained violin and piano pieces and some opera overtures; one that I still remember well was " The Light Cavalry" by Franz von Suppe.

My friends and I related our summer experiences and everyone seemed to have had a great time whether it was in the mountains or on the beaches. We all had noticeable tans. Some of my friends wanted to know how I felt during my malaria attack. I described only what I remembered feeling during those days of uncontrolled chills and fever, and the delirium and development of deafness after the injections of quinine. It became clear that I was the only one who came down with that calamity.

Our teachers appeared relaxed and in the best of health; this by no means meant that they were going to be any less demanding or menacing. As the weeks rolled on  we were introduced to our new classes, and among them to new concepts of biology. Our biology teacher was Mr. Kairis, a smallish man with glasses, a well-trimmed moustache and graying hair. He was a dedicated person, who made it his mission to teach us biology not so much by enumerating facts but by explaining why certain things were happening. He introduced us to genetics and to chromosomes that we saw only in pictures. He tried valiantly to explain to us the stages of early embryologic development but without a textbook it was very frustrating.

You can imagine his excitement when in 1953 he received a

preparation of slides, which showed the different stages of cell division and the formation of the corn chromosomes, that I had prepared as a graduate student in a course of genetics at the University of Illinois, the year before. In a letter he sent me he stated: "...I received the microscope slide preparations. I thank you very much. It is very moving for teachers when our students remember us. In these post-war times when the criterion of what ever action is taken by a person is motivated by the possibility of personal gain, your gesture has greater value for me". Mr. Kairis made his classes enjoyable and most of us were looking forward to his clear and erudite lectures or his lab sessions when he would try to explain the morphology of cells, as we looked through a monocular microscope at preparations of onionskins.

Next to biology, the art class was one my favorites. The art teacher, Mr. Rengos, was a short fellow, with gray, frizzy hair and thick eyeglasses. He was soft-spoken and eager to answer questions about sketching or painting. He was not only an effective teacher but also an accomplished painter. I particularly enjoyed his classes because we were given the opportunity to be creative. Using plywood we were taught how to fashion fruit or candy containers that were cut out, with lacy holes made by using a fine, wire saw and then fitted together into a four-sided bowl on a stand. Mr. Rengos also taught us how to draw still life and how to use the technique of perspective. I enjoyed painting with watercolors and he was very instructive and patient with me.

Mr. Kamilieris, our music teacher, was a tall, balding man who enjoyed his work and was determined to teach us, in addition to authentic traditional Greek songs, songs by Schubert, that were translated into Greek. Some of the songs that the class enjoyed singing were, unknown to us then, arias from Italian operas. I discovered, some years after leaving Greece for the United States, while listening to music on the Evanston Radio Station, that the song "Xenitia" ("The Strange Land") was a translation of the aria " Ai Nostri Monti Ritorneremo...", from Verdi's opera "Il Trovatore". Although the Greek translation was not too close to the Italian libretto, the Greek verse was a sorrowful lamentation of the man who left his native country and was now longing for it. The song begins by the man equating himself to a migratory bird " Sta xena dernome, kinigimeno, pouli panderimo xoris folia...." ("In a strange land I wander like a hunted bird, desolate, without a nest..."). Invariably, whenever a group of college students, who like me, had migrated to the United States from Greece after the war, would get together and I would sing this song, it would bring tears to our eyes. Most of the class enjoyed Mr. Kamilieris' sessions and earnestly participated in the choirs he formed to sing a variety of songs that had their beginnings in the war of independence of 1821 against the Turks. Almost all the songs were sung *a cappella* since the only instrument Mr. Kamilieris used was a small harmonium that he used mainly to set the key he wanted our wide range of voices to follow. I clearly remember some of the wonderful voices among our classmates. Christoforidis, in addition to his athletic skills, had an alto voice that was easily distinguishable from the rest of our group. Equally notable was Asimis' voice that was complemented by my voice, which began to change to a semblance of that of a tenor.

In October the weather was still mild and the days sunny and warm. This gave us the opportunity to take part in the sports, that the school permitted us to play, with great enthusiasm and zeal. Our school yard also served as the "athletics stadium". Mr. Michailidis, our gymnastics teacher, was also a very dedicated person who enjoyed his job. He was responsible for all the athletic activities and it was obvious that his goal was to make us good athletes. He had no assistant coaches and he tried to instill in us the importance of trying to excel in what we were attempting to do. The tall students in our class, like Alexis Maniatis, Sotiris Tziridis and Alekos Andreadis, were asked to concentrate on basketball, whereas the shorter ones, like me, Kostopoulos and Christoforidis, were trying to excel in track and field. Unfortunately, none of the students in our class had the makings of a star. The one that came the closest to achieving fame was Christoforidis, who surpassed everybody in the broad jump and especially in the triple jump. He was not only fast and amazingly agile but he mastered the scissors' technique in the triple jump, which propelled him further and gave him a few extra centimeters in the air.

Our class enjoyed a carefree life, full of intellectual stimulation, trying earnestly to master Algebra, Geometry, French, Latin and Greek, Physics and Chemistry in a world far away from the killings and destruction of life that was consuming most of Europe. This fragile tranquility of our life was shattered on the morning of Monday, October 28th, 1940, when Italy invaded Greece. October 28th was the last day of school for the academic year 1940-1941.

*"We make war that we may live in peace".*
Aristotle
*"In war: resolution. In defeat: defiance*
*In victory: magnanimity.*
*In peace: good will".*
Winston Churchill
*"War is the father of all, king of all. Some it makes*
*gods, some it makes men, some it slaves, some it makes*
*free.*
Heraclitus

# The 1940s

## 6. Echoes from the Cobblestones

### The early days of the war with Italy.

On the first day of the war with Italy I began to get ready to go to school. My mother helped me get together my clothes and my newly resoled shoes. The new shoes that my parents bought me for Easter some seven months before had been worn out and they were given to the cobbler, whose shop was across the street from our house, to be resoled. It was customary in those days to put rows of metal studs on the new soles so that they would last longer. On my way to school, as I was walking on the cobblestone streets, every step I took made a distinct clapping sound that produced a small echo in the narrow passageways. This pleasant experince will conrast several months later with the unpleasant echo emanating from the boots of the German

85

soldiers. I was pleased with my newly repaired and shined shoes and as I entered the schoolyard some of my friends commented that they looked like new. Next to a well fitting, warm, suit having a solid pair of shoes was considered an essential adjunct.

All the students entered their designated classrooms and without much fanfare our teacher informed us that the school would close indefinitely. We were dismissed and told to go home.

The news of Italy's attack on Greece caused a great deal of concern and fear among the general population. However, within days a new atmosphere of defiance, of patriotism and of war readiness overtook the whole nation. Men were called to arms, reservists had to report to their units and soon the streets were full of trucks and buses carrying newly drafted soldiers to assembly points. Within the first few days after the initial attack the Greek forces were able to stem the march of the Italian army and quickly pushed them out of Greece and back into Albanian soil. The newspapers were full of reports of heroism of the advancing Greek army units; the first maps of the newly occupied areas in Albania made their appearance. Argyrocastro, Koritsa and Hagii Saranta were cities that were now in the hands of the Greek army units. All this was accomplished by the heroic action and determination of an inadequately equipped army and the altruism of the Greek villagers who aided in every way they could, carrying food, clothing and ammunition up the rugged mount slopes to the infantry units. Pride and delirium were evident in young and old, but especially in the young who were now singing parodies of popular songs which made fun of Mussolini and the Italian army.

Earlier in the month my mother and Chris had come to Thessaloniki to seek medical advice for a complication which afflicted Chris as he was recovering from malaria. Although the signs and symptoms of malaria subsided he had developed mild encephalitic signs, which were common in serious cases of the disease. Fortunately, within two to three weeks he recovered. My mother decided, and the rest of the family agreed, that it would be prudent for her and Chris to stay in Thessaloniki. She very wisely considered the possibility of any future medical complications with Chris' illness would be better handled in Thessaloniki than in Alexandroupolis. In the meantime my father was still looking after the mill in Alexandrououlis.

It did not take long before we were reminded that the war on the Albanian front had several facets. Although the battles were raging several hundred miles away, and the rumble of guns was buffeted by the mountain range of Pindos, Thessaloniki was alerted by the sirens announcing an impending first air raid by the Italian air force. However, the initial alerts were not followed up by actual bombings because of bad weather and it was more than a week later that the first bombing occurred. That morning I was visiting Uncle Elias and at the sound of the sirens everyone in the office ran to the basement along with everyone else in the building that housed mainly law offices. As the people entered the basement they huddled against the walls. Larger groups gathered at the corners talking and discussing legal cases oblivious of the bursting bombs that were falling a few blocks away and near the harbor. In about twenty minutes the sirens sounded again to announce the end of the raid. Instead of going back to the office I decided to walk home. The downtown streets were bustling with people who tried to get to their places of work. Although there was no panic in the streets, the stores were quickly emptying of shoppers. People were getting on streetcars and buses as they tried to get to their homes; their faces strained and worried, not knowing the fate of their houses and families.

My mother was visibly moved when she saw me walk into the house. She was shedding tears of joy as she hugged me. Chris was anxious to know where I had been hiding during the raid and I explained that I was at Uncle Elias' office and hid in the basement with the rest of the people in the building. My grandparents and Aunt Helen admonished Chris and me not to venture too far from our immediate neighborhood since our house was almost two miles away from the seaport, the most likely target of the air raids.

One day Chris and I went, with our mother's permission, to visit Uncle Elias' office since there was a lull in the air raids and because of the presence of an air raid shelter in his building. A few minutes after noon, we left Uncle Elias' office and began to walk towards Egnatia Street. As we approached the corner of Egnatia and Venizelou streets the air raid sirens began to howl and we both ran to the entrance of the nearest office building. At that moment we noticed a soldier on a motorcycle suddenly gunning his motor and speeding eastward on

Egnatia Street. We quickly went to the basement where several other people had gathered. Within a few minutes of getting there we heard three powerful explosions. From the loudness we surmised that they had come from not too far away. After several minutes the air raid was over and Chris and I began to walk on Egnatia Street towards our house. About two blocks from the building where we sought shelter we noted the aftermath of one bomb explosion. A building at the corner of Egnatia and Hagias Sofias Streets was partially demolished and in front of it on the street was the body of the soldier who sped away as the sirens sounded the alarm; his motorcycle could not outrun the airplane or escape the deadly bomb.

This was the first war casualty I witnessed. The other explosions we had heard came from bombs that fell on Plateia Hagias Sofias. They destroyed part of the belfry of the church and the façade of a beautiful building across from the church. The site of the explosions was about one half mile from our home.

The family began to discuss possible areas in the city or suburbs that we could move to avoid the air raids. It was decided that we move in with family relatives in the suburb of Saranta Ekklesies, where we had lived two years earlier. For a few days we were far away from any explosions and we felt quite safe. As we had learned from newspaper descriptions, the performance of the Italian air force was dismal, and when the bombers were chased by the Greek fighter-planes, they were forced to unload their bombs anywhere in the city.

During one of the air raids we happened to be buying things at the local grocery store of the suburb. When the sirens sounded we all rushed into the storage room behind the store and huddled next to each other. The motto "strength in numbers" did not apply here. No sooner did we get to the makeshift "shelter", we heard the rumbling of the bombers and in sequence the explosions of two bombs; one of them was so close that it knocked the only door out and a cloud of dust flew in. After a while the sirens sounded the "all clear" and as we walked outside we heard the sounds of planes in the distance. We could clearly see a Greek fighter plane chasing a lumbering Italian bomber. We all stood there shouting and cheering on the Greek pilot to "go ahead, give it to him". After a few minutes both planes were lost from our view as they disappeared in the horizon.

The day following the last raid we returned to our home on Apostolou Pavlou Street. In the afternoon of the same day the Italian planes returned. This time we ran to our basement and took pots and pans with us to cover our heads. As we huddled with our make shift helmets against the wall we had created a ludicrous theatrical "tableau".

When the raid was over, Chris and I ran out in the street. People were milling around and many were saying that the bombs fell near the harbor and that a bomber went down. Groups of people began to walk towards the seaport and Chris and I followed. As we approached Plateia Aristotelous, we saw a large crowd around what appeared to be the site of a smoldering crashed plane. As we came closer, we could smell the unmistakable odor of burning flesh. Although we were familiar with the smell emanating from a lamb roasting on a spit, this smell was different. It was a penetrating, pungent odor that made its way into our clothes, an odor we could still smell for some time after we got home. The blackened body of the pilot could be seen in the sitting position, burned to a crisp. Several people were milling around the wreckage, commenting on the fate of the poor man. Some people looked through the remnants of the plane and picked up a few fragments. We walked around the body a couple of times, picked up a couple of bomb shrapnel and a small piece of plywood and returned home. It was a common practice to collect shrapnel or small fragments from fallen planes as souvenirs. The image of the unfortunate burned pilot has never been erased from my memory. This was the second wartime victim I had witnessed so far.

In the meantime, the war was raging on the Albanian front. The Greek army continued to advance and the newspaper reports were giving detailed accounts of the battles. However, it wasn't too long before we began to see reports in the newspapers of dead and wounded Greek soldiers. Soon disabled soldiers made their appearance in the streets of Thessaloniki, some with a leg missing, others without a foot or with the toes of both feet missing, the latter a result of frostbite. Snow and ice were covering the mountainsides where most of the battles were being fought and frostbite injury was the most common form of injury after an Italian bullet. All the advances on the war front were gained at a heavy cost. The third victim of the war was my father's cousin, Athanasios Kallitsis, who walked into our house one day with his left leg missing. He was on crutches and one could easily see from his clumsy gait that he was still trying to familiarize himself with his wooden assists.

As the war progressed day-by-day, discussions in our house at dinner time inevitably gravitated on what might lay ahead. Schools were closed and future educational plans were put on hold. Food supplies were for the time being adequate but, with employable people drafted into the army and industrial production shifting towards military preparedness, we wondered how soon were we going to see food lines. My father who was still in Alexandroupolis, looking after the mill, earned enough to support our family. The thought was entertained that we might consider storing food, such as oil, wheat, sugar and rice. I was only 13 years old and with school out, Big-Pappous and Uncle Elias asked whether finding a job might be a thing to think about. My young age and my inexperience limited the possibilities and the options that were available to me. Nothing more was said for more than two years, when at times after school I would go out and sell cigarettes and candy and at times bread rolls.

In early December, Uncle Elias informed us that within two days we were going to leave Thessaloniki and move to Vavdos, the vacation place in Chalkidiki. On a Saturday afternoon we boarded a bus that was requisitioned by a high official in the Greek Security Police, Mr. Solon Tsaoussis, who lived in the same apartment-building as Uncle Elias.

The two friends and their wives, along with two other couples in the building, played cards frequently and participation in this tiny card club helped forge a special friendship. We left Thessaloniki in late afternoon and the bus was almost full. In addition to my mother, Chris and myself, there were my grandparents and Aunt Helen, Mr. Tsaoussis's wife, her son Themis, Aunt Stasa and her Aunt Akrivi and three more relatives of Aunt Stasa's who completed the passenger roster. The distance from Thessaloniki to Vavdos is about 37 miles. Because of security reasons the headlights had to be covered except for a narrow slit that allowed a narrow beam of light to show. The darkness and the fact that the road was not well known to the driver, prolonged the trip.

We first stopped at Hagios Prodromos to let off Mrs. Tsaoussis and her son Themis `before we continued on to Vavdos, arriving around ten at night. The individual families made it to their rented houses for a long awaited restful night.

## Life away from the Air Raids

We spent the next seven months in Vavdos, away from Thessaloniki and the constant threat of air raids. We lived in a closed environment, next to the mountainsides, with the frequent fog and the gray clouds that gave us a celestial cover. Life was tranquil, timid, providing little opportunity to satisfy wants and desires of children and adults. We were like obligate tourists who lost our ability to dictate the events of the day or night. Movement in or out of the village was minimal. Rarely a new family would move into Vavdos from Thessaloniki and equally rarely a family would leave to go back to Thessaloniki; some, however, moved to Athens or to one of the islands in the Aegean Sea.

The nights were eerily quiet; there were no street lights since there was no electricity. The kafeneion, however, was always full of customers, busy with one game or another, either card playing, chess, checkers or backgammon. Every adult in the kafeneion smoked and it was impossible to make out the faces of the players unless you were standing next to a table. I still carry with me the picture of the kafeneion owner, sitting at one of the tables, playing cards and smoking one cigarette after another. The cigarette never left his mouth until the long cylinder of ashes that hung precariously from it eventually made it to the floor and the butt would begin to threaten his thick gray moustache. He would then take out a fresh cigarette, light it with the butt still in his mouth and start smoking it after having stepped on the tiny remnant. Yellow stains on his fingers and the lower edge of his moustache formed unmistakable signs of his passionate habit.

Weekends were awaited with noticeable excitement. Practically the whole group of tourists gathered to sit at the only café-restaurant in the village. The most distinctive feature of the place was a massive, hundreds of years old platanos, a plain tree. Its trunk was at least five feet across. What was more impressive was the spread of its branches that covered the whole outside area of the restaurant. The tree survives even today.

Families would gather and sit at tables under the massive tree. There was always a cool breeze and in the spring and summer months the area under the tree was the most desirable spot. The lighting came from special kerosene lamps that operated with a pump that lighted a lacy sack made of an incombustible substance, known as amiantos, the Greek equivalent to asbestos. The white incandescence emitted by the lamp was very bright and two such lamps were sufficient to illuminate the whole area outside the restaurant. A similar lamp illuminated the inside of the restaurant. The highlight of the evening was the music and the dancing that followed the meal. Couples would dance to the tunes of current Greek and European popular music and especially Italian and Spanish. Young children like myself would simply enjoy listening to the music and watching the dancing couples. One young man, several years older than us young teenagers, who had a good voice, would at times take the cone out of the phonograph, use it as a megaphone and sing popular songs. The one that made a hit with us was the Spanish song "Granada". This was a perfect example of improvisation for at that time there were neither microphones nor amplifiers available at the restaurant. Electricity would come to the village some years later.

For most of my classmates formal education ceased with the closing of the schools after October 28, 1940. Some classmates were fortunate to have parents with the financial means to hire private tutors and continue lessons in mathematics and physics. When we moved to Vavdos I remember taking the classical Greek, the French and the algebra texts with me. With no teachers available to spend time with me or with my brother Chris, I began reading and doing exercises by myself. I must admit that Aunt Helen was a tremendous help in checking my progress in algebra and French. She taught me a little poem in French that allowed me to remember the names of days in French. "Bon jour Lundi, comment va Mardi, tres bien Mercredi, je vien de la part de Jeudi, dire a Vendredi, de se prepare Samedi, pour aller au bal de Dimanche." Unfortunately the lack of formalized teaching and supervision made my review sessions less and less attractive and more sporadic. There was one activity, however, that my friend, whom I had met the previous summer in Vavdos, and I enjoyed very much and unhesitatingly performed; that was listening to the news at noon from radio Athens and then transmitting it to the old folks at the kafeneion.

My mother was the busiest person of everyone in the family. She cooked, baked bread and did the laundry. The neighbor behind our house had a brick and clay oven and baked bread twice a week. She allowed us to bake our loaves along with hers and in return we gave one of our larger loaves to her. To do the laundry my mother needed to bring water from the fountain in the middle of the village, one block away from our house. This was my responsibility, which I performed, though grudgingly, without fail at least once a week. The drinking water was plentiful and clean as it came from a spring in the mountain. We had a large storage vat in the house that we filled with water for drinking and cooking. Although charcoal for cooking was available at the grocery store, Chris and I were asked frequently to go into the hillsides and cut down shrubs that were used for making fire to heat water for washing clothes and taking baths.

There was plenty of meat at the butcher shop and vegetables, olive oil, rice and beans in the grocery store. Our main meals were served in the afternoon and consisted of meat and potatoes, or bean soup, or chicken and rice but everyone's favorite was avgolemono soup (egg and lemon soup). On rare occasions someone from a nearby village that happened to be by a lake would bring fresh water fish and the whole supply would be sold immediately. Eating fish was a very welcomed change in our standard diet. For us the amount of food was adequate and it appeared that subconsciously, by gaining weight, we were preparing ourselves for the period of starvation that fell upon us the following year.

Compared with our prewar period we were living under restrictive conditions, if not primitive. If at night we had to visit one of our friends or relatives we had to use the wind-proof kerosene lamps to illuminate the paths back to our house. We were constantly under the specter of future deprivation of food and clothing and this forced us to improvise. To save our good shoes we began wearing slippers made of felt and galoshes on top of them. It took but a couple of months before the soles began to wear off and a few weeks later before holes appeared on the bottoms of galoshes. We were forced to buy another pair of galoshes for Chris and me, still considerably cheaper than a pair of new shoes.

One product that came out from the region of Vavdos was honey. The hills all around grew thyme and it was said that the honey elaborated by bees feeding on thyme was the best. When spread on freshly baked bread, the combination tasted heavenly. Most of the beehives were kept on the slopes of the hills on either side of the main road leading in and out of the village. Chris and I came by the apiaries frequently, either to buy honey or just to kill time.

We were never molested by the bees but one time after Chris and a couple of other friends began to walk back to the village, I lagged behind, admiring the sunset on the horizon, when suddenly I heard the drone of a swarm of bees. I quickly looked behind me and all I saw was a small dense, dark cloud racing towards me. Knowing what they could do, I panicked and I began to run as fast as I could. As they came closer I took out my handkerchief and started to wave it around my head. I can't remember how far I had run but suddenly, as if they hit an invisible wall, they stopped and as a unit they made an about face and flew back, away from me. I, however, did not take any chances and continued to run until I caught up with the rest of my friends. They casually asked "ti epathes, pou hathikes" (what happened to you, where did you get lost")? I related to them my encounter with the swarm of bees and they all looked at me with some degree of disbelief. I was more intrigued not by the bees chasing me but by the fact that they suddenly stopped pursuing me "en masse" and returned to their hives. The only explanation I could give was that they had reached their feeding boundaries and instinctively they stopped pursuing me.

The news from the war front in Albania reached us daily by radio and from the newspapers Makedonia and Fos, which were arriving in Vavdos with regularity. Although, we were well secluded and away from the sites of air raids, occasionally we were treated to a silent display of bombs bursting and sending clouds of dirt and smoke in the area of what was then the military airport Mikra east of Thessaloniki. This view was afforded by the fact that just west of Vavdos and beyond the foothills of Mount Holomondas opened the Plain of Galatista and Vasilika, which continued on to the Gulph of Thermaikos.

The year 1941 arrived without much noise and fanfare. The

Kefalides family increased with the arrival from Alexandroupolis of Uncle Sophocles's wife and children, Aunt Anastasia and my cousins, Nicos (short for Nicolaos), Michael and Soula (short for Evdoxoula). Nicos was 13 years old, Michael 5 and Soula 3. Uncle Sophocles was drafted and was somewhere either in the fighting front or guarding the northern frontier against invasion through Yugoslavia or Bulgaria. With the arrival of cousin Nicos the number of boys in our group increased, which allowed us to do many more things together. Climbing the mountainside and exploring new paths was a frequent activity. One of the desires we had as youngsters was to be able to enter a cloud and walk through it. Since the upper portion of the mountainside was almost always covered with white fluffy clouds in the winter months, we had no trouble finding one. One morning we ventured up into the mountain and we entered a white cloud. The experience was somewhat disappointing; it wasn't what we expected. We noticed immediately that the visibility was diminished but we could still see each other. We did, however, observe that the air was cooler towards the ground and around the numerous ferns that grew luxuriously all over. Having satisfied our curiosity we returned to the village.

A custom that was prevalent in many villages of Greece then and probably persists in some even today, is the way the village people celebrate the rite of baptism. The only church in the village was on the outskirts of Vavdos and up on the mountainside. The baptism took place inside the small church and unlike the present day custom where the mother hands over the child to the priest and during the ceremony the priest hands the child over to the godparent, the mother in the villages stays home and awaits the arrival of a messenger who would run to the house and announce the name of the child. The mother shows her pleasure and elation by giving the messenger a sum of money commensurate with the family's financial standing. I am not certain whether the gift is greater when the infant is a boy.

On one such occasion, I went to the church to attend the baptism, but since speed was of the essence in reaching the waiting mother before other children did, I stayed just at the entrance of the little church and close enough to hear the name pronounced by the godparent. The moment I heard the name, which happened to be "Eleni", I took off like lightning and began running downhill towards the family's house jumping like a gazelle over the rocks and bushes, to announce the name to the anxiously waiting mother. I succeeded in being the first to arrive and I blurted the name "Eleni"; the mother gave me a big hug and a ten-drachma coin, a significant amount of money in those days. I don't remember how I spent it, but I spent it. Within less than a year, the occupation brought with it an ever increasing inflation and the ten drachma coin was worth one hundredth its original value.

*In peace, children inter their parents, war violates the order of nature and causes parents to inter their children.*

Herodotus

## 7. Germany Invades Greece and Uncle Sophocles is Killed

### The Invasion

On April 6, 1941, German troops began an assault on Yugoslavia and Greece. By April 17, Yugoslavia capitulated against the superiority of the German forces. The Metaxas defense line was covering only the border between Greece and Bulgaria. The Germans poured through the undefended Monastir Gap into Greece. From Bulgaria, that was by now on the side of the Axis forces, the Germans pushed southward against the Greek defenses and into Thrace and Macedonia. The Greek forces were outnumbered and outgunned and although they put up a valiant fight the northern front collapsed and the German tanks moved south and into Thessaloniki on April 11. By April 23, Greece capitulated and its government moved to Cairo, Egypt.

News of these tragic events reached us quickly in Vavdos. Discussions in the kafeneion centered around the takeover of property and production facilities by the Germans and Italians. Slowly, many people began to move from Thrace, that was now occupied by Bulgarian forces, to Thessaloniki and points west and south. Before long my father left Alexandroupolis and joined us in Vavdos. The family began to discuss plans about moving back to Thessaloniki.

A number of the first Greek soldiers who were discharged from the army began to show up in Vavdos. Some were from the village itself and others from neighboring villages. The soldiers were asked about the fighting on the northern front. They all admitted that it was hellish, impossible to mount a sustained resistance. As more and more soldiers began to pass through the village my grandmother and my Aunt Anastasia asked whether they had met or heard anything about Sophocles Kefalides. Some said they hadn't and others that they saw him outside one of the pill-boxes of the Metaxas line. The lack of any definitive answers as to whereabouts of Uncle Sophocles created a sense of despair, which was beginning to show on the faces of my grandmother and of Aunt Anastasia.

Slowly, the days rolled into weeks and no new soldiers were coming through the village. If he is alive, my Aunt would ask, why didn't he get in touch with the family?. Was he injured and was he being hospitalized? It was impossible to get answers to such questions from Vavdos. The desperation on the faces of all the members of the family was clearly evident. There was no wailing, no chest beating, just quiet sobbing, and dabbing of tears as they came down the cheeks. Big Yiayia would retreat in the corner of a big room, sit on a chair and silently pulverize coffee beans in a cylindrical coffee grinder. Aunt Anastasia also spent most of her time in silence, sobbing quietly. The realization that Uncle Sophocles might have died on the war front was gradually emerging in our minds.

Finally, the family decided to take a rare approach to the quest of the whereabouts of Uncle Sophocles. It was decided to ask the aid of a Medium. One night we gathered around a large table, we held hands and in the darkened room the lady Medium invoked the "I call the spirit of Sophocles Kefalides". After several minutes and several attempts there was no contact with the spirit and the meeting ended, as my grandmother and Aunt Anastasia broke down in tears. Eventually the family accepted the fact that Uncle Sophocles was killed in the days of the German assault and sometime later the Greek government officially verified the event.

About a month into the occupation, a German officer, a soldier and an interpreter visited Vavdos in a military vehicle. While the soldier stayed with the vehicle, the officer and his aide went looking for the village administrator. Since this visit was unannounced it was not surprising that we saw the administrator coming out of the Kafeneion followed by the officer and the interpreter and heading for the village hall. No doubt the German officer interrupted a very important game of backgammon, which was soon to be resumed since the visit did not last long and the foreign visitors departed.

All the time that the officer was with the village administrator, a group of boys stood by the military vehicle looking and scrutinizing the German soldier. This was our first look at a genuine German soldier, in his green-gray uniform, wearing his helmet, a holster with a pistol, and mid-calf boots whose soles were reinforced with metal studs. Since none of us spoke German and not surprisingly neither did the soldier speak Greek, we exchanged smiles and grins until at one point I made a remark, probably slightly derogatory, that made all the boys around laugh. This immediately caused the soldier to reach over, grab the top of my head and rub it with his thick and roughened hand. Was it a reaction to the other boys laughing that somehow upset the soldier or that he understood me; I found one or two years later, more German officers spoke Greek than we suspected.

Near the end of May 1941, Uncle Elias visited Vavdos and suggested that we make long term provisions by preparing partially cooked pieces of meat embedded in fat and sealed in large six gallon tin cans. Big papous bought the meat, usually beef or lamb and pork and my mother, with the help of Aunt Anastasia and Aunt Helen partially cooked the cubes of meat and mixed it with melted fat before pouring it into the large tin cans that were then sealed with solder and a hot soldering iron. We also bought blocks of Greek white cheese, about 4 inches square, and preserved them with brine in the same kind of tin cans. My mother baked several loaves of bread, which she cut into thin slices, and then re-baked them until they became dry, thus making the typical rusk (paximadi in Greek). With several cans of preserved meat, cheese, bags of rusk, wheat, raisins and a few jars of honey we returned to Thessaloniki at the end of June 1941.

It gave me a great sense of relief to be back in our home in

Thessaloniki where so many amenities were at hand, compared with the living conditions in Vavdos. It was good to see the family together again, living under the same roof. My father found a job with a harvester company. The job took him some distance out of the city making it difficult to commute every day, especially when buses ran infrequently. He managed, however, to come home on weekends.

The threat of air raids was for the time being almost non-existent. We couldn't predict when the British planes would start bombing German installations. I spent a few hours every day helping Aunt Stasa in her dental office doing little chores such as removing used dental instruments, washing them and placing them in a small autoclave to be sterilized or running errands, such as taking dental impressions to the dental technician's laboratory or picking up completed work and bringing it back to the office. Most of the time though I stayed in the waiting room listening to the radio or reading books that I would select from a large selection. Among the books that I had enjoyed reading was one by Pierre Loti " The marriage of Loti", which described life in Tahiti in the latter part of the 19th century. With time Chris and I re-established our contacts with boys in the neighborhood. Besides reading, there was very little else left for us to do except play backgammon or checkers.

When curfew was imposed, it was not possible to stay out beyond ten o'clock at night, unless one wanted to explain the reason for breaking curfew to a German patrol.

Movie theaters were still in operation and going to the cinema was one of the most popular recreational activities left for many people. America had not entered the war yet and it was possible to see, in addition to German and Italian movies, pictures from the United States. As time went on, moving pictures became the staple of the family's entertainment. Aunt Helen, and to a lesser degree I, would be delegated to go to a movie theater and then return home and relate the whole story. Aunt Helen had an uncanny ability of remembering many details and recounting them with the precision and the emotional flair she acquired studying law and helping her brother, Uncle Elias, in certain of his cases. She would sit in the middle of the sofa and the rest of us would snuggle around her and hang onto every word she uttered. It was one of the most pleasurable experiences of that period I have carried with me. My contribution to the family's recreational menu was not as eloquent but somehow it filled the need. Whereas Aunt Helen emphasized details, I concentrated on summarizing scenes and the effect was not as satisfying.

The presence of the German troops was not immediately evident in the streets as they were housed in their barracks and in the numerous high-rise apartment buildings they took over displacing the tenants to other apartments in smaller houses. One morning as I was coming out of our house, which was about one block from Egnatia Street, I heard music coming from a distance, that sounded strange. I could make out the sound of drums and brass instruments and as I approached Egnatia Street I saw a German military band playing a military march. One instrument that was a novelty to me was the percussion lyre, having colorful tassels on either side, with shiny metal plates that the soldier-musician hit with a metal bar. The band was followed by a regiment of what I estimated was about 100 marching soldiers. They marched with precision, their boots coming up and then hitting the cobblestones with force to complete the goosestep. With each boot hitting the cobblestones a myriad of echoes emanated from the metal studs that covered the boot soles. As I walked on the pavement, the echoes from my studded shoes were drowned out, and I then knew the German army was in Greece.

## Feeling the effects of the occupation

The first summer after the German invasion was not like any other. The difference was not that overt and was not felt by everyone equally. The German forces did not yet make massive arrests or kill civilians indiscriminately. These were to come some months later.

The customary vacations to the mountain villages that the people enjoyed taking in previous years were put off. Uncertainty about the quality of life in the distant villages and the beginning of travel restrictions forced many people to stay in their homes and in the environs of Thessaloniki. Those who had close relatives in other towns or villages ventured to visit them and spend several weeks with them. Our family stayed in Thessaloniki after having spent seven months in the mountain village of Vavdos. Chris and I met with our friends in the neighborhood and I was anxious to find out whether any of my classmates were back. I was glad to find that Alekos Marketos,

Yiannis Asimis and Ippocrates Socotes were back in Thessaloniki. We got together three to four times a week and spent the time discussing the conditions of occupation. Our main concerns centered on the fate of our schools. The fact that Peiramatikon was an educational facility did not exempt it from being taken over by the Germans, since they had already taken over many apartment buildings in the center of the city that they felt met their needs. The Peiramatikon was a new building and its layout was ideal for an office facility. Although in the fall of 1941 classes started at the Peiramatikon, by the fall of 1943 the Germans took the school over.

All the teachers and classmates were back. The teachers refrained from discussing with us the effects of the occupation. They felt that their primary responsibility was to continue teaching the same courses that the Department of Education had outlined before the occupation and continued to dictate during the months after the new school year began.

We were beginning our fifth year of the eight-year Gymnasium but actually it was our fourth year since we completed only one month of the latter. Our teachers displayed a remarkable ability to continue teaching with the same dedication and diligence that characterized them in the previous years. We were certain that they were affected economically the same way as the majority of the population since they were generally dependent on their government salaries, which were being eroded by the uncontrolled inflation. What was impressive about them was that they seldom if ever took time off because of illness or of the need to cope with their family demands. In the three and a half years of occupation we saw a group of teachers whose zeal to teach remained undiminished, although with time we noted that their suits became tattered and their faces gaunt. Actually, their economic situation was not as good as that of some of our classmates whose fathers were professionals, doctors, lawyers or businessmen, who were able to cope better with the period of famine that was affecting the whole country.

As we were leaving the fall months of 1941 behind, the news from Athens was reaching us that the famine there was in full swing. The capital was suffering from severe lack of food. Athens with its port of Piraeus accounted for one-fifth of the country's population before the war. As the occupation took hold, many families from other parts of Greece, returning veterans and the occupation forces contributed to a massive increase of the city's population and the lack of food became even worse. The galloping inflation led many storeowners to hoard their food supplies and thus reduce the amount available for sale in anticipation of a price increase in the near future. Athens depended heavily on the foodstuff produced in the countryside. With almost complete breakdown of transportation between the capital city and the countryside villages, the food supplies dwindled fast. Stories of long lines of people waiting outside stores that still sold food supplies were rife. Slowly as the cold winter set in, the sight of starving people, adults and children, roaming the streets was soon to be replaced by that of many dying of starvation.

The situation in Thessaloniki was not as acute as in Athens during the summer and fall months of 1941. There were food supplies still available. During this time many farmers resisted giving away their farm products to government agents. But as they were in need of cash, they would bring a variety of produce to the city that they would sell either wholesale to shopkeepers or individually to passersby. The big Square of Vardaris, in the western end of the city, was the usual site of makeshift markets where many farmers would unload their supplies of wheat or corn, olive oil, potatoes, chickens and eggs or honey.

As the new year of 1942 was ushered in, a very cold and bitter winter settled over the city. The apartment buildings that had central heating and an ample supply of coal managed to weather the cold. Houses like ours depended on traditional stoves that burned wood or braziers that burned charcoal. The latter were usually placed in the middle of the room and provided additional warmth. Unfortunately, people would succumb to carbon monoxide fumes, if the room was not adequately ventilated. One day Aunt Anastasia who was sitting close to a brazier with her room door closed began to feel dizzy and nauseated. Fortunately, her daughter Soula, who was also in the room but not near the brazier quickly reacted by taking her mother out of the room and into the open air.

Although our house had a large size living/dining room, it was too cold to stay in it. The bedroom that was occupied by my grandparents and Aunt Helen served also as a living room for all. Our bedroom with two beds, where my folks and Chris and I slept, was without heat also. We avoided going to our bedroom unless we needed to retrieve books or clothing. At night, when Chris and I were ready to go to bed, we usually procrastinated until one or the other would get into bed first to warm up the sheets that felt like sheets of ice. We survived that cold winter and all the subsequent ones. In 1943 we installed a new wood stove in our bedroom and I must admit it made going to bed less traumatic.

The severe winter of 1942 contributed heavily to the high morbidity and mortality from the famine of that year. The effects of starvation revealed themselves in more ways than one. One of the most common sights that I saw was mothers with their babies or older children huddled against the wall of a building on the sidewalk, begging for food. Mother and children would be clad in tattered clothes, the bellies of the children usually swollen from edema due to malnutrition. Since these people had no homes or places to spend the night, they would either try to find shelter at the entrances of large buildings, outside churches or remain on the same spot on the sidewalk. It was not unusual to find a mother and child dead the next day on the same place they occupied the day before, or only one of the two surviving. Another common occurrence was to see someone barely walking in front of you and suddenly falling to the pavement, dead from malnutrition, or if not dead immediately, still alive on the sidewalk with eyes wide open, fixed into space, unable to ask for help. A less painful sight was the long lines of people waiting outside centers that gave gratis a bowl of soup or rice and a piece of bread, usually made of corn flour. The support of these centers came from church groups, welfare societies and the Red Cross. Unfortunately, since the supplies were limited, the facilities would close down after a few days. Information gathered from different sources after the war estimated that from 300,000 to 500,000 Greek citizens died directly or indirectly as a result of the famine during the period from the summer of 1941 to the fall of 1944.

Young boys and girls, between the ages of 12 and 16 years, when their skeletal and muscular development begins to make notable strides, were denied essential nutrients, protein, fat, carbohydrates and vitamins. If meat was available, the price was so high that many people could not afford it. Olive oil was and still is an important ingredient of the Greek diet. With time, however, during the occupation olive oil was replaced by vegetable seed oil, including sesame, corn and cotton. When olive oil was still available in the market, it was sold from barrels. Customers would bring their empty liter bottles and buy one or two "okades" of oil. (One oka is equivalent to 2.5 pounds or 2.5 pints). This amount of oil would be enough for three to four meals for a family of four. It was therefore necessary to find ways to buy larger quantities of oil and store them. To accomplish this task one had to search the black market, a market that initially was physically covert, non-identifiable by street and number and manned by shadows.

Buying olive oil became rather risky because one was not sure about the honesty of the vendor. It was easy to mix olive oil with vegetable oil and sell it with the price for olive oil. There were even times when the uppermost layer of a can's contents was oil and the rest water. These shady vendors quickly disappeared after the sale of "olive" oil and were never to be seen again. In the majority of cases, honesty prevailed, especially because people frequented the same site and recognized each other. If one were lucky to find a seller of a six-gallon can of oil, one would be obligated to pay the inflationary price, not in drachmas, since their value was constantly eroding, but in British gold sovereigns. The person, who either had a supply of sovereigns or had enough drachmas to buy them, again in the black market, could afford to purchase the big can of oil. Although one would expect to buy gold sovereigns at the bourse, this was not possible in those days. However, on the street in front of the bourse building it was possible to see young boys with their hands in the pockets of their short pants jiggling their sovereigns. The exchange took place quickly and without much haggling.

The quantity and type of vendors increased as the number of people with special needs also increased. The black market became so pervasive that it replaced the standard means of purchasing for one's needs. Not only people of the middle class would be on hand to sell you any kind of food product but men and women of all classes and ages would roam the streets of downtown Thessaloniki and would set up "shop" anywhere, on the sidewalks, in the alleys around the neighborhood of "ladadika", as the area of wholesale oil vending was known then.

People would be selling a piece of furniture, such as a desk or chair or cooking pots and pans, in exchange for consumables, such as wheat, sugar, rice or even soap. Farmers coming into town from the western and northen villages, bringing carloads of sacks full of drachmas were a common sight. They were headed to furniture stores, shoe and clothing stores, provided they did not make the mistake and fall victims of card sharks in Vardari Square, where these charlatans were frequently stationed. They would set up a small tripod on top of which rested a wooden tray. On the tray they placed face down three playing cards, one of which was a King. When a person approached they would lift the cards so that the customer would see the King as well as the other two cards but as they replaced them on the tiny table they would change their sequence. The object was to guess which of the cards was the King. The clever "croupier", as he was shifting the cards, would say "Etho o papas, eki o papas, pou eine o papas?" ("Here is the king, there is the king, where is the king?"). At times they would allow the poor player to win once or twice, to raise his confidence in the game or have one of their buddies win, to convince the player how easy it was to pick out the card with the King. Many farmers lost their entire supply of drachmas trying to figure out under which card the King was.

The winter of 1942 found the whole family united. Our number increased to a total of eleven people with the addition of Aunt Anastasia and her three children. The uncertainty of everyday life weighed heavily on everyone. Our food reserves were adequate and we managed to get along with all the supplies we had prepared the year before. We prepared our own bread from wheat we had taken to be ground to a small neighborhood mill. Baking ovens were uncommon kitchen home appliances in those days. Most houses had small fireplaces that were used to prepare simple meals, such as boiled rice, fried eggs, soups and the like. To prepare a more complicated meal, such as lamb with potatoes or orzo or chicken with rice, one used large wide pans that required a baking oven.

Right next to our house was a bakery whose owner, Mr. Spyridakis, baked bread that he sold to vendors and was also happy to bake the meals that people in the area brought to him. He got up very early, about four o'clock in the morning, to knead the dough and prepare koulouria, (pleural of koulouri), which are rolls in the form of a ring covered with sesame. He sold the koulouria to vendors who picked them up between five and six in the morning and sold them while walking on the streets or staying at a busy corner. He also baked regular small rolls, about six inches long that he also sold to vendors. The reason the vendors went out so early in the morning was the fact that most workers went to work on foot and for breakfast they would buy a koulouri or a small roll of bread. The smart vendors would select posts as far east on the main avenues as possible since most workers moved westward to get to their shops and factories.

In the summer of 1943 my grandfather suggested that I go out in the early hours of the morning and sell bread rolls to the people going to work. This venture, like all of my other "business" affairs, was not very successful profit-wise. I would get up about 5 o'clock in the morning, go to Mr. Spyridakis bakery and purchase a number fresh rolls, put them in a large basket and select a spot on Egnatia street a couple of hundred feet west of Kamara, in front of a small school that the Germans had already requisitioned. After about two hours, having sold only a few rolls I would return home and around noon I would go to the city center and try to sell the remainder of the rolls to people dining in restaurants or taverns. Since bread was scarce, restaurants did not serve it with their meals and my showing up was a welcome chance to buy one. In the area that I frequented other vendors were also moving about.

Frequently, German officers would be visiting the shopping area and one time an officer asked me to stand in front of a donkey, that was hitched to a cart, and hold a roll of bread near the donkeys nose. I did and he photographed me, the bread, the donkey and the other young men that gathered around the cart. What we did not notice at that moment was the presence of a small boy, around four to five years old, with a distended belly, standing a few feet away. The German soldier thanked me and went on his way and I went on mine. I had forgotten the incident.

Some five or six months later, during spring break in 1944, I was selling raisins on a table that was supplied with a balance and a few paper bags. At one moment, a German officer in khakis and carrying a canvas satchel stopped by the table and began talking to me in German, as if trying to explain something. My first reaction was that of distrust and suspicion, that he probably knew something about my involvement in the underground. Thoughts of running away or pretending to be sick raced quickly through my mind, thoughts that I quickly dismissed. All this time his demeanor was quiet and calming and did not appear threatening. Finally he uttered the word " photograph' and the phrase I recognized "Kommen sie mit mir" and I finally decided to follow him.

We walked towards Hagias Sophia's church and we reached a small, one story building exactly behind the church. That small structure was a shop used by a sculptor who made marble crosses and small statues that were used in cemeteries; the Germans had requisitioned it and converted it into an engineering drafting shop. The officer walked to his desk reached into a drawer and produced a picture. To my pleasant surprise, I recognized the picture of me holding the roll of bread in front of the donkey. He gave me the photograph with an unmistakable smile of satifaction, realizing my relief and surprise. Unfortunately, I did not know enough German to ask him how he recognized me after all those months. We shook hands and I went back to my table of raisins that a young neighbor boy was guarding for me. I learned later as a medical student that the little boy with the distended belly in the picture was most likely suffering from Kwashiorkor's disease, a disease of malnutrition.

The total number of breads I sold was not enough to turn in a profit and invariably I ended up returning home with the remainder of the rolls, which were promptly consumed. One might say we ate my profits. The thing that put an end to this enterprise of mine was another incident involving this time a German soldier. As I have noted the place I stood early in the mornings to sell the rolls was in front of a small school that was now being occupied by German soldiers. As I was calling the people going to work to buy fresh rolls my shouting must have awakened one of the German soldiers who opened a window and the shutters, thrust a rifle through it and shouted in German something incomprehensible to me. The tone of his voice and the sight of the rifle convinced me quickly that the fellow meant business. I picked up my basket and went back home, thus putting an end to my first business enterprise.

The uncertainty of our existence was dramatically demonstrated when one day in early spring we were told that Uncle Elias was arrested by the Gestapo along with other lawyers and taken to a concentration camp in the outskirts of the city called Pavlos Melas. Before the war the place was used as an army barracks. The whole family was at a loss as to the reasons for the arrest. We found out some days later that the secretary of the Thessaloniki Bar Association gave the Germans, upon their request, a list of lawyers who had socialist leanings or were involved in socialist activities. Uncle Elias represented the labor unions in a number of litigations and was well known for his activities. Everyone in the house was upset and felt totally helpless. We knew from many sources that the majority of the inmates in Pavlos Melas were sent to the firing squad and we had no illusions about Uncle Elias' potential fate. Big Yiayia was still mourning the death of Uncle Sophocles, wearing a black dress every day. It was difficult to come up with comforting words to assuage her grief and sadness in the face of a recent loss of a son and at the prospect of losing another.

A few weeks passed since Uncle Elias' imprisonment at the concentration camp and to us it was this had the appearnce of a hopeful sign. At least he was not immediately marked for execution. Although the children in the family were kept out of the details of such events, we were pleasantly surprised one day to learn from my grandfather that Uncle Elias was released and was free to return home. The rumor among the members of the family was that a lot of gold sovereigns were paid out for Uncle Elias' release. The relief and joy was evident on everyone's face, especially that of Big Yiayia's and Big Pappous'.

The summer of 1942 came with a noticeable change in the weather. The temperature and humidity were high. We kept all the windows open in the house. The bustling noises from the traffic on Egnatia Street, especially when heavy German army trucks were going through, were easily audible through our open windows. Since their arrival, the Germans had begun to requisition high-rise buildings throughout the city, especially those in the center or those with a view of the sea. They were promising the families they displaced to relocate them in another apartment somewhere else in the city. Our house had a second floor with three bedrooms, a living room /dining room, a kitchen, a bathroom and a balcony that overlooked Apostolou Pavlou Street. The tenants of our second floor apartment moved elsewhere and we had placed a sign outside the house indicating that an apartment was for rent. The apartment remained vacant for about two months.

One hot afternoon we heard the sound of a military vehicle rumbling down the street and suddenly coming to a screeching halt. We looked outside and saw that it was stopped in front of our house. A German officer, probably a lieutenant, accompanied by a short man with obvious scoliosis, in a brown striped suit, came out of the car and knocked on the main door. Our first reaction was to decide whether there was something we needed to hide. The only incriminating object was my grandfather's revolver, which we had hidden in the roof of the house, but with easy access only to members of the household; it was tucked safely in a secret place. Aunt Helen asked me to go and let the men in. The man in the brown striped suit, obviously the interpreter, told me in Greek that they wanted to see the apartment that was for rent. Aunt Helen and I led them to the second floor and they proceeded to inspect every room, exchanging comments in German, which we could not understand. After a few minutes the German officer through his interpreter indicated that they would bring a family, whose apartment in the center of the city they had requisitioned. I, in my youthful defiance, bristled and blurted out "We will rent the apartment to whomever we please".

Aunt Helen looked at me, puzzled and bit her lower lip. The German officer, without waiting for the interpreter to translate my remarks, looked at me and in perfect Greek told me "Do you know what happens to those who defy the Third Reich?" I was stunned on two counts, first by the threat and second and most importantly by the fact that this foreigner spoke almost unaccented Greek. I replied with a terse word in German I had learned "Jawohl" and left the room.

Within two days following the German oficer's visit, the Sklavounos family moved in. The family included the father, Konstantinos, the mother, Lily, a daughter, Nicolette, about 14, a son, Alkis, short for Alkiviadis, about 7, and the mother's aunt. The family was a lovely group of people, polite, learned and happy to have found a decent apartment. Their moving into our house was a blessing-in-disguise as subsequent events two years later would show.

Mr. Sklavounos was a tall, handsome man with dark hair and a thick black moustache, who smoked cigarettes using an ivory cigarette holder. He was very pleasant and polite. His wife, Kyria Lily, was short, a little plump, with light brown hair and very pleasant with an attractive smile. The daughter, Nicolette, had straw blond hair that came down to her shoulders, light brown eyes and she was very beautiful. The boy Alkis had blond, curly hair and was also very pleasant. Kyria Lily's aunt was a bespectacled, old lady, with gray hair and also with a very pleasant disposition.

The move of their furniture to the second floor was not anything out of the ordinary until a small truck arrived carrying a good size piano. It could not be taken up to the second floor through the stairway because of its size, so the movers had to set up a pulley on the balcony that led to Nicolette's room and, after a great deal of maneuvering, it was brought in. Immediately, Nicolette sat down and played a sonata from Mozart. It was an unexpected and welcomed change in our drab existence and we all applauded. Our family soon established a nice rapport with the new tenants, who were quiet, pleasantly interactive and conversant. Mrs. Sklavounos, the teacher, and Aunt Helen, now a lawyer, had always topics of common interest to talk about. Mr. Sklavounos, who owned a high-class café in the center of town, was also always pleasant but did not bother to engage in non-specific chitchat unless it was a subject of importance. I frequently found opportunities to talk to Nicolette about school and her interest in music and I was impressed by how bright she was. She admitted that although she found playing the piano a rewarding activity she did not see herself developing into an accomplished pianist, especially because of the inordinate time required in practicing for it. My interaction with Alkis was minimal but Chris found more time to spend with him.

Uncle Elias' concern for the welfare of the family remained undiminished. The members of the family who were in dire need of help were Aunt Anastasia and her three children, Nikos, Michael and Soula. Because the family lost its only breadwinner in the war, Aunt Anastasia was eligible to receive a government annuity. Thanks to Uncle Elias' efforts to get through the necessary bureaucratic machinery, the annuity became effective in the fall of 1941. However, inflation was rampant and the amount of drachmas she was paid was gradually losing its buying power. Uncle Elias, being in the legal business, became aware of a law which gave war victims the right to share in a farmer's crops provided the family shared in the labor. Uncle Elias found a farmer in the village of Zorbas, which lay one hour west of Thessaloniki by horse driven wagon.

Aunt Anastasia and the three children moved to the village and lived and worked there on and off for two years during the planting, harvesting and threshing seasons. Only Aunt Anastasia and Nikos were able to work in the wheat fields, while Michael attended first grade in the village school and Soula stayed home. The arrangement provided for wheat grain to be given to the family instead of monetary compensation; part of the grain was ground into flour for the family's needs and part was sold or bartered for other types of food, such as eggs, chickens, sugar, milk and butter. The remainder of the wheat and any other food products not consumed by the end of the planting season in 1942 were brought to the house in Thessaloniki where they became part of the common pool of comestibles.

Preparing bread for the whole family was the task of my mother and Aunt Anastasia. They would prepare the dough and kneed it in a big trough. When ready, the dough was placed in a large, round pan about one and a half inches deep and 22 inches in diameter. It was then taken to Mr. Spyridakis bakery who baked it for a small fee. Big-pappous handled the allotment of the bread for each day. He would cut small slices out of the pan and weigh them on a scale, giving everyone about 120 grams (4 oz.) for the day. Everyone was careful not to eat the whole amount in one sitting. Meat and cheese, rice and potatoes were always on our table throughout the year, though in small quantities.

In the summer of 1943 in addition to Aunt Anastasia and her family, my mother, Chris and I worked on the farm. The farmer's house was big enough that an extra room was found for us. There were now five of us working in the fields and helping with the harvest, threshing and the back breaking job of picking the heads of the wheat plant that broke off as the stems were cut with the sickle during the regular harvest. The summer heat was almost unbearable as the sun beat down on us hour after hour. We found some relief by sitting for a few minutes under a plane tree and drinking some water. We walked up and down the rows of the plowed ground, picked the wheat heads one by one and dropped them in gunnysacks. We carried the sacks back to the farmhouse and the next day we took each one of them and beat them with a heavy wooden club to free the kernels. Following this, the sacks were opened and the seeds were separated from the chaff by throwing small platefuls up in the air, allowing the seeds to fall on a sheet while the wind carried the chaff away. After several such cycles, the seeds were almost completely separated from the chaff. When the wheat-head gathering was over, we probably had accumulated several kilos of grain, a small amount compared with the whole harvest but a significant addition to our daily needs.

My cousin Nikos and I also helped with the threshing. The threshing was carried out on a circular area of ground that was covered with a thick layer of harvested wheat. A wooden platform about two and one-half feet wide and five and a half feet long, with rows of flint stones on its underside, was hitched to a horse and the driver, in this case my cousin or I standing on the platform, guided the horse around the circle tens of times until it was clearly evident that the wheat kernels were freed from the head and the stems were chopped up into pieces. The horse we used was familiar with the process and required little if any prodding. One time, however, the horse became startled and began to trot faster and faster. As I tried to restrain it, it took off and the reins of rope burned my palms resulting in the loss of skin. It took more than two weeks before my hands healed and I could work on the farm again.

It was almost the end of August when we left the village and returned home. Again through Uncle Elias' efforts we rented a vineyard for that season in the northwestern end of the city. When we took possession, the grapes were almost ready for picking. The vineyard had several rows of large, white, sweet grapes and a number of rows of equally delicious red ones. The disadvantage was that the vineyard was right at the edge of a large road named Langada that began on Vardaris Square and led north and away from the city. All sorts of vehicles and people traveled this road. Our job was to make sure that the grapes were not stolen during the night since it was easy to scale the wire fence that protected the vineyard. My cousin Nikos and I spent several nights sleeping on the ground under a small apple tree. Despite the fact that it was hot in the daytime, the nights in the countryside were quite cool and we needed light blankets to break the night chill. One of the most pleasant surprises was the discovery that during the night the grapes became chilled and when we had them during breakfast their sweet taste was enhanced by their cold, crisp texture.

During the day several passersby stopped over at the vineyard and bought a few "okades" of grapes; everyone usually preferred the white ones. We carried home several bushels and the whole family enjoyed them well into fall. My grandfather decided that it would be wise to make some wine and also ouzo. He arranged for large amounts of red grapes to be brought to the basement of the house where he set up a large vat for the pressing. We used the very primitive way of expressing the juice out of the grapes, our feet; except for my grandparents and my father, we all participated in the task and seemed to enjoy it. The barrel was large enough to allow two persons at a time in the stomping and pressing of the fruit. The juice was allowed to run out through a spigot, was collected and placed in an aging barrel. I don't know which process Big Pappous used to bring about the correct fermentation, but the end product was delicious and a bit on the sweet side. The family enjoyed drinking the wine during meals and although young boys were not allowed to drink, my grandfather served us a small amount in a demitasse on rare occasions. Chris, cousin Nicos and I, however, managed to get to the storage room, where the wine barrel was kept, on the pretext that we were going to cut wood for cooking and for the coming winter months. We each carried a demitasse in our pockets and after we finished drinking two or three of them, we were full of vigor and willing to cut the wood without a grudge.

The next event was the preparation of ouzo. After pressing out the grapes, the remaining skins and the stems were distilled and the alcoholic liquid was collected in large flasks. This is called "tsipouro" and by adding the proper amount of anise it is converted into ouzo. Since no one besides grandfather drank ouzo in the family, he decided to take a small barrel, that held about eight gallons, fill it with ouzo and sell it to the taverns in the village of Zorbas. Big Pappous was gone for more than a week and when he returned, he was a changed man. He appeared quite happy and contented. He explained that he sold only a portion of the ouzo, and the larger part of it he shared with the young men in the village during friendly gatherings in one of the taverns. He was about 82 years old when he had his last such fling.

*Fig.1. Paternal grandparents. Standing, right, grandfather Nicholas Kefalides, and to his left, grandmother Evdoxia. Great grandmother to the right of Evdoxia. To the right of grandfather is his brother. (Picture taken ca. 1890 in Kirk-Kilisse, Turkey).*

*Fig. 2. Maternal grandparents. Sitting, right, Parthenis Aimatides and Maria, left. (Picture taken in Alexandroupolis, ca. 1926).*

*Fig 3. Easter Sunday picnic. April 15, 1928. From the right, sitting, my father Athanasios, my mother Alexandra, her parents Maria and Parthenis, my father's parents Evdoxia and Nicholas. From the left, sitting, Aunt Zografia, my mother's sister, and her husband, Uncle Stavros. Next to Uncle Stavros, friends of the family. Standing, on the right, Aunt Helen and to her right, her friend Chrysothea. Standing on the left, Uncles John and Thanasos, my mother's brothers. Almost every one is holding Easter eggs, ready to crack them.*

*Fig 4. Seashore picnic, Alexandroupolis, 1932. My mother , on the left, Aunt Zografia, on the right and a friend in the middle. Sitting on the sand, the author Nicholas, my brother Chris and cousin Annoula.*

*Fig 5. Family portrait, ca. 1936. Front row, from the right: Annoula, Chris, Maroula, Annoula's sister, my maternal grandparents, my parents, Aunt Zografia and Uncle Stavros, Uncle John next to my mother and me, in front of the tree.*

*Figs. 6-10, are from Uncle John's movie of the family in Alexandroupolis when he visited Greece from America in 1932.*

*6. That's me, at age 5 with Uncle Elias, my father's brother*

*7. Chris in the foreground, me behind Uncle Elias, Aunt Helen on the right next to my mother. Big-Pappous Nicholas, on the left.*

*8. My father in the foreground, Annoula behind my father, the back of Chris, and me in front of Chris. My mother and Aunt Helen in the background.*

*9. Big-Pappous, Nicholas.*

*10. Big-Yiayia, Evdoxia.*

*Fig. 11. Carnival, Alexandroupolis, 1936. I am dressed as an apache and so is my friend George on my left. His sister Aphrodite between me and Chris who is dressed as an Evzone. The two sitting boys are Chris's friends.*

*Fig. 12. In Big-Yiayia Evdoxia's back yard. Alexandroupolis, December 1933. I, in front, cousin Nicholas, Annoula and Chris.*

*Fig. 13. Uncle Triantafilos and me in Komotini, summer 1935.*

*Fig. 14. Family portrait. Alexandroupolis 1937.*
*First year student in the 8-year highschool, at age 10.*

*Fig. 15. Thessaloniki, summer 1940. Aunt Helen and me.*

*Fig. 16. German troops enter Thessaloniki, April 11, 1941.*

*Fig. 17. Classmates and friends, at a picnic in Seih- Sou, a wooded hill, in the northern outskirts of Thessaloniki. Back row, from the right, George Karavas, Aggelos Kaloyeropoulos and me. Front row, sitting on the left, Alekos Marketos and behind him Yiannis Asimis.*

*Fig. 18. Same picnic. Dancing pairs. Me on the right, Marketos on the left and Kaloyeropoulos in the background.*

Fig. 19. Our 1943 high school class. Front row, from the right, me and Kostopoulos. Second row, behind us, Kaloyeropoulos, Mihalopoulos and Saporta, a Holocaust survivor. Between the two teachers stands Kostas Melissaratos, wearing glasses. Third row, from the right, Ioulios Iosifidis, Tasos Oikonomou, Yiannis Asimis and Alekos Marketos. Next to Marketos stands Vasos Demetriadis, Alekos Maniatis, Alekos Andredis, Nikos Triantafillou, and Roulis Tziridis, in white pants.

Fig. 20. Thessaloniki, winter, 1943. Marketos, right, and I are carrying clandestine leaflets to one of the nearby high schools.

*Fig. 21. Thessaloniki, spring, 1944. The German officer who took this picture asked me to hold the bread close to the donkey. I made sure it did not touch the donkey. The bandage on my left knee was applied following a fall from a bicycle. The little boy on the left has a distended abdomen, characteristic of low protein intake, very common during the years of starvation. The condition is known as Kwashiorkor disease.*

*Fig. 22. Thessaloniki, late summer 1942. A group of our class. Fron row, from the right, Angel, one of the Jewish friends who perished in the concentration camps of Europe. Ioulios Iossifidis, in the white hat, and George Gratsanis. Standing, from the right, George Kostopulos, Joe Saporta, the other Jewish student, who survived the Holocaust. me, one who attended our school only for one year and whose name I forget, Alekos Maniatis and George Karavas.*

*Fig. 23. Athens, May 1947. Waiting for the American visa to be issued.*

*Fig. 24. Athens, May 1947. With a friend from Thessaliniki, who was active in the resistance during the occupation.*

*Fig. 25. May 1947, crossing the Atlantic on the liner "Saturnia"*

*Fig. 26. New York, Astoria Long Island, May 1947. My cousin Nicholas, the son of
Uncle George, who emigrated to America in 1920.
The two ladies are friends of the family.*

*Fig. 27. Evanston, Illinois, summer 1947, with Uncle John and Aunt Bettie in their back yard.*

*Fig. 28. Lima, Peru, 1958, with Dr. Manuel Bocanegra, in front of the Burn Unit of the Children's Hospital.*

*Fig. 29. Jane, 1960, the year we came back to Chicago from Lima.*

*Fig. 30. Birthday party for little John and little Doxa with Aunt Helen, Uncle Minas and my grandmother.*

*Fig. 31. I am standing next to my new 1960 Chevy, while visiting Evanston.*

*Happiness depends on being free and freedom depends on being courageous.*

Thucidides

*There is no easy walk-over to freedom anywhere, and many of us will have to pass through the valley of the shadow again and again before we reach the mountain tops of our desire.*

Jawaharal Nehru

## 8. The Sweeping Loss of Freedom

The German occupation and its consequences were felt in all aspects of our lives. The famine was spreading and the difficulty in finding food was fueled by the rampant inflation. The black market was thriving as the general public was trying to find ways to cope with their daily needs. While in the early days of the occupation the black market fulfilled those needs to some degree, with time it turned into profiteering activity. One welcomed sight in those difficult days was the occasional arrival of supply ships carrying food supplies from the International Red Cross. Soon after their arrival there would be long lines of people waiting to get a scoopful of rice or sugar at distribution centers. I distinctly remember the arrival of one such ship, the "Theophile Gautier" in the harbor. (Some years later I read that Theophile Gautier was a 19th century French poet and novelist.) Our most precious commodity, our lives, was fast becoming a precarious quantity. People were executed by the Germans, first in small numbers, and then by the tens and hundreds.

The victims were either innocent people, killed in retaliation following the blowing up of a bridge or the killing of a German soldier or for sheltering British soldiers after the major part of their expeditionary force had left Greece for Egypt.

As the resistance against the forces of occupation increased so did the arrests, imprisonment and executions. The Germans created the so-called "Tagmata Asphalias", the "Security Battalions" who went around arresting people, sending them to prison and executing hundreds of them simply because they were suspected of resistance activity or because someone informed on them for personal reasons. One of the goals behind their creation was to shift popular sentiment away from the Germans for their atrocities to the Greek Security Forces that were equipped and funded by the Germans.

## Unexpected Calamities

During the occupation the odds between the state of being left alone and that of being killed were wide and variable. Life was uncertain and could be wiped out from one day to the next, from one moment to another. Thessaloniki was the center of intense military preparedness on the part of the Germans because the Allies landed in Sicily in June 1943 and the Germans expected a second hit in the Aegean.

German army truck traffic in the streets of Thessaloniki increased noticeably. Army vehicles were speeding down the main avenues not obeying the speed limits. One day, in August 1943, while waiting for the light to change on the corner of Egnatia and Hagia Sofias streets I was behind a mother and her little girl of 5-6 years of age. A German army truck came up Egnatia Street and without slowing down turned right into Hagia Sofias Street and over the sidewalk where the mother and her little girl were standing. The right side of the massive truck hit the little girl with brute force killing her instantly, spilling her brains on the pavement. The mother began to wail while holding the lifeless body in her arms. The German driver came out of the cab of his truck and appeared visibly shaken. He was trying to say something to the grief stricken mother but it was of no use. She did not understand German and he could not speak a word of Greek. Soon a Greek policeman arrived and took information from the people who witnessed the fatal accident. After a while the crowd began to leave the site as an ambulance was arriving. No one knows what was the fate of the German truck driver or of the mother. In those days it was difficult to press charges against the occupiers and expect a favorable outcome.

In the spring of 1943 the Germans began to segregate the Jewish citizens of Thessaloniki into ghettos. They forced them to wear the yellow star of David. Many of the Jewish people were sent to labor camps, in the environs of the city but between March 15 and early June the majority of the Jewish citizens were deported to the concentrations camps in Europe and the last trainload left around the beginning of August.

The Jewish community represented about one fourth of the city's population. Many of its members were professionals, doctors, lawyers, merchants, manufacturers, industrialists and laborers. Many of them had considerable wealth and the larger percentage of them lived in beautiful homes. All this peaceful tranquility was shattered by a simple decree of the German command. I happened to visit one of the ghetto areas with my Aunt Stasa who with Uncle Elias had several friends and colleagues who were Jewish.

One evening my Aunt and I took a bus to the eastern end of the city and after entering the ghetto we went to a house that was occupied by several families. The mood in the house was solemn and depressed; the people spoke in low voices and some walked around aimlessly. The man we came to see, Mr. Nachmias, appeared in the living room where we were waiting, embraced Aunt Stasa, shook my hand and sat in an easy chair. Aunt Stasa had prepared a couple of dental bridges made of gold. She removed the temporary bridges, prepared an adhesive substance and inserted the gold bridges in place. I had no idea why this man needed gold bridges at this time. I, of course, as well as many of the Jewish people did not have a clear idea what their ultimate fate was going to be. They were probably hoping the gold bridges might come handy in the near future, maybe to bribe a guard or buy some food. After Aunt Stasa satisfied herself that the bridges fit well, we said goodbye to the people around us and left. We walked out of the house feeling depressed and returned home without saying much to each other. As Aunt Stasa entered her apartment and I was ready to leave, she whispered "I don't think we will ever see those friends again".

A number of the Jewish people in Thessaloniki were descendents of those who were thrown out of Spain during the Inquisition in 1492. After the year 1500 the population of Thessaloniki doubled due to a large extent to the migration of Spanish speaking Jews. Many of those who were expelled from Spain ended up, in addition to Thessaloniki, in other places such as Istanbul, Sarajevo and Alexandria. The Jewish newcomers acquired Ottoman citizenship but some kept their Spanish identity as well and when that part of Greece was freed from the Ottoman rule they also acquired Greek citizenship.

In our class at the Peiramatikon Gymnasium we had two Jewish students, Jo Saporta and Angel Marcel. Jo was tall with brown hair, green eyes and a very pleasant but quiet demeanor. His family had kept their Spanish citizenship. Angel was rather short, of slight build, with dark hair and blue eyes and a face that was rosy, and studded with freckles. Angel was quiet and did not appear to mingle with any particular group of the classmates. Unlike the Saporta family, the Marcel family did not have Spanish citizenship. Jo Saporta lived in an apartment in the center of the city, near the seashore. Angel Marcel lived in a house in the eastern part of the city.

The fate of the Jewish people of Thessaloniki, who were shipped to Europe, was unknown to the general population and to the Jews themselves. Before they were sent off to Europe, they were segregated into specified areas from which only few with special permits were allowed to come into the center of he city. Those who came into the center of the city, apparently to take care of special affairs, were very easily distinguished from the other pedestrians because they were required to wear a yellow star on their jackets. I could see on Tsimiski Street a few of them walking in pairs, the second person also a Jew, apparently acting as a designated guard. Although the opportunities to escape were available to anyone who wished to do so, their family ties were so strong that many of them refused to leave. Some, however, did so and managed to join the guerilla forces in the mountains and thus survive the war and occupation. For those who were daring enough and could find the money, escape to Turkey or Palestine was an option. A number of Jewish individuals or whole families were taken in by Greek families in villages outside Thessaloniki or in some of the islands along the Aegean Sea.

The option to escape was offered to our classmate Angel Marcel but he refused because he did not want to leave his family. His fate followed that of the many thousands who were deported to the concentration camps, never to return. He left with the early deportees in March 1943.

The fate of Jo Saporta and his family was different. Because his family retained their Spanish citizenship, they were not segregated into a ghetto. In June 1943 the Germans offered to take all the Jews with Spanish background back to Spain. However, the fear that they may also be deported forced Jo's father to arrange for an escape to Athens where they managed to hide in an apartment. In time, however, they were discovered and the whole family, father, mother, two sons and a daughter were shipped to Bergan-Belsen concentration camp. Fortunately, the whole family survived the holocaust and after the war they settled in France. During my visit to Paris in 1959, I visited with Jo and his brother who gave me a sketchy account of their ordeal. Jo got married and had three children and now has several grandchildren. My wife and I visit him and his family whenever we are in France. Jo and his wife, Lina, travel to Greece to attend the Gymnasium class reunions. Jo became a successful businessman and managed with a partner to patent a new way of making yarn, something that allowed him to retire comfortably. Jo is a unique individual not only because of his intellect but also because he is a warm and caring person and a dear friend.

My Uncle Elias, who always came up with business schemes for me and my cousin Nikos suggested that I meet with an enterprising young Jewish man who was selling silk square (10 x 10 inches) handkerchiefs. It was late February 1943 when I and my Jewish partner met in Vardari Square. We got onto a horse driven flat carriage and drove westward on what was known as Monasteriou Street; it led to the western suburbs and villages. After about one hour's drive we reached an old railroad station that was teeming with German soldiers resting on the grass or on benches next to an endless number of railroad cars. The Jewish partner quickly informed me that these soldiers were going south towards Athens and that this was a rest stop, not only for them but also for the train engine that needed to be supplied with coal and water.

I couldn't at the moment figure out how my business partner knew about the train's arrival. Later I found out that informants along various stations passed information to the resistance groups and that was how Uncle Elias and the Jewish man knew about the train's arrival. It was easy to see vendors selling cigarettes, candy and sandwiches. The souvenir handkerchiefs we were selling had on one of the corners stamped pictures of the White Tower of Thessaloniki, of Mount Olympus and even of the Parthenon. Beneath each of the pictures was inscribed in German "for my mother", "for my father", "for my sister" or "for my wife". My Jewish friend failed to instruct me on how to advertise the souvenirs. I kept saying in German "fur meine Mutter", fur meinen Vater" etc, until some of the German soldiers began to laugh. I was puzzled and I did not realize what was going on until an older German soldier indicated that I should say "fur ihre Mutter: "fur ihren Vater", etc. I quickly realized my mistake and changed my chant to the proper German form. Despite the correction in my advertising technique, at the end of the day I couldn't entice more than four or five soldiers to buy silk handkerchiefs. I failed again in my new business venture to make a profit despite Uncle Elias' good intentions.

My father found a job outside the city, working in the wheat fields, operating a combine. He would leave early in the morning and would return in late afternoon. The mode of transportation was a bus that, because of the lack of gasoline, was running by gazozen. Gazozen was a cylindrical device that burned charcoal. It was located on the right side of the vehicle just in front of the entrance door. At the bottom of the cylinder was a mechanical fan that was operated by hand to fuel the fire and the fumes produced by the burning of the coal were funneled into a combustion chamber that made the bus engine turn. The same device was also used in all the taxis that were functional. The only vehicles that were running on gasoline were those operated by the Germans.

I have already mentioned the disregard of traffic regulations by the German forces and its consequences. Another traffic incident hit very close to home. The bus that my father took to return home stopped on Egnatia Street only a block from our house and a few yards from the arch of Kamara. One afternoon, after he got off the bus and was waiting for other passengers to get off, a German truck suddenly swung around to the right of the line of traffic to bypass the bus. In doing so the truck hit my father in the back of his right leg and threw him down.

The truck driver did not even stop to see what happened. Neighbors who were passing by recognized my father, as he lay on the ground, his pants torn and the leg around the right knee bloody. Fortunately, a few yards from where the accident had happened the Clinic of the Social Security Administration was located. The neighbor and another man helped my father to the Clinic where he was given emergency treatment and sent upstairs to a patient room. In time, the family was notified of the accident and my mother visited my father who was in obvious pain. He was given some sort of an analgesic and was able to fall asleep. The following day we were informed by the Clinic that he was in need of surgical care and that he had to be hospitalized. We did not know how to proceed and we were all at a loss.

Near us was the Municipal Hospital of Thessaloniki, whose director was Dr. Konstantinos Maniatis, the father of one of my classmates, Alexis Maniatis. Their home was only a few blocks from our house, just behind Hagias Sophia's Church. I waited till two in the afternoon before I visited Dr. Maniatis. When I arrived, a tall and elegant looking lady greeted me at the door. I recognized her immediately as Alexis' mother. She had a distinctive foreign accent, since she was born and raised in Germany before coming to Greece as Mrs. Maniatis. Dr. Maniatis trained as a surgeon in Germany. After I explained that I was a friend and classmate of Alexi's and detailed the reason for my visit, Dr. Maniatis appeared in the living room accompanied by Alexis. Dr. Maniatis immediately understood the situation and without hesitation assured me that he was going to send the hospital ambulance to transfer my father to the Municipal Hospital.

The ambulance arrived at the specified time and the driver, who also served as a nurse, took a stretcher and beckoned me to follow him to the second floor of the Clinic where my father was recuperating. Since there was no elevator in the building, the driver and I realized that to carry a heavy man, like my father, down two flights of stairs on a stretcher was going to be a serious task. Somehow, we managed, as he and I marshaled our strengths, to accomplish what initially appeared as an impossible task. My father's wound that ran across the whole length of the back of the right knee was surgically treated, severed tendons were sutured and the wound closed. After two weeks he was released. Initially he required a cane to help him walk but after walking around for a week or two he was able to manage without it and was able to return to work.

The urgency to keep working in the summer time and in early fall was clearly felt by my cousin Nikos and myself. Since we were young and unskilled we were forced to resort to simple business endeavors. It was not uncommon to see young boys selling candy and cigarettes out of a shallow, square wooden case that was hanging from their necks. My cousin Nikos was the one to start first with a new endeavor and soon he began to sell candy and cigarettes. It did not take long before I got my case, cigarettes and candy and began my rounds in the center city area.

We purchased our cigarettes in packs of 20 or in cartons of 100 loose cigarettes. Many people either could not afford a pack or did not smoke more than three or four cigarettes a day and simply asked for that number. The place one could buy cigarettes wholesale was the black market in the Square Dikasterion. Most vendors would have their supply of cigarettes in large leather cases and produce them on request. Bargaining was common and competition fierce. The vendors never stayed in one spot and they constantly moved around, always wary of the police, who at times raided the area and made a few arrests. One did not ask "what are you selling?" but simply stated what one wanted. The probability was almost 100% that they were carrying it or they would point to another fellow black marketer who had it. Besides cigarettes one could buy soap, tooth paste, matches, flint-stones for cigarette lighters, saccharin, and quinine and atabrine (quinacrine), the last two sold as anti-malarial drugs.

Working the downtown streets, cigarettes sold better than candy and they had a greater margin of profit. Invariably, I would enter nightclubs and taverns where many of the customers were German soldiers. As a rule all the night clubs were dimly lit, the darkness allowing the soldiers to smooch with their Greek "girlfriends". It wasn't unusual to see a young lady sitting on the lap of a soldier, his fly open and his penis resting limply on her tiny palm. At times I wondered who was the real conqueror?

## The constant loss of simple freedoms

Curfew was imposed early after the conquest of Greece and by ten at night people had to be in their homes. The Germans periodically issued new regulations, usually to restrict freedom of assembly or travel or the prohibition of pamphlet distribution. Generally such regulations were published in the papers and at times were posted on the walls of public buildings.

One day, around five in the afternoon, I left home with my case of cigarettes and candy and headed towards the center. I reached Hagias Sophia's Street and I proceeded south towards the seashore. I was approaching the Hotel Majestic that was now occupied by the Standortkommandatur, the military police. These men had a distinctive metal plate hanging from their neck with the identifying words of their official function. We called them "petalades" from "petalon" meaning a metal plate. As I neared the entrance of the building, I shouted "cigaretta, carameles", ("cigarettes, candy"). Immediately, a military policeman called me over and as I eagerly approached him, glad that I had my first customer, he beckoned me to follow him inside. At the same time, a short man, with an unmistakable kyphosis of his spine, appeared and began to talk to me in Greek, obviously a Greek interpreter. He proceeded to remind me that it was forbidden to advertise aloud one's products after 5:00 P.M. I told him that this regulation was new to me and I was not aware of it. He indicated that "it was published in today's afternoon paper 'Apogevmatini". When I pointed out that the paper did not come out before 5:00 P.M. in the afternoon, he said, "You broke the law and you must pay a fine". When he quoted the amount in drachmas and I did the math, I realized that the amount was equivalent to the value of everything I had in my case. I was very upset not only because of the excessive fine but also because I did not have much cash on hand. Whether spontaneously or on purpose, I began to cry. The policeman came close to me and in German told me not to cry while the Greek interpreter sped to translate it.

Quick as a flash the policeman dipped his hand into one of the cartons that had the loose cigarettes and came up with a handful. After that he gave me a big smile and let me go without charging me an extra fine. My relief was indescribable. I finished my rounds early that evening and I headed home, to the comfort of my family. The surprising thing is that the German policeman became an unexpected friend; every time he saw me on the street with my case, he would mimic me by saying "cigaretta, carameles", he would dip his hand into one of the cartons and with a smile would come up with 6-8 cigarettes and then go on his way. I made sure I did not advertise my products after 5:00 P.M. Today, we would be calling this interfering with the freedom of speech. In those days we were prevented from exercising many more freedoms but, somehow, we found ways to overcome the restrictions.

There is a Greek saying, which states: "O trelos eide to methysmeno kai fovithike", ("The madman saw a drunk man and was frightened"), probably implying that the drunk man was more irrational than the mad man. In the episode I am about to tell you I was to experience the wrath of a drunkard.

As usual my cousin Nikos was first with innovative ways of selling things. One day he showed me a wooden disc, about 8 inches in diameter that was mounted at the end of a wooden handle. The wooden wheel was painted red and was divided into twenty equal pie sections. Each pie section had numbers from 1-20 painted in black at the periphery. The low numbers were repeated more frequently than the high ones. For example, numbers l, 2, 4 and 6 appeared three times each, 8 and 10 twice, 14, 18 and 20 once. At the periphery of each pie section was a small nail. When the wheel was spun around, the nails would hit a small piece of cardboard making a clicking sound until the wheel stopped, resting on a pie section with a number in it, which equaled the number of peanuts the player was entitled to receive. The peanuts were kept in a small rectangular wooden box with a handle in the middle. Each spin was worth a fixed number of drachmas and I can't remember how much each spin cost but for the same amount of drachmas one could get 1 peanut or up to 20. The game was well known to the denizens of the taverns and restaurants. People tried their luck and ended up winning a few peanuts or a lot and did not mind paying the required amount of drachmas.

One evening, as I was winding down my rounds I decided to enter a tavern on Komninon Street a few yards off Tsimiski Street. The tavern was small with a counter, a broiler behind it, a cabinet with bottles of wine and ouzo and eight small tables. As I entered, a man, who was sitting alone at a table and drinking his ouzo, called me over. He tried his luck, got a few peanuts and paid me. The next call came from a man sitting at the end of the room. He was dressed in a German soldier's uniform. A bottle of wine was at his table. He spun the wheel and the first time he got two peanuts. He tried again and this time he got only three.

I could see he was becoming agitated. He went for a third spin and got again only two. Suddenly, he got up and started shouting at me in a language that I could tell it was not German. In his drunken stupor he slurred his words and I couldn't place the language; it could have been Serbian or Croatian, not surprising since the Germans recruited people from those countries to serve in the various fronts, especially the Eastern front. He began shouting at me, his bloodshot eyes, fixed on my panic stricken eyes. He suddenly pulled out his pistol, a Luger, and thrust it up against my stomach. As I began to walk backwards, with his pistol boring into my abdominal muscles, I felt totally helpless and utterly scared. While he ranted, I kept quiet and I was hoping to reach the exit before he pulled the trigger. As we approached the bar counter, he grabbed the wheel and brought it down on the counter, splitting it down the middle in two equal parts. I was still holding on to the box of peanuts. Everybody in the tavern was frozen with fear, holding their breath, and not knowing what this drunken soldier would end up doing. Without warning, as we approached the exit, he pulled the pistol away from my stomach, made an about face and went back to his table. Obviously, finishing off the bottle of wine was of more immediate concern. I also made an about face, ran out in the street and did not stop running until I was a couple blocks away. I stopped to rest and I was out of breath, the panic still overcoming any attempt to calm myself. I finally reached our home, completely shaken.

After hearing my story, my parents and the rest of the family decided that these business ventures were not worth the dangerous risks they engendered and they agreed that putting myself in harms way was not the way to "keep me out of trouble". The next day I went to the tavern to pick up the fragments of the wheel and the owner was very apologetic about the previous night's events. He handed me the pieces of the broken wheel and said, "you were lucky". How true!

## Joining the Ranks of the Resistance

Signs of early resistance began to appear as early as the summer of 1941. Pamphlets calling on the public to resist the foreign conquerors were distributed. In May 1941, an ammunition warehouse was blown up in the town of Diabata, outside Thessaloniki. In the beginning of summer, the railway engine depot in Thessaloniki was destroyed. These early acts of sabotage led to the execution of hostages held by the Germans. The various pre-war political parties began to organize armed resistance units. Behind these acts of sabotage was Eleutheria (Liberty), the first resistance organization that was founded in May 1941. The formation of this early group included the local KKE (Communist Party of Greece), members of the Socialist Party of Greece, and a group of Venizelist officers, led by Dimitrios Psarros and Captain Mercuriou. In the summer of 1941, the first guerillas appeared on the scene. Other resistance bands appeared in western Macedonia. The first raids by these groups against the occupying forces resulted in severe German reprisals. An ambush on a German vehicle outside of Thessaloniki on September 22nd was followed by the burning of several villages on Mount Kerdyllia and the execution of their entire adult male population.

The most significant Greek resistance movement was established in Thessaloniki in April 1942 under the name "National Liberation Front" (Ethniko Apeleutherotiko Metopo or EAM). In due course followed the formation of EAM's military arm, the National People's Liberation Army (Ethnikos Laikos Apeleutherotikos Stratos, ELAS). Young high school students in the big cities and the countryside as well as university students in Athens and Thessaloniki joined the resistance movement. Of all youth organizations of resistance, the most active one was EPON (Eniaia Peneldadiki Organosi Neon-Unified Panhellenic Youth Organization). EPON was founded in February 1943 by several underground resistance and party organizations. Members of EPON carried out many important tasks: they painted resistance slogans on the walls, distributed leaflets, delivered defiant messages at night across rooftops through cardboard megaphones or through magazines that were rolled into a cone. They took part in demonstrations, helped transport supplies and delivered secret messages.

In the general public, the existence of the various resistance organizations was well known. A large number of people were considered sympathizers, individuals who were not taking part in any of the activities, such as distribution of leaflets, writing on the walls or joining large demonstrations but did declare among friends that they were hoping for the successes of the resistance forces. At least in the large cities no one was forced to join one or another of the resistance organizations.

In our Gymnasium we knew of several students in the upper classes who were active in the EPON. Among our classmates the one who I knew was a member of EPON was Alekos Marketos. In late fall 1943 Marketos asked me if I wanted to join EPON. I clearly remember the event. It was a cloudy drizzly November day, as Alekos and I were walking east on Hagiou Dimitriou Street. As we approached the movie theater Aigle, he asked me if I had heard of the Youth Organization EPON and I said I had. His asking me to join did not come as a surprise since he knew that members of our family, such as Uncle Elias and his wife Aunt Stasa were members of EAM.

I felt excited at the prospect of being involved in the resistance and I accepted unhesitatingly. I proceeded to ask what was I supposed to do and Alekos outlined some of the activities that members of EPON were involved in. These included distributing leaflets that urged people to resist the conquerors, announced upcoming events during national holidays, such as walking in large groups and putting wreaths on statues of heroes of the war of independence. Writing messages on the walls was a frequent night activity. Another activity that I particularly liked was to climb on the old walls and hiding behind one of the battlements announce the latest news of the war in the European and Russian fronts.

Our group selected me as the speaker on all occasions and the means of delivery was a simple megaphone, the German magazine "Signal", which the Germans published in the style of "Life". I would roll the magazine into a cone and speak through it. The messages were short and terse after which I would unroll the magazine and the group would blend with the people in the street. The constant participants in this type of activity included in addition to myself, Alekos Marketos, George Kostopoulos, Thanasis Mihalopoulos and Yiannis Asimis.

One such event took place on a starry night on Good Friday, in early spring of 1944. We selected the hill behind a neighborhood where blue collar workers lived. I began by saying "Prosohi, prosohi, edo i phoni tis EPON" ("Attention, attention, this is the voice of EPON"),

145

and immediately continued with the message "keep the fight against the conquerors alive" and proceeded to give them good news of the advances of the Allies in the war fronts. The neighborhood consisted of small one-story homes and as my voice was coming from the hilltop it was amplified in the quiet of the night. For the first time people opened their shutter-covered windows and started to clap their hands and shout "bravo", ignoring the regulation of maintaining darkness. At the end of the announcement I unfolded the magazine and we began to move back trying to get on the main road.

The area we were in, is known as Seih-Soo, a small forest covered with pine trees. The terrain was uneven and there were several crevices all around which because of the complete darkness, were not easy to see. Suddenly, as we were walking in pairs, we heard a loud thud and in quick succession a second one. We all stopped and called on Marketos and Mihalopoulos since they were walking ahead of the rest of us. Initially we head a grunt, which helped us approach the edge of the crevice. Marketos was on his feet but Mihalopoulos was still on the ground. Carefully we found a path that led to the bottom of the crevice. As we joined our friends, we helped Mihalopoulos get up and asked them both if they had pain anywhere and whether they could walk. There were no obvious injuries. We found Mihalopoulos' glasses lying beside him with one of the lenses and the frame broken.

We quickly got back on level ground and Mihalopoulos surprised us all by asking "Where am I, what are we doing here, who are you"? I reminded him that we just sent a message with "televoa" (megaphone) as we called the cone shaped magazine. He did not understand what I was saying. I told him it was holy week and that it was Good Friday and people were returning from their churches after they had attended services. It was customary for people to keep their candles lit as they returned home. From the vantage on top of the hill one could see the streets in the old city full of little flames as the people slowly moved uphill. Although Mihalopoulos could see the lit candles, he still could not make the connection. All this time we kept walking towards the road that led to Hagiou Dimitriou Street. Suddenly, as we were approaching Marketo's house, Mihaloupoulos slapped me hard on my back and shouted "Now I remember, you are Kefas, (my shortened last name Kefalides) and you are Marketos, now I remember what we did".

146

The relief in everyone of us was obvious and immeasurable. What surprised us again was that Mihalopoulos was more concerned with how he was going to explain the broken eyeglasses to his parents rather than with his temporary amnesia. Fortunately there was no permanent damage to his brain. In fact, he went on to receive a degree in Civil Engineering from the Polytechnic University of Athens.

The activities in EPON became more frequent. Writing slogans on the walls was done usually with two individuals, one standing at a corner to watch for any approaching Greek police or German patrols and the other writing on the wall with blue paint a popular slogan "Zeto i Eleutheria" ("Long live Freedom") or "Thanatos stous Germanous" ("Death to the Germans"). Our group was never caught painting on the walls, although there were instances where Greek police patrols intercepted other wall painting groups. If one was caught but managed to get rid of the can of paint before hand and asked what he was doing, the standard answer was "I was urinating on the wall", not an uncommon practice in neighborhood streets at night. The activity that required serious planning was the preparation for large demonstrations. These were usually organized and led by university students that included men and women. Members of EPON were always taking part, carrying placards and chanting resistance songs.

Marketos was the leader of our group and he arranged for business meetings with his superior, who in this case was a woman who went by the code name Anna, a University student. When I had first joined EPON, Marketos suggested that I should select a code name. I was surprised when he came up with three names, not from the ancient pantheon of Greek heroes or heroes from the Greek revolution of 1821 against the Turks but from the French revolution and the names were Danton, Marat and Robespier. I chose Danton but I don't remember ever using it. Everybody called me Nikos or Kefas, short for Kefalides.

Some of the activities we were asked to perform were more dangerous than others, not by themselves, but because the potential of being discovered and being caught was there and the result could have been imprisonment and even execution. One day I was told by Marketos or by another higher ranking individual, I don't exactly remember, to go to the old city known as Koule-Kafe, where an underground printing shop was operating, to pick up a large upright basket full of leaflets and bring them into the city, at the home of our friend Lakis Theodosopoulos. Lakis' home was only one block from our Gymnasium and we often had clandestine meetings there. I was given exact directions on how to find the house with the printing machine. To get there I had to wind up through narrow streets, covered with cobblestones, where the houses were small, one-story dwellings and where one could see small shops, little taverns, grocery stores and an occasional pharmacy.

When I arrived at what I recognized was the designated house I knocked at the door, which was at the street level, and when it opened, a man's voice from behind the door asked who I was and what I wanted. I gave him my name, the name of the person who sent me and the purpose of my visit. I was asked to enter into a dark basement and without much fanfare I was given a large basket full of leaflets, which were covered with a bed sheet. The door closed behind me and I began my descent towards the center of the city following the same path through the narrow streets I used earlier to climb up to the printing "shop".

It was mid-afternoon and the hot sun was beating on my head. As I walked, rather slowly, I tried to look as casual as I could, another person going home with the day's shopping. It was lunchtime and the taverns and small restaurants had set up tables on the sidewalks in front of the stores. The customers were busy eating and drinking not caring who was going up or down the street. As I approached one of the taverns I spotted two Greek policemen having lunch. My fear of being discovered was quickly manifested in my stomach feeling tight and the sweat on my forehead becoming more profuse than the hot weather justified. To my great relief the policemen were too busy eating their meatballs and drinking their ouzo to notice a young boy in short pants walking past them. Walking casually, I reached the next street where I turned quickly to the right and into another street and continued rapidly on my way with my precious cargo.

The moment I reached the Theodosopoulos house I was let inside where Lakis' older brother relieved me of the basket and thanked me shaking my hand and patting me on my back. To me this was a mission that had a lucky ending. I wished that I would not have to do it again and I didn't. However, the circumstances of our daily life were such that they generated other missions, in which I was involved, that were equally dangerous.

On March 25, 1944, the day people celebrate Greek Independence day, several of he classes of our Gymnasium attended the services at Hagia Sophia's church. Through the proper channels members of EPON were notified to gather, at the end of the church services, in the square in front of the church and proceed down to the waterfront promenade and continue eastward to the marble bust of Admiral Votsis that stood in front of the White Tower. A large group of high school and university students, men and women, gathered quickly and marched in the direction of the White Tower. I joined a small group of students who helped a young woman climb on the marble bust and place a wreath over the head of the admiral. To everyone's pleasant surprise there was no attempt either by the Greek police or the Germans to interfere with the procession or the placement of the wreath. As quickly as the procession formed earlier, it was dissolved just as fast after the placement of the wreath.

The higher administrative office of EPON was recruiting large numbers of university students into its ranks. The university students were very bright, very active and very innovative in their attempts to create recreational and cultural activities for the people in the poorer neighborhoods. The surprising thing was that these activities were taking place legally. In fact the Mayor's office of Thessaloniki, as well as private individuals and some business concerns supported them financially.

In the midst of these laudable practices, there were activities that could not be easily explained. The following incident exemplifies the situation that probably was spawned at the higher echelon levels of EPON's administration and delegated to the subordinates to be carried out. The activities that attracted large crowds were demonstrations that protested the treatment of workers, the attempt of the Germans to lure people to sign up for work in Germany or in occupied countries of Europe, or frequently protesting the lack of food or the loss of access to basic needs. These demonstrations frequently went undisturbed but the Greek police and sometimes the German forces tried to disband the crowds by shooting in the air and if that failed then by aiming their guns at the crowds. Injuries and sometimes deaths were inevitable.

I was once caught up in one of these demonstrations and when the shooting started near the Square Diikitiriou I ran to the first high rise apartment building I saw and entered the lobby. There, a young man I knew asked me to follow him to the yard in the back of the building and from there he helped me scale the wall, separating the neighboring building, and jump into its garden. From there I simply walked out into a street, a block away from the site of the demonstration.

On other occasions the enthusiasm of participating in a demonstration was short lived. It was the middle of spring 1944. The plan was to congregate in a small square in the neighborhood of Koole-Kafe, in the old city, where I was to give a speech. The crowd was modest, about sixty people, I gave my oration and the crowd became very enthusiastic and began to clap. Next to me stood Marketos and Mihalopoulos. One of the organizers shouted: " We will march to the Square Diikitiriou". On the north side of the square was a big building that housed one of the German Administrative Commands.

As we began to walk towards the Square Diikitiriou, I noticed that the crowd began to thin out, people simply ducking away at side streets, until, when we reached the Square, there were not more than five of us. Marketos, Mihalopoulos, Sokotis, a neighbor of Marketos' and me. In the square there were many people promenading. Across from the square, at the gate of the German Administration Building was a German soldier standing guard at the gate. The five of us stood in the middle of the square and before I realized two from our group hoisted me on their shoulders and we all began singing the Greek national anthem. Within a minute the square began to empty of the people promenading there and before we finished singing, the square was empty except for the five of us. Marketos' neighbor, who was wearing a cap, threw it on top of my head with the purpose of shielding my face and I began to give the same speech I had given a half an hour earlier at Koole-Kafe. What was amusing was the fact that there was no audience to hear my message. I finished my oration, got down on the ground and we all began to walk away from the square.

There are seven different streets leading away from the square and as we were walking away from it I kept throwing glances at the German guard, but he appeared to not be interested in us. Marketos' neighbor and I walked slowly, not to arouse suspicion. When we reached the street that followed a northeast direction, we said good-bye to each other and ran for our lives. This affair demonstrated the unreliability of the crowd in a demonstration, the determination of some to complete the task and above all the defiance of the enemy in the face of potential serious danger.

One spring afternoon of 1944, after playing soccer in the square in front of the Achiropoiitos Church, a couple of the boys were asked to approach two of our friends, Marketos and Kalogeropoulos. I was several feet away from the spot where the discussion was going on and I could not hear the conversation. One of the boys they were talking to was my brother Chris and the other was Mihalopoulos' brother Nikos. Before I had realized, the two boys were gone and I did not bother to inquire where they had gone. In time everyone left the Church square and I walked to my mother's brother's house in the upper part of the city, where I was spending the nights. One reason for moving to Uncle John's house was that the Germans requisitioned in late Fall of 1943 our Gymnasium, Peiramatikon and we moved to an old building in Koule-Kafe, the Manos School, which was very near my Uncle John's house.

Very early the next morning my mother came to my Uncle John's house, woke me up and in tears told me that Chris did not come home the night before. She told me that something bad had happened to him and that I was responsible for it. She instructed me to find Chris without fail.

Right there and then I began to think and act under the subconscious drive that had as its main and only purpose to find Chris. I left my Uncle John's house and went immediately to Marketos' home. It must have been 6:30 in the morning when I reached Marketo's home. I told him that Chris did not go home the night before and I asked him whether he knew what happened. Without hesitation he told me that he was sent to a house in the upper city just behind the old walls to meet a man by the name Mr. Apostolides and deliver a message. Alekos gave me the man's address. I indicated to him that it would be wise to leave his home and hide someplace. I immediately returned to Uncle John's house where my Aunt Despina's sister, Olga, also lived. I asked Olga to go to the homes of some of our classmates and friends who were members of the group to warn them that Chris was probably caught and that they should hide. I notified the remainder of our group, including Thanasis Mihalopoulos, Yannis Asimis and Angelos Kalogeropoulos.

I was moving about like an automaton. I went back to Koule-Kafe and found Mr. Apostolides's house. I knocked on the door and a middle-aged man opened the door. The moment he saw me, his right hand reached for his right hip pocket. Although I did not see a gun, I am certain he was getting ready for any eventuality. I introduced myself and told him that my brother visited his home the evening before. He did not deny it, all the time keeping a calm and polite attitude. He explained that Chris came the evening before, knocked on his door and when his wife answered he proceeded to read her the message he was given, namely that Mr. Apostolides should stop harassing the neighbors because the resistance forces would kill him. Mrs. Apostolides was startled by such a pronouncement coming from a fifteen year old young boy and very cleverly suggested that they go to the tavern that they owned across the street and give Mr. Apostolides the message himself. Here was a totally naïve and inexperienced boy following his instinct to do his duty. After he repeated the message to him, Mr. Apostolides beckoned to two Greek undercover policemen,who were drinking in the tavern, and handed Chris over to them.

Mr. Apostolides, in his very cool attitude recounted the events of the previous evening emphasizing the fact that he was very concerned and frightened by Chris's message and so he felt compelled to hand him over to the police. I repeated to him that my mother and the whole family were very saddened and concerned with Chris's arrest and felt totally helpless. With a sandwich wrapped in newspaper and a copy of the Old Testament in my hand- we had religion class that day- my plans were to return to school later that morning.

We began to walk toward the center of town and all this time not once did it occur to me that I might also be walking into a lion's den. Mr. Apstolidis assured me that he was going to try to find him. Each time we came upon a police station, he would go inside to inquire about Chris's whereabouts and then return to tell me that he was not there. The idea that I should simply walk away and disappear did not once enter my conscious mind. I lacked the true clandestine mind. I had promised my mother that I would try to find Chris and that was one of the overriding thoughts in those moments. Another thought that I distinctly remember I contemplated was that I needed to get close to Chris to find out what they had done to him and how much did the police find out. The next to the last police station we stopped at was only two blocks from our house, across from the Sindrivani Square, so named because of a beautiful marble fountain that adorned its center. I knew the name of this police station as the "Special Security Police". After some time Mr. Apostolides came out and told me that there was one more station he was going to try and chances were that Chris would be there.

We proceeded east on Egnatia Street for about a quarter of a mile and we stopped outside a large white, three-story building. Mr. Apostolides went in and when he came out he told me "he is in there". I asked whether I could go in to see him and he nodded. We entered the building together, he pointed at an office and after I entered he left.

Here I was, in the presence of a high official, with three silver stars on his epaulettes indicating that he had the rank of a captain. He was sitting behind his desk, looking at me with a serpentine calm, when suddenly he lashed at me and asked who I was and what I wanted; things he already knew. It was probably an attempt to startle me and maybe confuse me. He asked me which school I attended and who were my friends. I replied "Peiramatikon", and "all my classmates" to his questions. He wanted to know what my friends and I were involved in during off school hours and I replied "playing games and going to the movies ". At one point I indicated that I had to go to school that morning and pointing to the copy of the Old Testament I told him that I was going to miss my religion class. He looked at me with a half smile and with a slight bobbing of his head he told me "you are going to miss a lot of classes, don't worry about this one".

He stopped talking for a moment, lit a cigarette and as if flipping the pages of a book he changed the subject and started asking me about Elias Kefalides, my uncle. I knew that Uncle Elias was a left wing follower and that with the aid of the Greek police he had been arrested by the Gestapo. I also knew that he and Aunt Stasa had left Thessaloniki for Athens in late 1943. I replied that I did not know where he was. His next question was "Did he go to the mountains?" implying that he had gone to join the revolutionary army ELAS (Greek Popular Liberation Army). Again I said emphatically, I did not know.

My interrogation had suddenly changed direction, as a policeman came into the room and announced that the prisoner was across the hall. The officer asked me to follow him and when we entered the room I saw Chris. He was standing quietly with his head bent downward. His face and eyes puffy. There was another officer in the room and with a rough and commanding voice asked Chris "Who is this?" pointing at me. Chris did not reply and I could see that he was visibly disturbed, not knowing what to say. Obviously, he did not want to implicate me by saying that I was his brother. I, however, broke the silence and said "I am his brother", at which point the officer who accompanied Chris slapped both sides of my face, hard, saying, "I did not ask you!" I did not know what the point of the meeting with Chris was, but after that short encounter we were both taken to adjacent prison cells across the yard of the main building.

The prison cells were small, about 4 x8 feet, with concrete walls, and a metal door with a small window having two vertical metal bars. There was no chair, box or bench to sit on. The only item in my room was the remnant of an overused small broom. To rest, I had to sit on the cement floor and to sleep, I rested my head on the little broom. For the first time since our arrest Chris and I exchanged words through the door windows. I asked him how he was and what happened after he was brought in. He was interrogated extensively and was beaten severely by hand and with a horsewhip. The whereabouts of Uncle Elias was of primary interest to the Police as evidenced by an after midnight visit by a police officer who woke me up to ask me again where Uncle Elias was. Waking up a prisoner from a deep sleep is a method often used in situations like ours. The moment after being awaken, a person is more likely to reveal information that otherwise he might not; it is a moment when one's guard is down. I had said before "I don't know" so often that instinctively I said "I don't know".

Even though members of the resistance were arrested with regularity and imprisoned, whether by the Greek police, the Gestapo or the Security Battalions, members of our group were never advised or schooled on how to behave when we were interrogated; what we should say and how we should say it. What to say if we were asked about our activities, our circle of friends, the whereabouts of people we might have known or of members of our family.

On the second day after my arrest we were moved to a room in the sub-basement of the main building. It was a fairly large room with a wooden floor and regular windows that opened on the inside. Iron bars ran up and down the windows.

That afternoon our mother was allowed to visit us. The reunion was very emotional and she broke down crying as soon as she entered the room. Here was a mother who did not exactly know the reasons for our arrest and imprisonment. She appeared visibly nervous because she could not openly ask the questions she wanted to ask; a policeman was standing outside our room by the open door. She kept running her hand up and down our backs and our arms, obviously an attempt at caressing us and may be to make sure there were no broken bones. We turned the conversation around and we began asking her about everyone in the house. Everyone was fine in our home but very saddened and deeply concerned about our state and our uncertain future. The only one who did not know of our arrest was our father who was working in the countryside and there was no way to get in touch with him. After about a half hour our mother's visit ended, she left a basket containing a fresh change of clothes, fruits and bread with cheese and returned home. We did not see her again until she visited us a few days later at the Vayianos concentration camp.

On the morning after our mother's visit another member of our group was brought into our room. Angelos Kalogeropoulos was taken from his home that same day. Early in the afternoon a policeman came into our room and put handcuffs on all three of us. With a rifle hanging from his shoulder he asked us to get out of the room and proceed outside the building and into the street. It was a hot sunny summer day in June 1944 and the walk was slow and lumbering. The three of us, Chris, Angelos and I were walking ahead of the policeman who was following also at a slow pace. We asked him where he was taking us and he replied in a terse fashion "Sta grafia tis Gestapo" ("To the Gestapo offices").

We all had heard of the Gestapo and its activities in the city. We concluded that our immediate destination did not bode well. We had heard of their brutal treatment of prisoners and their executions. We were walking through old neighborhoods. The streets were quiet as most people were taking their afternoon siestas. Suddenly, Angelos, I am sure in jest, said to the policeman that if he wanted he could escape at the next corner. The statement took Chris and me by surprise, for three reasons. First of all, it was daring, something Angelos would likely dare say, but I wasn't sure whether he would carry it out. Second, he had a slow lackadaisical walk and I couldn't see how he could outrun the policeman and third, the policeman had a rifle. Without losing his composure, the policeman turned to Angelos and pointing his rifle at him said "You try that and I will turn your ass into a sieve".

We all fell into a soporific silence until we arrived at the building that housed the Gestapo. The policeman led us up a stairway into a large office that was illuminated only by the daylight pouring through the windows. At the end of the room we could see a woman with blond hair and high heels alongside a man interrogating a young person and with each question beating him, the woman with a leather strap and her associate with his fists. The questions had to do with the whereabouts of a boat. Every time he replied, "I don't know", the beating continued. For a moment I asked myself whether we were going to be given the same treatment. Within a short time the woman approached the policeman and spoke to him in Greek. As she stood near us I noticed that she was a beautiful, attractive woman and I asked myself how could a beautiful person like her behave with the sadistic brutality she displayed towards the prisoner.

The policeman gave this woman what appeared to be our files and walked into another room. Soon a tall blond man in civilian clothes approached us. After exchanging a few words in German with another man, he beckoned us to follow him. We went out in the street, still in handcuffs, and walked north to what we soon found was the Vayianou concentration camp. As we walked, the German guard gave us another surprise. He reached into his pocket, pulled out an automatic pistol and rocking it in his palm he said in perfect Greek "If you have any notions of trying to run away, look at this" pointing at his pistol. I don't know whether the policeman who took us to the Gestapo offices mentioned the small episode with Angelos Kalogerapoulos or whether the Gestapo did not trust their fearful reputation to explain the German guard's attitude.

Vayianou prison was an old building. It was a psychiatric hospital with its isolation rooms, its windowless rooms, and its iron bars. When we arrived there, the German escort handed us to a Greek policeman who took Chris and me to a room already occupied by another group of five prisoners. Angelos was taken to a separate room. There were separate rooms where women were held as we discovered the following day during our recess period. Men and women were not allowed to come in contact; as we were returning to our rooms after spending a half hour in the yard, the women were being herded out of their rooms. That same afternoon a policeman gave us a buzz haircut

Our lives in the concentration camp were very restricted. We were kept locked in a room with only a skylight and we were allowed a few minutes every morning to clean up. The only memorable person among the inmates in our room was an older person, probably in his early sixties. He was tall and well built. He enjoyed talking about his experiences in the village where he lived. He was a farmer and worried about the fate of the crops in his farm. The German court found him guilty and he was sentenced to die. Although he tried to amuse us with funny stories, frequently he would admit his concern about being sentenced for execution. He told us bits and pieces about his interrogation in the Gestapo offices and mentioned the young, beautiful lady who used a wide belt to beat him and how the buckle came up to his face once and broke one of his front teeth. Many of the inmates in Vayianou were kept there until they were taken to the concentration camp Pavlos Melas where in most instances they were executed. The old man related that his interrogation was close-ended. He used the analogy of the white-black handkerchief. "If they showed you a white handkerchief and asked you what color it was and you said 'white', then they would beat you. After persistent questioning, if you changed your answer and said "black" then they would beat you again", implying that the answer they wanted was irrelevant to the question. The old man, however, never told us what they wanted to know.

The days at Vayianou continued without much change in our daily routine, save for the fact that our mother brought us, on two occasions, a basket with fruit, bread, cheese and clothing. One afternoon, near the end of the second week of our internment and during our recess, a policeman opened the main gate and an older lady stuck her head through. I immediately recognized Mrs. Kalogeropoulos, Angelos' mother. She acknowledged my presence and told me in a very excited and happy tone "Ilthame na paroume ton Angelo" ("We came to take Angelos out"). While she was waiting at the gate, Angelos came to the courtyard carrying a bundle of his belongings; he said goodbye to us and walked out the gate into his mother's arms. The guard closed the gate and Chris and I looked at each other with mixed feelings of puzzlement, hope and dread, with hope the overriding one. We continued our milling around in the courtyard and within fifteen minutes of Angelos' leaving, a policeman approached us to tell us that we were free to go. We went to our room, picked up our belongings and said goodbye to our roommates, especially the old man, whom we never saw again.

Chris and I began walking along a long street towards the streetcar depot where the cars that went through Kamara were stationed. As Chris and I were walking we heard young children's voices shouting "Niko, Naki" ("Nakis, a diminutive of his second name Parthenis") and as we turned to look back we spotted our mother running towards us, also shouting "Niko, Naki". Chris and I began to run towards our mother until we reached her and fell into her embrace. She told us that she came to Vayianou to bring us fresh clothes and food and the guard told her that we were set free. Fortunately, there were a couple of young boys playing in the street in front of Vayianou and our mother inquired if they had seen the two of us leave the prison. They told her that the two brothers were walking towards the streetcar line and they took off trying to reach us before we boarded the tram. The excitement on our mother's face was indescribable between wiping her tears of joy and laughing nervously.

We arrived home to the surprise of everyone, since no one knew beforehand that we were going to be freed. The atmosphere was jubilant. The hugs and kisses were unstoppable. The only person missing was our father who had gone to work after his last visit home. During his last visit, the week before, as he was approaching our house, a neighbor lady, whose specialty was gossip, ran out of her door to greet my father and inform him that the Germans had arrested both of us. That came as a sudden shock to him, who only uttered the word "ksepediastica" ("I have been deprived of my children"), before he passed out.

One of the things I did after we got home was to change my clothes and underwear. As I was taking my undershirt off, a woolen undershirt that my mother knit for me, I noticed innumerable little creatures, imbedded into the woolen fabric. I immediately realized that they were lice. In the darkness of our prison room I had not seen them and was not aware of their presence. Instinctively I began to pull them out one by one and crush them in the "classical" way, between my two thumbnails. They were gorged with blood, my blood. When my mother saw what I was doing she asked me to stop and said, "We have a better way of getting rid of them, by boiling the shirt and then throwing it in the trash" and with this last act I got rid of any last vestige of physical association with the Vayianou concentration camp.

We soon began to ask ourselves who might have intervened to have us released from prison? Although it was not openly articulated, the consensus was that Mr. Sklavounos, who lived on the second floor of our house, used his influence through the contacts he had with the police.

It was inevitable that I was expected to behave myself after my release. I did not seek out my classmates who went into hiding. Two days after my release, I began attending classes in the Manou School where Peiramatikon was still in operation. The majority of classmates knew about my imprisonment and some asked specific details about life in prison. I was reticent in discussing any details and the questions ceased. Because of my shaved head, I decided to wear a trayiaska, the Greek equivalent of the paper-boy's hat. One of our teachers, Mr. Karasotos, called me over and asked me to take off my hat and not to wear it in school. In those days you did not argue with a tough teacher and I stopped wearing it. Angelos and I were the only two students with shaved heads and we were proud to display them. School ended in mid-July and by fall we were both sporting thick sets of wavy brown hair.

## Keeping busy with innocuous activities

The summer was full of sunny, hot days and I felt especially eager to explore activities I did not usually pursue. A few of my neighborhood friends and I started going o the beach. My swimming ability was not something to brag about and our frequent trips to the beach helped improve my performance.

Another activity that I began in earnest was painting in watercolors. Our house was surrounded by ancient and not so ancient structures. Within a few yards was the Arch of Galerius, the Kamara, as we knew it. In the opposite direction was the Rotonda. The old cylindrical Roman style structure that at times had served as a church, mosque and museum. A tall minaret, minus its uppermost section, stood in its courtyard. Behind our house and in plain view from the terrace was a Byzantine church and across from Kamara was another similar church. I began painting these structures with eagerness. The one that was a little more complex to draw and paint was Kamara with its complete and partially ruined arches and the sculptures on its outer walls depicting Roman soldiers in victory processions. The Byzantine churches presented the least challenge because of their symmetrical and simple architecture. The structure I had enjoyed painting most was the Rotonda. I had visited the inside and I was particularly amused when standing in the center of it I would whisper, speak loudly or clap my hands and the acoustics were fantastic; there would be a clear, crisp echo, repeating every sound eight times. It is for this reason that the Germans used the Rotonda to give piano concerts for small army groups.

The Rotonda was the object of not only the musically inclined German army but also of many soldiers who made it the object of their artistic endeavor. When I began painting the structures around our house, I used ordinary bond paper. One day, looking outside my bedroom window I saw a German soldier sitting on a small folding chair and painting the Rotonda and the adjacent minaret. He was using thick, rough-surface paper from a large pad. Next to him and resting against the wall of our house was a German submachine gun. For a fleeting second I contemplated finding a way to steal the submachine gun but the attractiveness of the drawing paper won out. I decided to go out of the house and approach the soldier-painter. He looked up at me, and with a smile he greeted me in German. I showed him my painting of the Rotonda and he appeared to be impressed. Then without hesitation, I pointed at his drawing pad and indicated that I wanted a sheet of paper. He immediately tore three sheets and gave them to me. I was overjoyed and I left thanking him in German, "Vielen Danke". The high quality of drawing paper made a tremendous difference in the way the colors were spreading in a continuous way as I painted. When I finished painting the Rotonda and the minaret anew, I could see clearly the better quality of workmanship. In the winter of 1945, after the liberation, our school had organized an art exhibit and I submitted three of my paintings. The art critic from the newspaper "Fos" liked my work and made some very favorable comments.

In the year 1944, another story was evolving. My mother's brother, Uncle John, gave me for my use a used blue striped suit and asked that

I take it to a tailor who could turn it inside out and adjust it to my size. Although, the suit was shiny from frequent cleaning and pressing, because of the high quality of the material, the inside was like new. Across from our house lived a tailor, Kyrios Vasos, short for Mr. Vasilis (Mr. Basil). The inside of his shop was visible from my room window and I detected some activity. He was thought to be a good tailor and that he did a good job when he was sober. He was always pleasant and eager to carry out an intelligent conversation. It was the middle of January when I walked into his shop; he took my measurements and examined the suit. He commented on the good quality of the fabric and told me that the suit would be ready within four to six weeks.

This very small and simple verbal exchange between two logical beings was to evolve into an epic saga. The four weeks came and left and then the six weeks came and left and there was no suit. Every time I would walk into Mr. Vaso's shop he would be busy doing something with the blue pieces of cloth lying on his worktable. Needless to say, he was always drunk whenever I visited his shop and he kept promising that the suit would be ready in a week or two. I could easily tell that he had no other jobs to finish and I concluded that the only reason for his delay was his constant state of drunkenness that prevented him from completing his job.

The weeks dragged and my visits across the street continued while Mr. Vasos was always apologetic and continually promising to finish the suit in a few days. I was becoming desperate and the thought of taking whatever he had finished to another tailor entered my mind but we had given Mr. Vasos enough of the promised cost for the job that we were reluctant to change tailors. The disparity between his promises and his actual working on the suit reached comical levels when one day as I was crossing the street to visit Mr. Vasos, he had seen me coming and as I entered he shop he grabbed an iron and began pressing the trousers with his left hand while holding a pot with his right in the act of urinating. The scene was pathetic. Mr. Vasos, drunk, his speech slurred, trying to accomplish several manual and physical functions with the dexterity of a dog chasing its own tail but never catching it.

The occupation ended and the liberation came on October 30, 1944 and my suit was not ready. Sometime in late November, Mr. Vasos informed us that the suit was ready. I went over to his shop and picked up the suit that looked like new, clean and well pressed. When

I entered our house my first task was to try it on. I put it on and stood in front of a mirror to admire the results of Mr. Vaso's sartorial skills. The jacket fit me perfectly, the lapels flat against my chest, the sleeves, the right length. Oh what a shock, when I looked at the trousers. I noticed immediately that the left leg was shorter than the right. My disappointment was indescribable. There was very little I could do. When my mother saw the sloppy job with the trousers, she said: Don't worry, I will fix them for you. I replied: "Are you sure mama you can do this"? She indicated that she would roll the bottom of the trousers to form a bouffant over short boots, in the style of the British and U.S. soldiers' uniforms. I bought a new pair of short boots and my mother very skillfully redid the bottoms of the trousers so that they would look even. However, even the masterful change by my mother could not assuage my deep disappointment. Not until early in 1945 and after the liberation did packages begin to arrive from America. Uncle John, my father's brother, sent us numerous packages with all kinds of clothing, including slightly used but elegant suits.

As the summer progressed my friends and I organized little excursions either to the beach or to the small, wooded hill of Seih-Soo, north of the city. During our visits to Seih Soo, sisters and girl-cousins of members of our group would accompany us. My cousin Annoula was among them and so was Sitsa, the sister of Lakis Theodosopoulos, whose whole family was involved in the resistance movement. We usually selected a flattened spot on the hill for dancing, placed a portable phonograph in the middle of it and danced to the modern tunes of the era, usually waltz and swing. After lunch we would all gather under a tree and sing popular songs. It was pure fun.

One morning while I was visiting with Nicolette, the daughter of Mr. Sklavounos, in the apartment above us, we began talking about the antiquities that surrounded the city and especially our neighborhood. The discussion came around to the minaret that was in the courtyard of the Rotonda and Nicolette, out of the blue, asked me if I wanted to climb the 120 or so steps up to the top. Since I had not tried this fete before, I accepted. We went to the Minaret and promptly began climbing the narrow, winding stairway with me leading the way. We reached the top and came out on the circular balcony, slightly exhausted. The view was breathtaking. We had never seen the city from a height of nearly120 feet. We looked around in the distance and we could clearly see the waterfront, the White Tower and the ships in the harbor. Looking to the north we could make out the walls behind the old city, the little forest of Seih-Soo and the Mount Hortiatis. To the east we recognized the University building and, behind it, the suburb of Saranta Ekklesies. Having taken in the spectacular views from the height of the tiny balcony we stated our descent to the bottom of the long, twisting stairway and out into the courtyard.

The year 1944 saw a flurry of air raid activity by the RAF. The main target was the seaport but frequently some planes strayed from their intended targets and the bombs fell on populated areas killing several people. During these air raids everyone from our family and the Sklavounos family ran down to the basement where we huddled against the wall and close to each other. We all managed to bring with us metal pots and pans, which we put over our heads for protection. Every time there was an explosion that was close enough to shake the house, we huddled closer together. The view of a bunch of young and old wearing metal covers on our heads was amusing and reminiscent of the characters in the "Our Gang" movies. The end of each air raid was met with great relief and each one of us returned to the job we were engaged in before we donned the pots and pans. During one of these raids bombs fell on the northern suburbs of the city in a neighborhood outside the old walls, where the roofs of the homes were covered with corrugated tin plates. As the flares shot out of the bombers illuminated the sky above these shacks, the pilots mistook them for military installations and unloaded their bombs. In one of these little homes there was a wedding celebration in progress and many in the wedding party were killed. The general public believed that little if any serious damage was inflicted to the German installations by these raids, although the loss of human life was disproportionately high.

Going to the movies or to an occasional stage-theatre was the principal form of recreation for young teenagers. The movie theater "Dionysia" was a favorite of mine as well as of other classmates for three reasons. It was located in the very center of Thessaloniki, it showed action movies and best of all it was owned by Tasos Oikonomou's uncle, his mother's brother. Tasos Oikonomou was not only an intelligent young man but also a truly caring friend. He would gladly help with school homework and would generously loan books from an extensive library that his father, a physician, had built. On top of all this he would almost never say no when asked for a favor and the favor we shamelessly would ask for was to ask his mother to give us a note telling the movie manager to let one or two of us in free. The movie manager had no say in the matter and would let us in grudgingly.

On two of these occasions, in late summer, as I was walking down the aisle with the theater lights still on, I came across Mr. Apostolidis, the Gestapo collaborator who handed Chris to the two policemen. Immediately he said "Hello" to me and asked me how I was. Fortunately I kept my cool and I replied "Very well". Both encounters had no apparent consequence. Within a few weeks, in early September 1944, I received information that suggested that a branch of EAM was planning to assassinate Mr. Apostolidis. I panicked because of the recent events of his involvement in Chris' arrest in late spring and the possibility of the authorities trying to link his death to us. The truth was that Mr. Apostolidis was an active member of the Gestapo and as he was menacing members of the resistance for some time, the police were expecting an attempt on his life from one of the resistance organizations. When I voiced my concern with contacts of the EPON about the attempt to eliminate him, I was told not to worry. Indeed, within a few weeks we heard and read in the papers that Mr. Apostolidis, a former captain of the Greek army, was assassinated, A day after the announcement we heard loud music coming from Egnatia Street. Chris and I walked over and we saw a funeral procession moving east, a casket draped with the German flag while a German army band played a funeral march. An important chapter in our lives was closed.

*The Greek people rose in defiance of an oppressive conqueror, for the liberation of the human mind and the liberation of the human body from the shackles and restrains of the murderous occupation and for the end of the indiscriminate killing.*

# 9. The Liberation

## The Germans abandon Thessaloniki

The time of the liberation of Greece and of Thessaloniki in particular was getting closer. The allied forces were pushing the Germans back to their homeland and the fear of their being cut off into the Balkan Peninsula forced them to plan an orderly retreat from Greece. On the other side, as early as March 1944, reserve units of the resistance forces of ELAS were moving into the neighborhoods surrounding Thessaloniki. Although the Germans had planned to evacuate by mid-fall, they never gave up their murderous and sinister way. On September 2, 1944, German units under the command of officer Fritz Schubert, killed 246 inhabitants of the village Hortiatis, near Thessaloniki, as reprisal to an attack by ELAS on a German army unit near the village. This barbarous act exemplified the determination of the Germans to respond with brutal force to any military activity against them, even as the occupation was coming to a close.

The resistance forces were battling not only German units, but the hated Security Battalions as well. As late as October 16, 1944, in the neighborhood Neapolis, the reserve units of ELAS in Thessaloniki fought a six-hour battle with a large segment of the Security Battalions,

The outcome was in favor of the reserve units, thus assuring control of most of the neighborhoods by the resistance forces. Gradually, during the second half of October, the main body of the German forces retreated toward the western borders of the city while it maintained control of the main strategic points, including the military airport at Sedes, the seaport, and the electricity generating stations. All through the period of gradual evacuation there was no serious attempt by the resistance forces to impede the withdrawal of the German forces.

On October 29, German army trucks were rumbling down our street, Apostolou Pavlou, toward Egnatia Street. The trucks were open and we could see soldiers sitting on side benches. As the trucks passed by our house, we could see the faces of the German soldiers, painting a subtle sense of satisfaction with their smiles, eager to leave the land they tortured and burned, that in turn repaid them with the heroic acts of sacrifice and altruism of its people. Many of the soldiers let streams of unused telegraph tape unroll from the open rear of the trucks. We knew inside us that it was a matter of hours before we could cry out "We are free, we are free".

On October 30, the withdrawal of the Germans was complete. In the afternoon of the same day large units of ELAS entered Thessaloniki. People flooded the streets carrying flags and placards, shouting "Long Live Liberty", "Long Live Greece", "Long Live ELAS". The people were beside themselves. The scenes in the streets resembled a delirium, a pandemonium, as people hugged and kissed and ran up and down the streets. For the first time, authentic metal megaphones made their appearance. No more "Signal" magazines rolled into cones. I was waiting for such an opportunity. I managed to get a megaphone, two and a half feet long, and ran out speaking to the crowds, through neighborhood streets, without fear of being arrested, or of being shot. Crowds were milling in the streets, singing patriotic songs well into midnight. In the days that followed, the air of freedom was felt by everyone, freedom of expression, freedom of assembly, freedom of the press, with innumerable publications appearing in bookstores and bookstalls on street corners. The next four months were full of rejoicing.

# Returning to our school

School classes were moved back to our own school, Peirametikon. A change in everyone's attitude was clearly evident. The teachers were more relaxed. They were more tolerant of students turning their work assignments in late. Some of the teachers would carry out routine conversations with students, something we did not experience before. Usually, during recess, the teachers would sit together on the hard benches and discuss their issues among themselves. The students stood together and talked about their day to day experiences. Now, however, there was an atmosphere of relief, of being alleviated from an oppressive weight. The teachers would smile when asking a question, the stern countenance having been replaced by a gentle expression.

All our classmates were back in school. For the first time we began to talk about our future aspirations. In a little more than a year we were going to be ready to enter university studies. The tendency was to follow one's parent's profession. Four of our classmates had fathers who were physicians and others had close relatives who were doctors, dentists or pharmacists. It is not surprising that after we graduated from Peiramatikon, seven out of seventeen applied to medical school and were all accepted. These included: Alekos Andreadis, Ioulios Iossifidis, Mimis Kajakides, Angelos Kalogeropoulos, George Kostopoulos, Tasos Oikonomou and myself. Future development of these seven varied widely, as later events would show. The remaining classmates followed different professions. Kostas Melissaratos became a pharmacist, following his family's tradition and Vasilis Dimitriadis a chemist; he spent his professional life working for Bayer Pharmaceuticals until his retirement. George Gratsanis joined his father in his typography shop and eventually took over the business when his father retired, while Sotiris Tjirides, though the son of a pharmacist, chose to follow an administrative career. George Karavas and Nikos Triantafillou became lawyers, following their fathers' foot steps. Alekos Maniatis, although the son of a physician became an electrical and mechanical engineer, while Thanasis Mihalopoulos, the son of a teacher, graduated with a degree in civil engineering. Alekos Marketos and Yiannis Asimes became mathematicians and taught in Gymnasiums reaching the rank of School Principals.

## Political extremism and unrest

By early December 1944, the political atmosphere changed in a rapid fashion. The political factions, representing either the right or the left wing were fighting the German and Italian conquerors but were also fighting among themselves and became more demonstrative of their intentions. The right wing conservatives who favored the return of King George embraced the forces that collaborated with the Germans and Italians and formed armed units, which included members of the Security Battalions. Athens became the center of armed engagement following the shooting into a demonstration of EAM followers by the police that resulted in several deaths. This initial encounter flared into an open shooting match between units of ELAS and British armed forces resulting in several deaths. The fighting finally stopped and a peace agreement was signed in Varkiza on February 12, 1945. The peace agreement called for ELAS to turn in its weapons within two weeks. The terms of the agreement were breached by both sides and this led to a new polarization of the opposing factions that resulted into a harsh civil war that lasted until 1949.

The end of the civil war was a severe political loss for the forces of the left but not a military one. The subsequent two and a half decades were characterized by a continual persecution, imprisonments, internal exiles and deaths of many followers of the left. One such victim was my mother's older brother Kyriakos. Uncle Kyriakos was married to Aunt Afentoula and they had three children. Parthenis who was born in 1927, Maria born in 1933 and Zoe in 1939. Uncle Kyriakos was a carpenter whose specialty was making quality furniture. He taught the craft to his son Parthenis. Uncle Kyriakos' family visited us frequently in the summers before the war in Alexandroupolis and Parthenis and I spent pleasant times going to the beach, swimming and exploring the various neighborhoods. With the onset of hostilities between Greece and Italy in 1940, Uncle Kyriakos was drafted into the army. He was already 45 years old and he was sent to serve in the County of Evros near the Turkish and Bulgarian borders.

After the invasion by Germany and the occupation of Greece, the District of Thrace was handed over to the Bulgarians. Uncle Kyriakos moved to the region of County Evros that remained under the control of the German army and from there he entered Turkey. While there he joined the resistance and moved back into Greece. His activities were clandestine, being mainly a liaison between the forces of EAM in the cities and ELAS in the mountains. The civil war found him on the side of the left and in 1947 he was arrested, imprisoned and tortured by the government forces. He was sent to different prisons and finally exiled to the Island of Giaros where he died at the age of 55. This is a tragic example of the persecution, terror, torture and eventual death that was the fate of many people who fought for their country against the foreign conquerors. Uncle Kyriakos death left Aunt Afentoula and her three children to fend for themselves. It was again the generosity of Hadji-Pappous, my maternal grandfather, who donated a Singer sewing machine to Aunt Afentoula to pursue her talent as a seamstress. This vocation saved her family in the next few years until cousin Parthenis opened his own business as a carpenter.

## Finding Aesculapious at the University of Thessaloniki

Our last year of the eight-year high school resumed in the fall of 1944 and continued until July 1945. However, we were not given our diplomas until December 20th of that year to makeup for the time lost during the war between Greece and Italy and the German invasion. With the end of the school year in 1945, came also the end of the eight-year high school system. I know that despite the conscientious and diligent efforts of our teachers, our education at the end of eight years was lacking in depth of knowledge of the major subjects such as chemistry, physics, biology and mathematics because of the intervening war years. Our teachers knew that the entrance exams at the University of Thessaloniki required the writing of a composition of "ideas" which meant interpreting a proverb or a saying. The rules required that the composition be written in "Katharevousa", the "clean language", the language used in government documents and emulated by many prose writers. The problem we faced was that all our course work was taught in the common everyday spoken language, the "demotike". During the last two months of our final year, our teachers of Greek made an effort to teach us how to write compositions in "Katharevousa". That effort seemingly had paid off because all those who applied to medical school from our class passed. I still remember the proverb "Opou akous polla kerassia fere kai micro kalathi", "Whenever you hear about too many cherries bring along a small basket"); in a few words, don't believe in many promises.

In the spring of 1946 we began our first year as medical students at the Aristotelian University. Medical School in Greece, as in other European countries, runs for six years, where the first two years deal with basic science courses and the last four with clinical studies. Our first year was short-lived because it lasted only three and a half months. We had the beginning of physics, chemistry, biology and anatomy. The main lecture hall was a large amphitheater at the bottom of which was a large bench with water taps and gas outlets for Bunsen burners. Our chemistry professor, Mr. Kavasiadis, and our physics professor, Mr. Empirikos, lectured from behind the bench. Mr. Kavasiades, in a black, dressy, three-piece suit, decorated with a gold watch chain crossing the middle of his rotund girth, carried out chemical reactions for the benefit of those sitting in the first ten rows. For those sitting higher up and in the uppermost sections of the amphitheater the professor's voice was barely audible and the test tubes where the chemical reactions developed, changed from colorless to blue or purple or red and finally became a monochromatic blur. I soon found myself sitting on the first row where I could hear well and see better.

The physics professor, Mr. Empirikos, lectured in a monotone, summarizing principles and laws of physics that were formulated in the course of the previous five or six centuries. The experiments, which he conducted on the lab bench, were simplified proofs of the laws of physics laid down by Newton. It was difficult to follow the professor's rambling and try to understand the principle inherent in the experiment because he parroted the expected results without an explanation of why it turned the way it did and why it could not turn out another way. The abbreviated version of our first year of medical school ended in July 1946 and promptly we were informed that in the fall we will have to start our first year all over again, thus joining the newly admitted first year medical students.

With the end of the war came the restoration of several of our suppressed freedoms. The old newspapers as well as new ones came into circulation. Hundreds of new titles in books were published and were available in bookstores as well as on tables on street corners where they were bought and read by the eager and avid public in large numbers.

In the summer of 1945, again at Uncle Elias' urging, I set up a table on a sidewalk in the city center, on Tsimiski Street, selling a variety of books, whose subjects ranged from novels to poetry, plays, philosophy, political doctrines and to current history of Greece. Next to the table I placed a chair and this afforded me a chance to read from any book I wanted during periods of low business activity.

The daily newspapers in those days were published with very few pages, usually 10-12. One of the big events we learned about from our reading was the dropping of the atom bomb in Hiroshima by the United States in the summer of 1945. The war with Germany had ended already and the dropping of a second atom bomb on Nagasaki resulted in Japan's surrendering unconditionally. The end of the "Hot War" was quickly followed by another, undeclared war, the "Cold War". This new development gave an opportunity for endless debates in the newly established United Nations on the emergence of new nations from former colonies, on establishing new borders between nations and other issues. Many of the resolutions were adopted but a number of them were "vetoed" either by the Soviet Union or the United States, when such issues reached the U.N. Security Council. The word "veto" was new in most people's vocabulary. My Big-Pappous read the newspapers daily and because of their small size he would read them twice and to kill more time, three times. One day, in a very serious tone he asked " My boy, I have been reading about all these people, Roosevelt, Stalin, Churchill and De Gaulle and I know who they are but I never heard of this guy Veto, who is he"? I quickly explained : "Veto is not a person.It refers to the power to reject a resolution by a member of the Security Council.

I remember Big Pappous commenting: "Where did you learn all these things"?

The summer of 1946 was one of the most memorable summers I spent in Greece. That year saw the beginning of reconstruction of the villages that were destroyed during the war and occupation. Engineering, architectural and construction companies were dispatched to the various parts of Greece that were severely affected and began their rebuilding by starting with the bare essentials, namely cutting down thousands of trees and making lumber for housing. One of the areas selected for deforestation was the Mount Meliton in the County of Chalkidiki, about 70 miles east of Thessaloniki. Uncle Elias, who always seemed to have the appropriate contacts, found out that one such company of engineers was going to be working in Chalkidiki and they were looking for a young man to manage the day-to-day affairs of the company. Uncle Elias recommended me and I was hired on the spot. The headquarters of the company was to be located in the village Neos Marmaras, a small fishing village by the sea, built by refugees who hailed from the town of Marmaras in Turkey on the southern coast of the Sea of Marmara, in northern Asia Minor. Soon, I met the chief engineer and his assistant, both from Athens, who described my job responsibilities. I was introduced to the local authorities as a medical student and would be the company's representative in the village. I was to stay in a rented room, in a house owned by an old lady.

On specified days when the engineers came to the village, I would arrange to have meals ready for them and hire horses to go up to the top of the mountain to inspect the tree cutting and sorting. Lumberjacks were brought in from neighboring villages and even from other parts of Greece to work on the project. The trees were cut and numbered and moved by horse or mule to a loading area on a main road where they were transported to special mills to be cut into lumber. Whenever we went to the mountaintop, we either had the horse owner act as a guide or, in his absence, we simply let the horses lead the way, since they were accustomed to following established mountain paths. The camp had a couple of tents used by the engineers and me. Most of my day was consumed cataloging the tree trunks by writing in a book the numbers painted on each log. Breathing the clear, crisp air on the mountaintop was a very satisfying experience and a distinct contrast from the aromatic taste and smell of the Lucky Strike cigarettes that I began smoking that summer.

My desire to smoke one morning was thwarted by the discovery that I had smoked the last cigarette in my pack the day before. I also discovered that the two engineers were nonsmokers. My senses of smell and taste at the age of 19 were quite acute so I decided to satisfy my desire to smoke by simply smelling the inside of the empty pack of Luckies, which I had tacked onto the center post of my tent. This makeshift, tobacco substitute lasted only two days as the pleasant aroma of the "Lucky" pack dissipated down to a barely perceptible odor. Fortunately, the following morning we moved down, back into the village and I supplied myself with another pack of "Luckies".

My free time, when the engineers were not visiting the village, was spent at a very leisurely pace. The morning papers from Thessaloniki arrived by bus in late afternoon and I caught up on the latest current events, sipping coffee at the coffee shop, which was located right on the beach and across the street from my apartment. In the morning, I usually went fishing at the pier, a very satisfying activity, since the fish were abundant and were constantly biting. Swimming was always a daily pastime and a great pleasure. The sandy beach was enclosed into a small cove providing an enticing place to rest and sun myself.

One of the regular customers at the coffee house was a retired high school teacher, who enjoyed playing chess and checkers with other customers. He noticed my eyeing curiously at the chessboard and asked if I cared to join him in a game. When I said that I did not know how to play he offered to teach me and within a couple of days he felt that I could test my newly acquired proficiency against his long expertise. He beat me in every game but after several days of trying I managed to win a couple of games, to my great surprise and pleasure. I fared better in backgammon, a game I played several times before and where the moves are based on simple principles of numbers and the chance of getting the right combination by throwing the dice.

Near the end of my two-month employment-vacation, while resting by my window and gazing out to sea, I saw a young girl, about my age or may be younger, approaching the window. The sun was reaching the horizon and was shining into my eyes. As she came close to the window the blinding light obscured her figure and all I saw was a hazy shadow. Soon the sun moved down and to the right, behind the coffee house and the tall trees. Suddenly, her figure became clear, as if I was looking in a mirror. She was pretty, and had brown hair and blue eyes. With a big smile and looking straight into my eyes she asked me what my name was and whether I was enjoying my stay at Neos Marmaras. Her name was Mary and she was from Thessaloniki. She was spending the summer in the village visiting with relatives. I found out that she was eager to enter the last year of Gymnasium in the fall and was looking forward to the following year when she hoped to enter the School of Philology at the University. After about thirty minutes she excused herself and went home.

At night, as I lay on my bed, I thought of the young girl and her beautiful face for sometime before I fell asleep. In the next couple of weeks, Mary came by my window three or four times to continue our routine conversations about school, our neighborhoods, our friends and our favorite recreations. She revealed that in the middle of September she was taking the boat back to Thessaloniki and her day of departure co-incided with that of mine. The trip to Thessaloniki was smooth, in a calm sea under a hot summer sun. As we sat on a bench we began to hold hands and, when the captain was busy steering the boat, we kissed each other, first furtively and gradually passionately. We reached Thessaloniki and we agreed to meet again the next day in front of the movie theatre Palace, near the White Tower. Our meetings became frequent, about once a week. When I revealed that I was planning to immigrate to America, possibly in a few months. She became visibly sad and even suggested that I drop my plans. We stopped seeing each other as I renewed my medical school studies in October 1946.

## Preparing for the trip to America

That was my last year of attendance at the medical school at the Univeristy of Thessaloniki. The family decided that I would be the one to be sent to America to study medicine. They convinced Uncle John, who now lived in Evanston, Illinois, a suburb of Chicago, to arrange for my visa to travel to the United States. As soon as this process was set in motion, all my concerns and those of the family were focused on completing all the necessary steps required for obtaining a visa and the boat passage to New York.

One of the first things I started doing was to go to a private tutor to learn English. He was a gentle, middle-aged man who had worked for Western Union in Malta for several years and his English was impeccable. To me he appeared to be a good teacher but as time had proven his system was not geared to conversational English but only to vocabulary and grammar. He was earnest in his efforts and his demand for payment was a kilo of wheat for each lesson. This payment came from all the wheat we had amassed in 1943 and kept in a large, wooden chest. We frequently used it to buy eggs, chickens, butter and other produce. Now it came handy in paying for my English lessons. Despite all the lessons, I had no opportunity to practice my English except on the rare occasion with some of my Peiramatikon classmates who were also taking private lessons. Our conversations were limited to short sentences, about the weather, our courses and our teachers or monosyllabic answers to short questions.

Uncle Elias was again the moving force in arranging the paperwork from the Greek side in fulfilling the requirements for my trip. Early in 1947 word came from the United States Consulate in Thessaloniki that I had to travel to Athens to go through the detailed process of obtaining the visa from the General Consulate. Uncle John in the USA was the person who was inviting me and I was going on a student's visa. I began writing Uncle John and asking details about my stay in Evanston, the school I was supposed to attend and what kinds of books I should bring with me. I was the product of war and a devastating occupation and in the course of four years I had developed a sense of independence, a limited respect for authoritative action and my expectation of equal treatment. My correspondence with Uncle John by letter was infrequent but it exemplified the issues that concerned me. A letter I wrote to Uncle John in Greek in late November 1945 is translated below:

Thessaloniki, 19 November 1945

My dear Uncle

After some time since my last letter, I am writing to you again, although I have not had your reply. We are all well at home save for a few minor health problems with the old folks. I trust that you are also well.

The packages you have sent us are arriving slowly: up to now we have received 25. Our joy and our gratitude are huge. The contents of the packages are very satisfactory both in terms of quality and selections of items.

On December 20 of this year I will be graduating from the Gymnasium and on 20 January I will be taking an entrance examination for the medical school at the University of our city. Regarding your preference of my entering the business school, I would have followed it, as it was your desire, but since this school functions only at the University of Athens and attendance there requires a large financial expense, I was forced to choose the field of medicine at the University of Thessaloniki. Another factor that contributed to my decision is the fact that a business school in Thessaloniki is not affiliated with the University and it is not in a position to yield the desired results nor is it in a position to guarantee a better future.

I began taking English lessons at the English Academy here in the city.

All of us would like to receive a recent photograph of you. Naturally we will send you ours.

Greetings from all
With Respect
Nikos

Another letter, written in Greek, describes the aftermath of war and occupation on the economic state of Greece and my attempt to make a case for going to the USA follows.

Thessaloniki, 16 January 1946
My dear Uncle
Again I am writing to you in an attempt to complete my previous letter on the subject that seriously concerns me as well as the whole family. To put it more precisely, it involves my future, which, depending on its ultimate outcome, will determine the fate of the whole family.

Uncle, if you could only think of the deprivation and loss that has resulted from the foreign occupation in the whole country and our family in particular, you would appreciate the state of backwardness and misery in our country. I would like you to understand that our country will take a long time to stand on its own and enter the stream of modern civilization. This in turn is a blow and a barrier to those who wish to move ahead and develop so that they could at the same time contribute their services to the general good.

For me, the need to study and to perfect myself as a human being is imperative because, in addition to other reasons, these are the immediate responsibilities towards my family. My father, after a few more years, I doubt that he would be able to provide for the family as well as he does today. For this reason it would be important for someone, after 5-6 years to be able to support this family. I could be the only appropriate person to fulfill that need.

However, in our country, the possibilities for advanced academic studies are hard to come by and especially for someone like me with limited economic resources. On the other hand, if the possibilities are not available in Greece, they are in America, in the place where many young men, some among my friends, have gone with the help of their relatives there.

I have all the desire, and urging of all the thirteen members of our family, to travel to America, where I could work and study at the same time. In this effort, I am certain that you, with the social prominence that you possess in your community, will be in a position to help me.

Presently, Uncle, I want and beg you for something, to arrange for me to come to America. I am sure that this is something that you wish to do and are in a position to accomplish.

You should be assured that I would not be a burden. I will work like you and I will study like you.

With this desire in mind, I end my letter with the unshaken belief that you will also agree.

Greetings from all

With respect

Nikos


Obviously, my letters had a positive impact on Uncle John's thinking about inviting me to migrate to America. Sometime in early fall 1946, the good news had arrived. In this letter, which was written in English, I ask him questions about preparing myself for the trip. The letter reveals my struggling with the English language and grammar.

Salonika    13/11/1946

Dear Uncle

I feel very excited at the thought that in another week you will read the first of my English letters. It will be very short, but I think it will satisfy you.

As I have told you in my earlier letter, our health is generally good. My grandmother cannot see well and she often stumbles here and there. On account of this fact she needs spectacles. I pray you send us as soon as possible a pair of these.

My English teacher suffers by otosclerosis. I beg you very much to send for him an ear instrument with batteries, if it will be possible. The money of this instrument he will give to grandfather. More particulars he writes to you in his letter.

And now you hear something of myself. I should like to know whether I must spend my time studying only English or at the same time to study my lessons at University in order to take examinations there, so that I may be promoted to my second year.

Please let me know when they will come my papers of America? Answer me in English.

My respects and love

Nikos

In the middle of April 1947, I went to Athens where I was met by Uncle Elias and Uncle Nikos Spyrou, also a lawyer and the husband of a cousin of my father's. Uncle Nikos was a very pleasant man, always ready to help and make my stay free of obstructions, as we went from one Greek government office to another and to the U.S. Consulate. My stay in Athens had its other satisfying moments when I was given the opportunity to visit the Acropolis, go around the elegant structure of the Parthenon, the Erechthion, with its magnificent Karyatides, the propylea, all the things that made me stand at awe, with pride for my heritage.

While in Athens I had the chance to visit my Uncle Thanasos, my mother's older brother, and his family, Aunt Lesvia and their daughter Nitsa (short for Elenitsa). Uncle Thanasos was suffering from tuberculosis that had affected his spine and was required to lie flat on a hard bed while he was hospitalized at a sanatorium. Tuberculosis was quite prevalent in Greece during the years of war and occupation. Many cases were active and required treatment and the most favored was to send the patient to a mountain resort where the air was fresh and unpolluted and the second most favored treatment was collapsing the affected lung by the process of pneumothorax. When Uncle Thanasos left Alexandroupolis I was only about five and I had only a faint recollection of him. My Aunt Lesvia and cousin Nitsa and I visited him at the sanatorium where he received us lying down on the narrow, hard bed. He greeted me with great emotion and as I bent over to kiss him tears were coming down his cheeks. My ten-year old cousin, Nitsa, a child of striking beauty, was very excited to see me; it was the first time we met. She and I spent the afternoon talking about our childhood experiences and every time I would mention the Gymnasium, the occupation and my plans to travel to the USA, she would beam with a broad smile and say "alithea"?, "really"?

When I left him to return to my hotel, I did not know whether I would have a chance to see Uncle Thanasos again. My first visit to Greece after I emigrated did not take place until 12 years later, in 1959, when Jane, my wife of 10 years, and I had a chance to visit Uncle Thanasos family. At that time Nitsa, now a 22-year old young lady and beautiful as ever, was a student at the University of Athens, studying philology. Unfortunately, though Uncle Thanasos survived his original illness, he died some 20 years later of pancreatic cancer.

The paperwork to obtain the Visa was moving along well with the help of Uncle Elias and Uncle Nikos, who knew how to cut through red tape. In the meantime, Uncle John from his end was able to contact the American embassy in Athens and facilitate the process. Quickly we found out that there were only a few formalities left and it was decided that I return to Thessaloniki to say goodbye to relatives and friends. Within one week after I returned to Thessaloniki my parents prepared me for the trip to America. My mother had purchased new underwear, new shirts and socks. A gray, fine, wool suit, which Uncle John sent from the USA, fit me perfectly. A pair of black shoes also from the USA complemented the outfit. On a daily basis, my mother and father were instructing me and admonishing me to be polite, to respect Uncle John and his wife, Aunt Bettie, not to argue and not to mingle with strangers. What a charge though, when the liner I was going to travel in was going to be full of strangers from diverse countries, but I agreed.

My job with the engineering firm the year before allowed me to make a good amount of money, which helped me with buying presents for Uncles Elias, Nikos and John for their untiring efforts to make my trip a success. Uncle John sent 50 dollars to be used during the trip across the Atlantic and after I had reached the USA. In less than 10 years I was again being separated from my parents and my brother. There were no tears or sad faces to fill the anticipatory atmosphere of our house. The family had the unshaken belief that I somehow would be a successful student and a successful professional and, like my Uncle John, I would be able to contribute to their welfare.

I set aside a day to visit Hadji pappous and Hadji yiayia, Uncle Stavros and Aunt Zografia and their daughters Annoula and Maroula to bid them goodbye and receive my grandparents' blessings. At home, Big Pappous and Big Yiayia were trying to convince me how lucky I was that I would live with Uncle John, not knowing of course what he was like as a husband and what he would be like as an uncle, a man who never had children.

One by one I visited my close friends, Alekos Marketos, Yiannis Asimis, Nasos Mihalopoulos, Ippocratis Sokotis, George Moustakas, Alekos Andreadis and Tasos Oikonomou. They all promised to write to me and I to them. Geore Kostopoulos went to Geneva, Swizerland to study medicine. His French was impeccable, since he had the good fortune to be taught by a private tutor for more than ten years. He sent me his address and I promised to send him mine. I was leaving behind a good deal of myself, the part that grew amid the ravishes of war and occupation, the part that was molded with the love of my saintly parents and the devotion of my grandparents and Aunt Helen, the part that would be irreplaceable away from Chris, the part that evokes ineffaceable sentiments of true friendship that grew out of the trying years of devastation and want with my classmates. I kissed my mother and father goodbye before I went aboard the ship that was to take me to Piraeus, the port of Athens.

The day after I arrived in Athens I got in touch with a dear friend from Thessaloniki, Vagelis Micromastoras. He was attending the Polytechnic School of Athens and was having fun. That afternoon, without hesitation he suggested that we visit a brothel in downtown Athens. I had no idea about the legality of such institutions but Vagelis assured me that they were legal. The experience was rewarding and since I was due to travel on the sea for two weeks completely cut off from the outside world I convinced myself without a shred of reluctance that I should indulge in a couple of more visits before departure which I unhesitatingly did. I thanked my friend Vaggelis for his wise suggestion.

As the day of my departure was getting near, I was required to go through a last official task and that meant I had to visit the American Consulate for an interview with the Consul General. I was ushered into his office, a large room, with what appeared to be massive, highly polished furniture and a big window looking out into the street. My eyes quickly fell upon the tall, blonde, blue eyed young man who stood up to shake my hand. His youthful look and his welcoming smile put me immediately at ease and after looking for a few minutes at what appeared to be my file he asked me "Why to you want to go to America"? I answered, "To study medicine". He said thank you, scribbled something, stood up, gave me an envelope, shook my hand and said, "Have a nice trip". Any nervousness that I may have allowed myself to surround me, dissipated and after thanking the young Consul I left the premises. I had my visa and I was ready to travel to the USA.

On the morning of Monday, May 5, 1947, the day set for my departure, I had a light breakfast and I went out to walk around the center of Athens. Near the Omonia Square I came upon a movie theatre that had a morning showing of a picture with Sherlock Holmes, starring Basil Rathbone; it dealt with German spies in the USA during World War II and his efforts to uncover their plot. I had enjoyed watching it and I felt quite satisfied with the plot and the acting. My main motive to go and see the movie was the nagging suspicion that I would not see a movie for at least two weeks. The last picture I saw before leaving Thessaloniki was one with Stan Laurel and Oliver Hardy, "Hondros kai Lignos" as we called then in Greece, (The Fat and Thin Man). When I got back to the hotel I found Uncle Elias and Nikos waiting for me quite upset and a little furious because they did not know where I was all morning and worried that something bad had happened. They were very relieved when I told them I went to see a movie and understood my concern to have to cross the Mediterranean and the Atlantic without the benefit of a moving picture.

Five in the afternoon, I clutched my envelope containing the passage ticket and my visa, I hugged and kissed Uncles Elias and Nikos and I boarded the passenger ship "Saturnia". By six o'clock we were on our way. Quickly, I found out where my bunk was and after stashing my small suitcase and a big box containing gifts for the relatives in the USA, I went back on deck and I stayed there watching as the last vestige of land from the southern coast of Greece faded in the horizon. After supper, I went straight to my bunk and laid down to rest, to shake off the excitement and worries that had piled up for the past few weeks, to begin the building of an emotional parapet that would keep the nostalgic yearnings buried away for at least two weeks.

The relatives in Greece asked me to take Greek delicacies to the relatives in America: they included fresh fig preserves, orange peel preserves, a bottle of ouzo and four bottles of Metaxa, a classic Greek brandy. All these items were stashed in the cardboard box; none of my relatives realized that liquor was a taxable item if the amount exceeded one bottle. This eagerness to please the relatives in the USA cost me 30 dollars in custom fees that I had to pay out of the 50 dollars Uncle John sent me while I was still in Greece. Despite the cost at the customs office, I felt that it was the gesture of people from a country that at this time had little else to offer besides their sincere thanks and affection and tokens of the things people still cherished in Greece.

The first night on the ship was quiet and I was lulled into a deep sleep by the rhythmic noise of the ship's engines coming from its bowels. The next morning found us outside Naples, Italy. We docked and were informed that there will be a layover of four hours and that we could go ashore if we so desired.

A small group of us decided to go into the city and see the sights. About a half hour after walking around, we came across a movie theater that was playing an American film, "Two Girls and a Sailor" with Frank Sinatra. We immediately aimed for the ticket booth and we settled for an hour and a half of relaxed entertainment, despite the fact that the picture was in English and the subtitles in Italian and none of us was too well versed in either, except for one in our group who was a Greek-American, and who was trapped in Greece when the USA entered the Second World War. He was able to fill us in on some scenes.

We returned to the ship and in about an hour we steamed away westward, leaving behind us the Mediterranean and making our entrance into the Atlantic. The view of Gibraltar was majestic. No wonder the ancients considered it the Pillars of Hercules, the bearer of the world, which is the world east of Gibraltar.

For the next twelve days, we were surrounded by the dark, green, sea and the clear blue sky, enjoying the beautiful weather lounging on the deck. In the evenings we would sit at one of the ship's bars and sip Coca Cola or, for those who preferred it, cognac. Lunches and dinners were pleasant occasions because the food was plentiful and tasty and we had the chance to talk with young men and women from Greece, Egypt and Italy. It was a mélange of three languages as we tried to converse in the language of the soon to be, our new country. During one of our evening dances I happened to be dancing with a young Italian woman, whose dancing style was a little on the "stiff" side and on two occasions, I stepped on her foot which made her exclaim what I thought was Italian "teekeereesee, teekeereesse". I surmised she was telling me in Italian "don't step on my foot" and I left it at that, trying to take slower, measured steps. Not until a few months after I had arrived in Evanston and began to walk around Chicago did I find out that what the young lady was trying to say was "take it easy", but with a heavy Italian pronunciation.

We arrived in New York in the late afternoon on Monday, May 19 after spending fourteen days on the ship, fourteen days of a carefree, relaxed and an almost aimless existence. We were informed that because of the late hour, we would not disembark until the following morning. Instead of going below, some of us stayed up on deck, looking at the big city in the distance. It was overwhelming and difficult to absorb everything all at once. The buildings closest to us were arrayed in a zigzag pattern, standing against the endless background like an old mural that changed shadows as the sun was descending behind us. At the base of the massive mural was a highway that ran from as far to the left and as far to the right as the eye could see and running on it were myriads of autos moving eastward one after the other, like a "comboloyi" ("a set of worry beads") or a massive rosary moved by the invisible hand of God.

That night we had a farewell dinner and dance. We ate and drank and I must admit to some unaccustomed excess. I remember drinking cognac until I felt relaxed, happy and then sad, so sad that I climbed up the steps to the open air deck and looking out into the starlit sky I cried "Metera, metera, pou eise?" ("Mother, Mother, where are you"?). Two of my friends who were with me did not hesitate long before they took me by the arms and led me to my bunk where they tucked me in and bid me goodnight. The following day I was going to meet Uncle George.

*We... are Greeks in this American empire... We must run the Allied Forces HQ as the Greeks ran the operations of the Emperor Claudius.*

Harold MacMillan, 1944

*In the United States there is more space where nobody is than where anybody is. This is what makes America what it is.*

Gertrude Stein, 1936

*I like to be in America,*
*O.K. by me in America!*
*Ev'rything free in America*
*For a small fee in America!*

Stephen Sondheim, 1957

## 10. Coming to America

### First encounters with my relatives

On the morning of May 20th 1947, we were told to collect our belongings and appear in front of the Immigration official who boarded the " Saturnia" for the inspection of visas.. The use of Ellis Island was abandoned some years ago. Everything went well. We were out of the ship and we finally reached the customs officials. They were inspecting everything we were carrying and in the process they discovered the four bottles of Metaxa brandy and the one of ouzo. I was informed that I would have to pay 32 dollars in import duty. I did and that left me with only 15 dollars from the 47 I had remaining after spending three dollars on the ship from the original 50.

As I came out of the customs office I spotted Uncle George in the waiting area. The joy and excitement were all over his face as he rushed to embrace me and kiss me on both cheeks. His deep blue eyes were filled with tears. His first words were " Did you have a nice journey? How are your mother and father? How are my father and mother?" He was pleased to learn that I had an enjoyable trip and that all in the family in Greece were in good health. This meeting would be in distinct contrast to the one I would have with Uncle John ten days later. We took the subway train to Astoria, Long Island. Again this was a first for me, riding on a subway train which soon became an elevated train.

We arrived at an apartment building made of red brick. I was immediately struck by the iron fire escape stairs zig-zaging on the whole side of the building; another first. The concept of personal safety was the concern of everybody, including the building owner, the community administration and the tenants themselves. We reached the third floor apartment and as the door opened we were greeted by Aunt Katina and my cousin Nick.

Aunt Katina was a tall, lean woman with dark hair and hazel eyes, whereas cousin Nick was also tall with curly blond hair and blue eyes. They both embraced me with obvious delight. They immediately took me to my room and asked me if I wanted to take a nap. I was anxious to talk to them and refused the offer. They bombarded me with questions about the lives of the relatives in Greece. Uncle George had not seen his family, save for his brother John who followed him to America, since he left Turkey for the United States 28 years ago. Uncle George, I found out, managed a restaurant and was thinking about retiring. His job was very demanding of his time and effort. Cousin Nick was in high school and Aunt Katina was looking after the house. Before I was ready to go to bed, I was given the opportunity to take a bath, the first in two weeks, to replace the daily showers on the ship. I gingerly stepped into the bathrub and eased my body into the bubbly water, letting out an exclamatory expression in Greek "A ti orea pou eine" ("Oh how nice it is"). The long, warm bath erased my desire to stay awake and I was soon in bed, sleeping comfortably.

The next morning, after a delicious breakfast, Uncle George took me for a tour of downtown Manhattan. As we were leaving the apartment building I was again struck by two peculiarities. In front of the building were two large metal barrels full of trash, having among the items intact glass bottles. I asked Uncle George "Why do you throw away these precious items?". He explained that there was no need to save bottles and cans since oil, vinegar, wine, soups, tomato paste and other comestibles came already packaged in bottles and cans. This was in contrast to my experience in Greece where we saved empty bottles to buy the same items by volume or weight that sometimes filled only a portion of the bottle. The other, equally surprising thing, was the abandoned children's bicycles on the sidewalk, left there during the night without fear of being stolen. Two obvious factors played a significant role, the fact that almost all kids in the neighborhood had some type of bicycle and then the sense of honesty and trust that characterized the children. In Greece, an abandoned bicycle would have been considered as useless and unwanted item. Needless to say, in communities today, whether in Greece or the USA, it would be unwise to leave something like a bicycle unattended.

We arrived in downtown Manhattan around noon. We walked up and down Fifth, Sixth, and Seventh Avenues. The size of the buildings was overwhelming and my head was kept in the upward extension, minute after minute, while Uncle George explained the significance of the names of the individual buildings: the Rockefeller building with its enormous Atlas at the entrance, the Chrysler building with its colorful spire, the Radio City Music Hall, and the Empire State building. For me, however, it was the short visits we made at various small grocery stores and restaurants along Sixth and Seventh Avenues that were exciting and full of curiosity. Each time we stopped at a store, Uncle George made sure it was owned by a Greek immigrant who, as soon as he recognized my Uncle, they would immediately break into a Greek dialogue but not without the admixture of pure English words or words that were especially modified to fit the Greek notion, such as "salivori" for "sidewalk", "samitsa" for "sandwich", "caro" for "car", "marketa" for "market".

Visiting all those stores I suddenly felt I was in the midst of a little Greece, a feeling that assuaged my nostalgic yearnings for my home. The visit to Manhattan ended with a late lunch at one of the Greek restaurants, where the owner treated us to avgolemono soup (egg-lemon soup), mousaka, an eggplant and ground meat dish, and Greek salad.

As I began to smoke a cigarette after dinner, Uncle George warned me that Uncle John did not approve of smoking. This admonition and warning put me on guard for the years to come every time I was contemplating lighting a cigarette and the probability of Uncle John showing up was better than 50/50.

The days in New York could not be complete without a visit to a couple of Greek family friends of Uncle George and Aunt Katina. Meeting someone who just arrived from Greece, especially after the years of war and occupation, was a rare opportunity for endless conversation and gossip. The first question they usually asked me was "How do you like America?" Here I was, three days in Astoria, Long Island and two trips to Manhattan, and I was asked to describe how I liked America. I did admit, however, that I was at awe at the enormity of the skyscrapers and the magnificent movie theater, Radio City Music Hall. During one of these visits I was presented with a fruit I had not tasted before, bananas. I was given an oversized and overripe banana and as soon as I began chewing it I found it too sweet. However, not wanting to insult our host, I ate the whole thing , something that  caused me to gag. I was left with a distaste for bananas which lasted for several years.

One of the Greek American families we visited was one that was trapped in Thessalonki after the United States entered the war and had to spend more than five years in Greece. Some time in 1946, the family returned to the United States. The daughter of the family, Anna, was a girl I met in Thessaloniki after the liberation while we both were taking part in the cultural and political activities of EPON. When she found out that I was also planning to travel to America, before leaving she gave me her address in the USA and to my surprise I found that she lived in Astoria. We visited Anna and her family and we spent a wonderful day reminiscing about our experiences in Thessaloniki in the aftermath of the occupation. It was a delightful encounter.

The visit that topped all visits in Manhattan was the day my cousin Nick took me for a tour of mid-Manhattan. We visited a few of the big department stores with their myriads of varieties of clothing, underwear, cosmetics, utensils and cameras, to name a few. The visits to Macys and Sacks Fifth Avenue were memorable.

We then proceeded to Radio City Music Hall, a gigantic theater. The movie picture shown on that day was the classic "Great Expectations" by Charles Dickens. The movie screen was enormous, nothing like the small screens I had been used to seeing in Greece. The sound was stereophonic and I felt surrounded by cinematographic ecstasy. This ecstasy was surpassed by what followed after the end of the picture, a stage show. Stage shows between picture showings were common in large movie theaters in the USA. The program was taken up by performances of well-known music bands, singers and comedians. At the Radio City Music Hall we were treated to a performance by the Rockettes, an ensemble of 50 beautiful, tall ladies with sculptured legs, who did synchronized dancing, kicking their legs up in a parallel line. I looked at awe at the display of 100 beautiful legs. I turned to my cousin Nick and I whispered, I know what I am in for – "Great Expectations".

At 6:30 P.M., on May 29, 1947, I boarded the overnight train to Chicago. Uncle George and Cousin Nick took me to Grand Central Station in Manhattan, an awesome, cavernous structure with elaborate decorations, staircases going up and down, a place I could have easily been lost in, had it not been for Uncle George who knew which way to go. He purchased the ticket and we proceeded to the gate. The time to say goodbye came again and I boarded the train. I found a seat by the window.

Before departing, a middle aged man came and sat beside me. He said "hello" and I reciprocated. Our conversation was limited. He soon realized my conversational English was at the monosyllabic stage and politely avoided complicated questions. I managed to tell him I was a student, going to meet my uncle in Chicago. He explained that he was a mechanical engineer. As the train continued on its planned course, I could see on the left side the green, lush countryside, the small towns with their typical water towers and big advertising signs along the roads that ran parallel to the tracks. As I sat in silence, not being able to formulate complicated questions about the meaning of all the things that were passing in front of my eyes my curiosity waned.

Night fell and all that was visible of the landscape was the starlit sky and the lights in the distant towns. The night turned out to be long and uncomfortable as I tried to fall asleep on the stiff seat of a moving and noisy train without success. As we were approaching Indiana and the first rays of daylight came through the windows, I sat up and began again to gaze at the scenery that was unfolding on the countryside. The land was flat and I could see miles and miles of corn fields and wheat fields and in some I could make out farmers already busy at work. My mind wandered to my impending meeting with Uncle John; I was trying to picture him from photos he had sent the family some years ago, in the operating room wearing his surgical cap or in his street clothes sporting a fedora.

My thoughts were interrupted when my engineer companion suggested that we go for breakfast. I gladly followed him to the restaurant car where we found a table for two, covered with a white tablecloth, napkins and metal silverware. The waiter brought us our menus and I spent several minutes lost in the array of choices that I hardly recognized. Finally, my eyes fell on "Omelet" which was the closest to "Omeletta" in Greek. I ordered it and the choice was rewarding. I enjoyed it along with toast, a glass of orange juice and coffee. At 9:00 A.M., Friday May 30, we pulled into the Union Station of Chicago.

## Coming to Chicago

Getting off the train, I came face to face with the man I immediately recognized as Uncle John. Dressed in a three-piece suit, in rimless glasses and wearing a Homburg, he was as I pictured him. With a big smile he said "Kalos Orises" ("Welcome"), gave me a hug and looking straight into my face he asked, "Pos ekapsess ta matotsinara sou?" ("How did you singe your eyelashes?"). I had smoked a cigarette that morning and in trying to light it I must have singed my eyelashes. Here was a man who had not seen me and the rest of his family in 15 years, and the first question he asked me was the state of my eyelashes. What a contrast from my first encounter with Uncle George. My reply was "I don't know" and we began to walk out of the station to take the subway to Evanston. A taxi took us from the Howard Street Station to 1509 Dobson Street, just north of Howard Street, the dividing line between Chicago and Evanston.

My arrival in Chicago coincided with the Memorial Day weekend, a national holiday. The scene at Uncle John's house was festive. Aunt Bettie, his wife, was very excited to meet me as was her father, Mr. Betsiaras and two friends of the family, Dr. Stavrianos, Professor of

History at Northwestern University and Mrs. Stavrianos, a Professor of Psychology at the same institution. We spent some time talking about my trip across the Atlantic, the political situation in Greece and the health of Uncle John's parents. Dr. and Mrs. Stavrianos, I quickly discovered, were very intelligent and well informed about world events and particularly of the internecine struggle between the left and right political wings in Greece. It was gratifying to find out that Uncle John and Aunt Bettie shared the views of Dr. and Mrs. Stavrianos on several political issues.

It did not take long for Uncle John to ask "What's in the box"? He sat cross-legged on the floor and began to go through the presents with the excitement of a young child. There were the bottles of Metaxa and Ouzo, the fruit preserves, two beautifully embroidered small tablecloths that Aunt Stasa made and sent to Aunt Bettie and a wool scarf that my mother knitted for Uncle John. The afternoon passed quickly; we ate lunch and I found myself dozing, unable to stay awake. I was shown to my room, all my own. The two windows faced west, allowing the afternoon sun to shine in. I had a closet, a beautiful mahogany desk covered with a glass plate, that Uncle John had previously used in his office, and a framed print of a Van Gogh self-portrait with the bandage over his left ear. A night stand was on the left side of my bed. All these items created a sense of awe, for it was the first time in my life that I had my personal room, with a modicum of privacy.

Uncle John's apartment was part of a building in an area of Evanston that was still only partially developed. To the west and north of the house, the landscape was empty prairie with only a few houses scattered here and there. To the east of Uncle John's house, all the way to Western Avenue, Dobson Street was completely built. During the memorial-day weekend Uncle John and Aunt Bettie took me for rides around Evanston and the suburbs north of it. I was impressed by the beautiful tree-lined streets, the elegant homes, the large and well manicured front lawns. The place that really caught my eye was the Northwestern University campus. A series of buildings arose along Lake Michigan in their Gothic architectural splendor, surrounded by tall trees with paths crisscrossing the grassy campus, where I would walk through as a student in two years.

Uncle John planned my daily life for the rest of the summer. The main goal was to learn English. If I thought I would go to a special school or have a tutor come to the apartment, I was mistaken. Uncle John bought me an English learning method entitled "English Self-Taught". He expected me to get up early in the morning, between 6 and 6:30 and start studying every day until eight, have breakfast and then continue until noon, when I would break for lunch. The afternoon was usually mine to do what I pleased, read, listen to music or go on a bicycle ride into Evanston. I soon discovered that Uncle John needed his seven to eight hours of sleep and when my alarm clock began to ring at 6 A.M. it was loud enough that it would wake him up, after which he could not go back to sleep. The solution to the problem was to wrap a small terrycloth towel around the alarm clock and keep my door closed. If the alarm clock was an intrusion on Uncle John's sleeping schedule, it was not of my doing, since he had suggested using an alarm clock.

I began making small adjustments to satisfy my Uncle and Aunt. Since Uncle John did not approve of people smoking, I avoided smoking in his presence. Aunt Bettie, however, knew of my habit and she frequently bought me a carton of cigarettes. When Uncle John asked me once point blank "Do you smoke"? I should have said "sometimes", instead of saying "no". Uncle John took my answer to mean "Never" and as time proved there was no room for "sometimes", which to him it was equivalent to lying. This was brought home about a year or so later when one evening, while taking a stroll with Aunt Bettie on Dobson Street. Uncle John had come home early. He was about a block away and saw us walking towards the house. The moment I realized he was approaching, I flipped the cigarette to the ground. In the dimly lit street he spotted the falling cigarette.

When we entered the house, he confronted me with the accusation that I was smoking and that I lied to him a year or so before when I told him that I did not smoke. He went into a tirade invoking honesty, trust and lying until I went to my room. The next day I avoided him and we were cool to each other. This situation dragged for another day or so until he burst into my room and declared that he was considering sending me back to Greece. This quarrel exemplified my inexperience in dealing with a simple issue that meant a great deal more to Uncle John, who was rigid and inflexible and who instead of trying to discuss the matter began to make illogical threats. Fortunately, Aunt Bettie intervened and whatever she said to Uncle John, he relented and we made up. He did not bring up the subject again and I continued to smoke but only in his absence. I quit on my own twenty years later.

My goal during the summer of 1947 was to improve on my English. I studied diligently and every night Uncle John would quiz me. He insisted that I not speak Greek and to converse with Aunt Bettie in English, though she spoke excellent Greek. She helped me with making use of the proper grammar and syntax in speaking and writing.

During dinner, Uncle John and Aunt Bettie enjoyed listening to the national news on the radio and after that to the radio programs. Invariably Uncle John would ask me what did the newscaster say and, naturally, I would begin recounting in Greek but he would stop me and say "in English". During the first couple of months it was frustrating since I was for the first time exposed to news analyses by seasoned speakers who used words and terms that were unfamiliar to me. Commentators who with time became names I recognized and admired were Gabriel Heatter, H. V. Kaltenborn, Walter Winchell and Edward R. Morrow. Initially I struggled and as time went on I began to recognize terms and regions, names of politicians, the various congressmen and senators and began to connect events and people involved in them. Listening to Uncle John and Aunt Bettie discuss the news from the radio or the articles from the New York Times began to help with my language improvement. What convinced Uncle John that I was making progress was my reaction to the comedy radio programs. He noticed that I began to laugh at the jokes, which on many occasions used idiomatic expressions.

## Starting College

September 1947 came and I was getting ready to enter college. Uncle John chose Wilbur Wright Junior College, a school that had three professors that had emigrated from Greece and two who were born in Chicago. This was very thoughtful of Uncle John because the knowledge that there were professors from Greece allayed much of my concern and anxiety of entering an American college.

Immediately, I was introduced to the concept of a liberal arts school. I registered for several courses, including English, Humanities, Mathematics, Social Science, Biology, Economic Geography, Accounting and of course Gym. In the first couple of months I made heavy use of my English-Greek Dictionary. I found the courses very interesting and the two that I enjoyed particularly were Humanities and Economic Geography. In Humanities we were introduced to the writings of some of the best writers of English literature. We were introduced to "Paradise Lost", an epic poem by John Milton, the "Rape of the Lock", a mock-heroic poem by Alexander Pope and the "Canterbury Tales", a poetic work of twenty-four tales, by Geoffrey Chaucer. There were two professors who read and interpreted for us the poems that constitute some of the finest examples of middle and neoclassical English. Their enthusiastic and erudite style of interpreting these writings helped many of us, for there were several other newcomers from Greece, to appreciate the early writings of English literature.

Shakespear's plays were reserved for the second year in the course of Public Speaking. The teacher was a dedicated person who tried to teach us how to deliver the many beautiful passages from the numerous Shakespearean plays. She insisted on the use of the proper pronunciation and on the proper inflections to convey the emotions of the speaker. All these lessons and exercises had a profound effect on my academic development. What especially pleased Uncle John and Aunt Bettie was the A's I was receiving in most of my courses which made it easier to get a tuition scholarship at Northwestern University where I started my third year of college studies in the fall of 1949.

Life with Uncle John and Aunt Bettie during the first year after my arrival was easy in that I did not have many chores to perform except that on Saturdays I had to help with the house cleaning. I was introduced to a new device, unknown to me before, the vacuum cleaner. The apartment was split level. The street level portion had a dining room, a kitchen, a pantry, a bathroom and a laundry room. I had to vacuum the stairway that led from the dining room to the second floor and the carpeting on that floor. My job also included cleaning the bath tubs and the sinks in both the upstairs and downstairs bathrooms. That was a small price to pay for all the privileges I was being offered. Other duties included going to the neighborhood grocery store to buy staples such as bread, soap, canned vegetables or soups. The trips to the grocery store gave me a chance to learn the names of the common food items used in the average household, selecting foods from a variety of choices and a chance to converse with the grocer.

In 1948 Uncle John decided to visit Greece, to see his parents and the rest of the family and to introduce Aunt Bettie to them. Another goal of his trip to Greece was to try out a business idea he developed. When Uncle John had an idea that to him appeared logical, he followed it with a passion. He reasoned that most Greeks in America would be longing to see their relatives in Greece after they had been cut off from them during the war years. His plan was to approach as many Greeks as possible in the United States and sell them on the idea that a movie of their family members in Greece, in their village surroundings, with their parents and grandparents busily working in their fields or olive groves, milking the sheep or goats, baking their bread in the typical village brick ovens, would be an enjoyable and less expensive substitute to having to travel to Greece.

In those days there were no marketing experts one could consult with for such simple adventures. Uncle John in his way was realizing his ambition to create a travelogue by photographing the daily life in the villages and towns of Greece. Cinematography was his hobby and this was an excellent opportunity to satisfy a noble cause. He therefore, planned the whole thing in his mind with Aunt Bettie's help.

Obviously, the most critical task was to get hold of as many names of Greeks living in major cities of the United States as possible. He was well known in Chicago proper and its surrounding suburbs. He and Aunt Bettie approached the Greek churches in the Chicago area and requested the names and addresses of their members. Some churches he contacted by letter, others by phone and the ones where some of his friends were members, he went personally to the church elders. Within a few weeks mail arrived at 1509 Dobson Street with the list of parishioners from the surrounding churches. Uncle John was very pleased with the response.

However, his zeal had awakened in him new entrepreneurial approaches and he came up with two new ones. In the one he suggested that I write an ad in Greek that could be read on the Chicago Greek Hour radio program on Sunday mornings. I wrote a very enthusiastic and rousing announcement, using all my literary talent I had developed in my Greek high school. In it which I described the process of Uncle John's contacting the relatives in the United States and emphasized the importance of having the opportunity to see their loved ones in Greece, in their daily activities, in Kodachrome. Uncle John who knew Greek well made some editorial changes and the ad was ready to be read by none other but me on the Greek Hour radio program. The ad was rather long maybe 3 to 4 minutes, and my delivery, sharpened by the night news deliveries during the occupation in Thessaloniki, made the listeners take notice. The radio station owner told Uncle John that listeners called to express their pleasure at the "good Greek" the new announcer was using.

To get to the radio station I had to take the Western Avenue streetcar at the start of the line on the cross-section of Howard Street and Western Avenue and travel south for one hour to the radio station. My announcement came on at 9 A.M. and as soon as I was finished with my delivery I took the streetcar back to Evanston. After two or three Sundays, the radio station owner suggested to Uncle John that I cut a record with the message and give it to the station so that I did not have to travel every Sunday morning. Cutting a record in a recording studio was another new experience for me. This was the pre-tape era and any mistakes in the delivery of the message, however minor, resulted in having to discard the record and cut a new one. Finally, I succeeded recording one that was flawless. We kept the records marked "NG", "No Good" and mailed the perfect one to the radio station.

The second plan of Uncle John's was to go through the many telephone books of various big United States cities, especially those with known large Greek communities and copy the addresses of people whose last names appeared to be of Greek origin. To accomplish this, Uncle John, Aunt Bettie and I spent three weekends at the Chicago Library where all the telephone books of major U.S. cities were kept on file. This was a monumental task. We targeted Greek names that were obvious, such as those that had typical Greek endings, like –idis, -ides, -poulos, -adis, -ades, -anis, -atis, -iris, -akis, -akes, -osas, etc. I can't remember how many telephone books we covered but with three of us working we amassed an enormous list.

The next task was that of putting all these names and addresses on metal plates so that we could address the envelopes. A typographer in the Chicago Greek Town, Mr. Damianos, was a friend of Uncle John's and he loaned him an addressograph. This was a large, metal embossing machine that used narrow metal plates for the addresses. The operator moved a carrier to the desired letter of the alphabet and pulled a trigger which resulted in the imprinting of the particular letter. We were now in the early summer of 1948 and since school was out I was given the task of making the hundreds of plates from the endless list of Greek names. It was a slow, monotonous and tedious job, which I did mechanically in practice and in spirit. To break the monotony, I began to sing a variety of Greek songs that I was able to recall freely. For effect and to drown out the rhythmic clicking of the addressograph, I was singing rather loudly and one evening, as Uncle John and Aunt Bettie were returning from the office, they could hear me from about a block away from the open windows. They concluded that I was enjoying my job so well that I was expressing it by singing and I did not try to dispel their pleasant impression.

The announcements, now written in both Greek and English, went out in batches. When all the envelopes were finally mailed, the long wait began. To Uncle John's disappointment and to our surprise only one Greek family responded positively, a family that lived in the south side of Chicago with relatives in Peloponnesus. The other surprise was the arrival of three or four letters from irate recipients who felt insulted that we would consider them Greek. With a little research we found out that many Lithuanian and Latvian names have similar endings as the Greek names.

With the movie project coming to an end, Uncle John investigated the possibility of me finding a part time job. A friend of his who owned a couple of movie theaters agreed to give me a summer job, as Assistant Manager, in one of the theaters in the downtown area. The job title was impressive and the manager was a friendly person of Greek origin. My duties, which began at 1 P.M., included taking tickets, seating people when the movie was on and on weekends cleaning up the gum from the carpet on the center aisle. My weekly salary was $50.00. I accepted the responsibilities and I was thankful for the opportunity to have some money of my own, in addition to the $10.00 Uncle John was giving me for my weekly allowance.

Uncle John was a successful physician and surgeon. He carried out his practice of eye, ear, nose and throat from an office on North Michigan Avenue in Chicago and operated in a hospital downtown, not far from his office. He was well off economically and this allowed him to invest wisely in the stock market which helped him increase his holdings. However, as the example of the filming of the Greek families demonstrated, his pet business ventures did not pan out. No sooner the first project was out, he began planning the next one.

In the 1940's Burton Holmes was the best known travelogue maker in the United States. He packed the theaters and even the Chicago Orchestra Hall. Uncle John decided that he would produce a travelogue on Greece. In early 1949 he began making plans to travel with Aunt Bettie to various parts of Greece and begin filming the sights and scenes of everyday life. Before leaving for Greece in the summer of that year, he bought a splicing machine with a viewer not larger than 5 x 4 inches. Again he relied on an amateur like me to carry out an important job that required the trained eye of a professional photographer or if not a professional, someone with some experience, which I lacked. My job was to take the canisters of exposed film that he was to send me from Greece, have it developed, run it through the viewer and look for faults in lighting, overexposed or underexposed areas, delete them using the splicer and then reconnect the film.

The summer of 1949 was full of anticipation. Uncle John and Aunt Bettie were getting ready for their long trip to Greece to film the life in the villages and towns. They were also planning to attend Aunt Helen's wedding to Mr. Minas Dafnis, a lawyer, an event they intended to film. Within two weeks after their departure I received two canisters with exposed film from Thessaloniki. I had it developed and I ran it through the viewer. I noted what I thought were scenes with faulty lighting and I sent a letter to Uncle John detailing the areas that needed re-filming. It was exciting to see scenes from my old neighborhood, the Kamara, the Rotunda, the markets in downtown Thessaloniki, the coffee houses, the shoe-shine boys and the crowds promenading on the "paraleia", the avenue by the seashore. Before long, additional canisters had arrived and by the time Uncle John and Aunt Bettie were back in Evanston, I had received a total of ten canisters, each containing a reel with 25 feet of film in it.

Upon his return Uncle John worked on the film he had shot and pooled the small reels into larger 100 foot ones. It took another three summer trips to Greece to complete the visits to Athens, the villages and towns in the environs of Athens, the towns of Peloponnesus, the islands of Crete, Rhodes, Kos and Myconos and a few of the towns in northern Macedonia. After a lot of editing and splicing the travelogue was ready for showing. The film was to be shown at the Chicago Orchestra Hall and Aunt Bettie was to be the narrator. The event was advertised in the Chicago daily papers as well as the local Greek paper, the Greek Star. The showing was a success, Aunt Bettie did an excellent job of narrating with her clear, well- modulated delivery and the full Orchestra Hall broke into thunderous applause at the end of the film. Technically and artistically the venture was a success but it did not result in more than another showing before the film was shelved for posterity.

After graduating from Wright Junior College in June 1949, I applied to Northwestern University in Evanston and I was awarded a tuition scholarship. My course work was more advanced, the chemistry and physics classes taking most of my effort because of the long lab periods. Since my aim was to go to medical school, I focused on science courses and I added anthropology, comparative anatomy and embryology. Admittedly, the course work was more sophisticated and more demanding but I enjoyed it. For the first time I was exposed to teaching assistants, graduate students and postdoctoral fellows, who assisted with the specific labs. All the teaching assistants were very knowledgeable and eager to help. The professors, who were lucid and articulate, gave the general lectures in the particular discipline. The three courses that were totally new to me and also very enjoyable were anthropology, embryology and comparative anatomy. They represented areas of biological science that I was not exposed to before and were preparatory for my future medical school studies. In anthropology, I was required to write a review of the famous book "Coming of Age In Samoa" by Margaret Mead." This was a new experience for me and I had to do a lot of library searching to be able to write an erudite review. The professor liked the review and gave me an "A".

## My marriage to Jane

The fall of 1949 saw a major change in my life. I met my future wife, Jane (Eugenia) Kutsunis and on November 24, Thanksgiving Day, we were married in Geneseo, Illinois, her home- town. The ceremony took place in a Methodist Church and was officiated by the priest of a Greek Orthodox Church located in the neighboring city of Moline. On my side of the family Uncle John, Aunt Bettie and my best man, George Papageorge, a friend and classmate from Wright Junior College, attended the ceremony. On her side, her father William, her mother Toula and her 14-year old brother George were present. In addition several friends of he family and many former classmates of Jane's were also there.

Part of the Greek ceremony requires that the bride and groom take three sips of wine, representing the blood of Christ, which was blessed by the priest. At the last minute we discovered that we had forgotten the wine and Jane's father dispatched George to the house to fetch a bottle of wine. At the proper moment the priest gave me a glass with what was supposed to be wine in it and ordered me in Greek "roufixe" meaning to drink with a slurping noise. The moment the liquid touched my lips I felt a burning sensation and I realized that what was in the glass was brandy and not wine. I took three quick sips and I warned Jane not to drink it but only to sip it. Obviously in the dark George had picked up the wrong bottle. Our honeymoon took place in Chicago, lasting only two days since I had to go back to Northwestern to resume my junior year classes.

The year at Northwestern was a rewarding experience. Jane moved to Evanston with me and got a job at Northwestern University working in the president's office. Finding an apartment commensurate with the salary she was making was difficult. We found a one- room apartment in a house owned by Mrs. Kaufmann. She rented individual rooms to college students and young couples. Mrs. Kaufmann was an older person in her 60's and ran the house like an army barracks. Noise had to be kept low in the room, no radio playing at night and no parties. Breakfast was prepared in the basement where we had to make our own coffee and toast. Life in the "Kaufmann Castle", as we called the place, was getting to be almost unbearable and we began to look for another place to live. We were fortunate to find an attic room with a bath and a kitchen nook in a house owned by Mr. MacDougal, a professor of journalism at Northwestern University. We rented the room for 50 dollars a month with the proviso that we would baby sit for their two young daughters, six and seven years old. The remainder of the school year went smoothly. Jane enjoyed her job at Northwestern University and I completed all my courses with a B+ average.

In the summer we moved to Geneseo to stay with Jane's parents. A change in my school plans was necessary as Jane's parents needed her to help with her father's store where ladies ready-to-wear was sold.

Mr. William Kutsunis was an immigrant from Greece, the region of Messinia in Peloponnesus. He had come to the USA in the early part of the 20$^{th}$ century to work on the railroads. After having saved some money he decided to go into business and opened a shoe store in Geneseo, Illinois. His business flourished and after a few years he opened a ladies ready to wear store. In 1926 he visited Greece where he married Toula (short for Panayotoula) Georgacopoulos. The couple returned to Geneseo and Jane (short for Eugenia) was born a year later. Jane was a bright, industrious student who excelled in English literature. She was awarded the State of Illinois prize in Extemporaneous Speech. She finished high school one year early, at age 17. Mr. Kutsunis' business went very well allowing him and his family to weather the depression years without the deprivations that afflicted many families. Jane's parents had another daughter who, unfortunately died at a young age and then a son George, who was born when Jane was eight. The economic difficulties during the war years were felt by the family and by everyone in the city of Geneseo. Mr. Kutsunis, however, persisted and his business grew, allowing him to invest in real estate. Today George owns seven ladies wear stores in Illinois and Iowa. His daughter Katie Andrios manages all the stores.

*Geronte: It seems to me you are locating them wrongly: the heart is on the left and the liver is on the right.*

*Sganarelle: Yes, in the old days that was so, but now we have changed all that, and we now practice medicine by a completely new method.*

Moliere: Le Medicine malgre lui.

*The desire to take medicine is perhaps the greatest feature, which distinguishes man from animals.*

H. Cushing: Life of Sir William Osler

# The 1950s

## 11. The Medical School Years.

When Jane and I moved to Geneseo, I registered as a senior at Augustana College in Rock Island, Illinois, located near the border of Iowa, and about 35 miles west of Geneseo. After a couple of weeks of total idleness I decided to look for a job just to keep busy. The area around Geneseo is part of the corn-belt region of the Midwest. It wasn't long, before I was hired by a local farmer.

The job required for us to stand on running boards on either side of a tractor and pull out the tassels from the corn stalks on alternate rows. The rationale for this type of maneuver was to accomplish cross pollenation between two species of corn that ultimately would produce hybrid corn. As we moved up and down the length of the cornfield, our hands had to move quickly to keep up with the speed of the tractor. The pay was below minimum wage but the job gave me a chance to be out in the countryside and earn some spending money. During the end of the first week, when the temperature was very high and there wasn't a cloud in the sky, I forgot to wear a protective hat and by the end of the afternoon I came down with a splitting headache, a flushed face and throbbing of my temples. When I got home, Jane put cold water compresses on my head and after about two hours of complete rest and a nap I woke up feeling better.

The episode of sunstroke put an end to my farming experience. Within a few days another job opportunity arose. An enterprising young man started his construction business and offered me a job, mixing cement in one of those small, portable mixers that held about 20 gallons of mix. The hourly pay was very good, $4.50 an hour and I did not have to go away from the town. Comparing the two jobs in terms of physical effort, this job was more demanding physically, whereas de-tasseling required only the moving of hands. When the cement reached the appropriate level of consistency I had to pour it into a wheelbarrow and take it to the area that was being cemented by other workers. I found the work satisfying and rewarding in terms of accomplishment. Unfortunately, the project lasted only three weeks and I found myself idle again until Sptember 1950 when classes at Augustana resumed.

## Finishing up my pre-medical studies

Augustana College, although a Swedish Lutheran institution, was an interdenominational liberal arts school that did not discriminate against religious preference or color. The teachers were all Ph.D.'s in their fields, enjoyed teaching and were the most approachable people I had met. This attitude, which was prevalent at Wright Junior College, at Northwestern University, and here, contrasted with the behavior of my professors of the medical school at the University of Thessaloniki, who had created a chasm between themselves and the student body.

I remember distinctly the weeks before leaving for Americaa when

I went to see Mr. Cavasiadis, the chemistry professor, to have him sign my attendance book, an official document with my name, photograph and the various courses I was taking. To enter the professor's office, one had to go through his clerk, a man who determined whether you merited the professor's time. As I approached Mr. Cavasiadis and was about to hand him the book I said meekly, "Mr. Cavasiadis", and before I could utter another word he got up and in a very authoritative manner said, "Leave and don't come back until you learn how to address your professors". The big mistake was that I addressed him as "Mr. Cavasiadis" instead of "Professor Cavasiadis". I left and went back the next day, met with the professor's clerk who agreed to present my book to the professor for his signature. The following day I retrieved my book with Professor Cavasiadis' signature. The signatures of the professors of my classes in physics, biology and anatomy were similarly obtained through the auspices of their respective clerks.

At Augustana I excelled in all my science courses, as well as in philosophy and French. About one month before graduation, in June 1951, I was informed that school policy required that all graduating students had to pass a swimming test. Without such proof I could not get my degree. I hadn't gone swimming for several years and I was wondering what sort of swimming tricks I was expected to perform. The day of the test came, I jumped into the pool and I began to swim. About half way down the full length of the pool, I decided to stop and rest and in doing so I decided to spin in the vertical position, a maneuver that caused me to lose my buoyancy and began to sink. The swimming instructor noticed immediately what was happening and he quickly tapped on my shoulder with a long pole and as I grabbed it I pulled myself to the surface and moved to the edge of the pool, where the teacher advised me to get out out of the pool and informed me that I had passed the test. In a college that was known for its adherence to rules and regulations, I was surprised that they did not inform us some time earlier that passing a swimming test was mandatory to getting one's degree. In June of 1951, I received by Bachelor's Degree in Chemistry.

It was during that summer when a letter arrived from Aunt Helen telling me that Big-Pappou had passed away after a bout with pneumococcal pneumonia. He was 90 years old. The sad news of my grandfather's death, although not totally unexpected, came as a shock. Previous letters indicated that he was doing well in his health; however the advancing age and the chronic bronchitis contributed to his decreased defenses. The news of Big-Pappous' death evoked myriads of memories- his warmth, his joy in bouncing me on his knees, his taking me by the hand and going for walks and visits to the city center, his telling me fairy tales, while I was perched on his lap, his coming from the mill atop his beautiful black horse. This nostalgic retrograde trip made it difficult to stop my tears, despite the comforting words from Jane. During visits in later years to Greece recounting with Aunt Helen and with other relatives experiences with Big-Pappous was a frequent and heart-warming event full of unforgetable memories..

In September 1951, I matriculated in the graduate school of the University of Illinois in Champaign-Urbana with a major in microbiology and a minor in biochemistry. That year was an eye-opener in terms of the quality of teaching, the quality of course work and of new concepts in biological science. Outstanding scientists taught the various science courses. Dr. Sol Spiegelman, a brilliant researcher taught microbial genetics. His formal lectures were followed by organized evening sessions that started after dinner and lasted until 10:30 P.M. Hypotheses were proposed and experimental designs were formulated. Dr. Spiegelman trained brilliant graduate students and fellows who worked endlessly and performed the most imaginative experiments.

One of the projects dealt with the production of bacterial mutants that lacked the ability to produce a given essential amino acid. This was accomplished by irradiating bacteria with ultra-violet light, which killed more than 99% of the culture leaving some able to grow in a complete medium, i.e. a medium supplemented with all the essential amino acids. Using the "replicate plating" technique, we would identify colonies that were deficient in one or another amino acid by demonstrating their inability to grow in a medium which lacked a specific amino acid. These mutants would then be grown separately and their metabolic properties studied further.

Another course that fascinated me was synthesis of viruses and specifically of bacteriophage that was taught by Dr. Salvador Luria, another brilliant microbial geneticist, who in 1969 received the Nobel

Prize in Medicine or Physiology. I vividly remember one day in the spring of 1952, while I was preparing bacteriologic media in the general lab, I saw Dr. Luria taking samples out of an International Preparatory Ultracentrifuge. Dr. Luria took a small plastic tube out of the rotor and with an excited voice, reminiscent of a young child who just solved a block puzzle, yelled at me, "Nick, Nick, look, I got it". What he showed me was what seemed like a speck of dirt at the bottom of the tube. That speck was his first evidence that he was able to synthesize bacteriophage. He quickly asked me not to discuss his findings with anyone, an obvious allusion to the fierce competition in the field. Dr. Luria's lectures on virology were fascinating because they were full of experimental data recently generated in his laboratory. Young graduate students, like Halvorson and Campbell were churning out the new data.

I still remember one graduate student whose name I cannot recall, working endless hours in a small cubicle, isolated from noise and interruptions, trying to isolate individual mutant yeast cells by using a hanging drop, a glass pipette drawn to the size of a fine capillary tube and a stage that was moving using a pneumatic apparatus. I was suddenly surrounded by dedicated people who constantly asked questions about metabolic properties of bacteria, genetic factors to explain the synthesis of bacteriophage, and mechanisms of bacterial resistance to antibiotics.

The courses in biochemistry and genetics again brought me face-to-face with giants in their fields. Dr. William Rose who discovered threonine, an essential amino acid and Dr. Rhoads, the professor of genetics who did original work in the development of hybrid corn. Dr. Rhoads taught our class how to make chromosomal preparations of cornflowers. The preparations were easy to make and we soon learned that we could identify the corn chromosomes from 1 to 10, based on their length and position of the centromere. When the notice from the University of Illinois College of Medicine arrived in early 1952, informing me that I was accepted in medical school, I was determined to find opportunities to carry out research while studying medicine. I had not thought yet what specialty I was going to pursue but I felt that if I could get involved in some research project I would make use of the laboratory skills I had acquired during the year in Champaign-Urbana.

## Medical school classes begin

The first year of medical school began in September 1952 with a class of more than 160 students. There were only five women in our class. The two courses that many students dreaded were Anatomy, because of the strange Latin and Greek names, and Biochemistry. Having had Latin and classical Greek in high school I found anatomy easier than most students.

Anatomy was the reason one of our classmates, one of the four assigned to our cadaver, was totally intimidated by the uncertainty of the structures that lay below the skin. He was standing across from me during dissection and as we were ready to make our first incision he asked me how deep he should go into the skin. Looking at our cadaver, an emaciated, thin lady, I suggested not to go too deep. I made my first incision and I was in the process of dissecting away the skin from the trapezious muscle when a shriek from our partner pierced my ear as he shouted, "Nick, I think I hit bone". I tried to quiet him and assure him that this was not surprising since the cadaver had no fat to separate the skin from the underlying muscle.

Although he was not squeamish about handling a dead body, his subsequent behavior revealed an obvious lack of confidence in his ability to handle the complicated concepts of the various courses. The anatomy episode was a harbinger of what happened at the end of the first year. He decided to quit medical school and join a pharmaceutical company working as a detail man, visiting doctors in their offices and hospitals.

In my mind, the most dynamic and memorable teacher in our first year was the professor of anatomy, Dr. Zimmermann, a native of Switzerland. He lectured with enthusiasm and tried to make the course as lively as possible even though we relied heavily on cadavers. He would draw the course of nerves and blood vessels on his white coat with colored chalk. One time he asked one of our classmates, Jerry Lewis, to take his shirt and undershirt off to show the distribution of back muscles on the student's athletic chest.

The course in biochemistry was taught by its chairman, Dr.

Richard Winzler. I approached Dr. Winzler and asked him for a job as a technician in his lab. He must have been impressed with my technical capabilities because in the summer following the end of the second year, he asked me whether I wanted to take up a project of my own and go for a master's degree in biochemistry. I accepted enthusiastically.

Living quarters were not easy to find on the medical school campus. A new apartment building was under construction and was to be ready in the spring of 1953. The University gave preference to married students and faculty and especially those with children. During the first quarter I lived at a medical fraternity house, which was very useful. Not only freshmen lived there, but also students from the more advanced classes who were always available and eager to help first year students with their academic problems. In early spring of 1953, Jane and I moved into a small apartment on Jackson Boulevard, not far from the medical center. It was a one-bedroom apartment with a small kitchen and a bed that was raised and pushed inside the wall. Within a month after we moved to the Jackson Boulevard apartment the University informed us that we could move into a "zero- bedroom apartment". Zero-bedroom meant one room with two sofa-beds, a table with four chairs, a coffee table, a galley kitchen and one bathroom. Our small apartment faced west and we enjoyed the afternoon and evening sun. Jane found a good job in downtown Chicago as a secretary to one of the vice presidents of Chicago Title and Trust Company. The elevated train that took her downtown stopped only a block away from our apartment building and made it easy for her to get to the station. Jane's monthly salary was large enough to cover our basic needs and left enough for entertainment and incidentals. The building had a large number of tenants from our class, which offered us opportunities for get-togethers to study, play cards and for dinner parties.

The first year of medical school ended with a sense of great relief. Jane and I took a two-week vacation in Geneseo where she helped in her father's store and I helped with odd jobs around the house.

We returned to Chicago, where Jane went back to work and I began working as a technician in the laboratory of Dr. Richard Winzler. This job was paying minimum wage and allowed students to continue during the school year if they were maintaining a B or better average. With the onset of the second year, I continued to work part-time in the afternoons. Dr. Winzler's laboratory was involved in the isolation and characterization of serum glycoproteins and their changes seen in acute and chronic disorders. In the middle of the school year, Dr. Winzler asked me whether I would like to try my hand at a project of my own. I was told that NIH funded medical student part-time research projects; I was happy to accept the offer.

My project was to develop a new method of isolating and characterizing orosomucoid, a serum acid glycoprotein. In 1954 the Germans marketed a small free-flow electrophoresis apparatus that used the Schlieren optical system to follow the purity of precipitated fractions. I had devised a precipitation and fractionation system, using magnesium sulfate to isolate orosomucoid from Cohn's plasma fraction VI. Since the major component of plasma fraction VI is serum albumin, I had to eliminate it by precipitating it out. After several such steps and with the aid of the electrophoretic apparatus that allowed me to follow the purity of orosomucoid I was able to prepare pure fractions of the desired protein. I was able to photograph the image of the curve on the screen of the electrophoretic apparatus with a built-in camera that used ordinary black and white film. Since I had only a few hours in the afternoons to work in the lab, progress was slow until summer time when classes were off and I could work full time. The protein I had isolated was so pure that with the help of Dr. M. Goodman and Mr. S. Silberberg of the Department of Pathology we produced high titer antibodies in chickens.

We used the antibodies to measure serum levels of orosomucoid in normal individuals and in those with acute or chronic diseases. These studies led to my Master's thesis and a publication in 1955, my very first, on the antibody serum levels of orosomucoid in health and disease. In 1956 I was awarded a M.S. degree in biochemistry, the same day I was awarded my M.D. In 1954 the Medical School gave each student a B.S degree in Medicine.

In 1956, in recognition of my research accomplishments I was given the Borden Research Award in Medicine. It was a competitive event and I was the one selected. Nine years after arriving in the United States I received four degrees and a research award. This would have been unheard of in Greece in those years.

The second year of medical school was very demanding in time and effort. New courses explored the functions of the various organ systems; physiology opened the secrets of cardiac, lung and kidney functions and pathology analyzed the causes of death by looking at normal and diseased tissue. Microbiology was the most fun for me since I already had a year of advanced microbial metabolism and genetics two years earlier as a graduate student in Champaign-Urbana. Pharmacology was a new area for almost the whole class and the mode of action of most of the commonly known drugs was unfolded in front of us, in lab experiments that used dogs and rabbits. Fortunately, we did not have to prepare the dogs for each experiment, something that was left to the specialized lab technicians. If I had to select the two most fascinating courses in the second year, both in terms of new information and answering questions of system functions I would have to choose Physiology and Pharmacology.

It was during the second year that we were introduced for the first time to patients. The course was physical diagnosis. We were allowed to wear a short white jacket with our name tag. Young faculty introduced us to patients suffering from a variety of diseases and went over their clinical and physical findings. The emphasis was on exposing us to patients with cardiac, liver, kidney, or eye problems, where the physical findings were obvious to the naked eye or easily discernible on examination.

All the excitement and fascination with the second year courses was suddenly overshadowed and waned as the day of the comprehensive exam was approaching, an exam that covered the material we were taught during the first two years of classes. It was a hard exam and I was pleased to learn that I passed it. I was relieved and I took that as an excuse to take a long and needed summer vacation before I returned to the lab to continue on my research project.

In 1954, a very important event took place in my life. I became eligible to apply for U.S. citizenship. In the application there was a space provided to indicate whether I wished to change my last name. In all the time that I had lived in the USA people kept mispronouncing my name or simply did not bother to pronounce it and called me by my first name. I decided to change my last name from Kefalides to Alexander, to honor my mother's first name "Alexandra". About two months before I was to appear before a judge, Jane and I attended a garden party. A young, ten-year old child, and her parents, who were attending the same party, were introduced to me. A month later we met the same family at another party and without hesitation, the young child said "Hello Mr. Kefalides", remembering my name and pronouncing it correctly. On the day I was to take the oath, the judge asked me if I wanted to make any last minute changes. I asked that Alexander stay as my middle name and to add Kefalides as my last name. In the process, I gained a new middle name and kept my family name.

The third and fourth years of medical school took us out of the labs and into the clinics. We rotated through the different services of the Research and Educational Hospitals and we were assigned to residents of the particular service such as internal medicine, surgery, urology, pediatrics, hematology, ophthalmology, otorhinolaryngology and neurology. The whole atmosphere on the wards and clinics was more relaxed and we were eager to see patients who presented with the signs and symptoms we were reading about in our textbooks. These were the years when we got to know our professors better. I began to know better the professors in medicine and surgery, as well as the residents in both services. The formal lectures were few and involved specialized topics with small numbers of students attending. In our senior year we occasionally took night call with one of the interns in our service, a practice that was preparatory for our internships the following year.

During he spring of 1956 a small group of my classmates and I traveled to a number of cities to investigate the nature and quality of the internship training programs in their major hospitals. It is true that we already knew the quality of the majority of the programs but we felt that we needed to get a first hand knowledge by visiting the specific hospital. During one of those trips we visited Wayne State University Medical Center in Detroit, Michigan. Some in our group were impressd and they began considering the Detroit hospital as a potential place for training. I had come to the conclusion that for my training aspirations I would rather stay with the University of Illinois Research and Educational Hospitals. Before leaving Detroit, John Kaminsky, the classmate who owned the Ford sedan that took us around, had suggested that we cross a bridge and visit Winsor Canada, since it was so close. We did and it was a memorable experience. That was the first and last time I have visited Canada. One of these days, Jane and I have vowed that we will make the trip to Canada as tourists.

Graduation day arrived in June 1956. The Schools of Medicine, Dentistry and Pharmacy as well as the Graduate School graduates gathered in the assembly hall and as each student's name was called we approached the stage where we were given our medical diplomas. I had the unique opportunity to march a second time to receive my Master of Science degree in biochemistry. My wife Jane and Uncle John were present at the ceremony. Hugs and kisses were in order as we met outside the hall. Uncle John took photographs to commemorate the successful outcome of four years of intensive study. Several of our classmates got together in small groups to congratulate and wish each other good luck in their internships. The majority of graduates selected hospitals away from the city and in different states. I was accepted into the internship program of the University of Illinois Research and Educational Hospitals.

The internship year was fantastic, as the excellent opportunities to develop independent actions under the tutelage of of brilliant faculty. I had decided to pursue a residency program in internal medicine and I had applied for it at the same hospital where I was accepted. However, the start of my residency had to wait three years. Having been deferred from military service because of my studies, I now had to join one of the services and I applied for the Air Force. Soon after I applied, my medical school advisor and friend, Dr. Mark Lepper, asked me to consider applying for the public health service at NIH (National Institutes of Health). The Chief of the Department of Medicine, Dr. Harry Dowling, asked me in his office and also urged me to consider applying to NIH. At that time I had little knowledge of the many functions of NIH. I knew that it was composed of several institutes carrying out research in several disease areas, such as arthritis, skin diseases, diabetes, cancer, blood diseases and cardiovascular disorders.

Over the years, as a grade school and high school student and later as a college and medical student I had developed an attitude of respect, admiration and a sense of obedience for some of my teachers. It was hard for me to say no to their suggestions and I sent in my application to NIH. In early spring the air force informed me of my acceptance in their program and NIH did the same the following day.

By this time, Drs. Dowling and Lepper described in general terms the nature of the project that I was supposed to be involved with. NIH had initiated a project to study the effects of salt solution in the prevention and treatment of shock during the first 72 hours following a skin burn. When I indicated that I had not worked with patients in shock, Dr. Dowling revealed more of the NIH project. The shock was no longer a problem for the burn patients but rather fatal septicemia, due to staphylococcus and pseudomonas microorganisms. The big news for me was that the project was being carried out in Lima, the capital of Peru. It sounded intriguing and challenging to say the least. I had never traveled outside the USA and Jane was very much against living in a South American country that she considered underdeveloped and very foreign. As much as I was becoming interested in the idea of joining NIH, Jane was set against it. The impasse brought in Dr. Lepper all the way to our apartment to persuade Jane to go with me to Peru. I wasn't present when Dr. Lepper talked to Jane but she related to me the arguments he used to convince her. He said it would be an excellent opportunity to run a research project and a great chance to further my career. Jane relented and I accepted the NIH offer. On July 1, 1957, we moved to Bethesda, Maryland.

*Let observation with extensive view, survey
mankind, from China to Peru.*
Samueel Johnson:
The Vanity of Human Wishes.

*A smell of burning fills the startled air.*
Hilaire Belloc: Newdigate Poem

## 12. Joining the NIH and Moving to Peru

My Chief at NIH was Dr. Sanford M. Rosenthal, a slight, balding, older
gentleman with a soft voice and a pleasant demeanor. His biochemistry
labs were located in the basement of Building 4, where he and his
colleagues conducted all their experiments. It was there that I was
introduced to Dr. Herbert Tabor, now Editor-in-Chief of the Journal
of Biological Chemistry, (JBC), and Dr. Carl Millikan, two scientists
who were involved in the burn project. I also met Dr. Leonard Warren,
the man who developed the thiobartrituric acid method for measuring
sialic acid (or neuraminic acid as it was later referred to) and published
it in the J.B.C., a paper that was the most highly cited methods work
in that Journal. The research project in Lima Peru was supported by a
intramural NIH grant, that is an grant supporting research by scientists
at NIH.

The burn project was the brainchild of Dr.Sanford M. Rosenthal.
In the late 40's he was working on the physiology of vascular shock
in rats and mice. He was able to demonstrate that crush injury or
tourniquet injury of the hind legs of rats produced shock and even
death in untreated animals. He was able to show that isotonic salt
solution given intravenously or by mouth prevented the development
of shock and subsequent death.

215

In 1950, the United States was faced with the possibility of having to take care of large numbers of civilian casualties in the prospect of nuclear attack or nuclear accident. At that time the Soviet Union and China were developing capabilities of delivering nuclear weapons and the United States had no centralized facilities where large numbers of trauma or burn cases could be cared for, save for the one such facility at the Brook Army Medical Center in Houston Texas.

In 1950, the Surgery Study Section of the National Institutes of Health published a recommendation in which it was strongly suggested that "The oral use of saline solution is adopted as standard procedure in the treatment of shock due to burns and other serious injuries in the event of large scale civilian catastrophe

. To carry out the clinical studies the government decided to go outside the U.S., to Central or South America where hospital facilities were few in the big cities and all burn cases were cared for in one or two hospitals rather than in every neighborhood hospital as in the U.S. The National Research Council sent out a committee of surgeons and scientists to visit the capitals of some of these countries and make arrangements to set up the clinical studies where saline solution would be tested and compared with plasma and other modes of therapy used in the particular country. The comittee settled on Lima, Peru, where all burn cases were taken to one of three main hospitals, the Men's, the Women's and the Children's. The arrangement was made with the then Dean of the Medical School of the University of San Marcos, Dr. Alberto Hurtado, who was a 1924 graduate of Harvard Medical School and an intern at Boston City Hospital from 1925 to 1926.

The project started in 1952 and its headquarters was set up at the Women's Hospital. The Director of the project was an American Public Health Service Commissioned Officer, Dr. Kehl Markley, a young surgeon. Except for Dr. Markley, all the project staff were Peruvian, including the hospital surgeons, the nurses, the physicians, who ran the biochemistry and microbiology labs and the pathologist who performed the autopsies.

The patients were placed on a particular treatment arm on an alternate case basis. The burn project was there to save lives and the American government was paying all the expenses. The financial arrangement was simple. The NIH grant went to the University of San

Marcos, where Dr. Hurtado kept an amount of dollars corresponding to the indirect cost (overhead) and the direct cost amount was deposited in the American Bank in Lima in the name of the American project director. This money was used to pay salaries for the surgeons, the nurses and nurse's aids, the chiefs of labs as well as for supplies for the clinical labs. Needless to say, all physicians were allowed to carry on with their private practices but whenever a new burn patients arrived, they were obligated to take care of those cases until their blood pressure was stabilized and the appropriate biochemical and bacteriologic tests were performed.

Dr. Kehl Markley ran the project until early 1957. After four and a half years as Director, he decided to return to the United States and remain at NIH indefinitely, working in the laboratory of Dr. Rosenthal, where he continued to study the mechanisms of death from shock in burns. In 1956 he had married a Peruvian lady, the sister of the leading neurosurgeon in Peru, Dr. Cabiezes.

Dr. Rosenthal and his colleagues began to look for ways to stem this trend of fatal septicemias and began experiments combining antibiotics with pooled human gamma globulin in mice that were scalded in hot water. The results demonstrated a significant degree of protection against infection and death from staphylococcus or pseudomonas. In 1956 an important scientific event occurred, the availability of the polio vaccine. Up until then, before the vaccine became available, pooled human gamma globulin was the only pharmacologic agent given to patients with polio to help stem progression of the disease. The American Red Cross was in control of all available quantities of the globulin and dispensed it appropriately. With the development of the polio vaccine the Red Cross was left with enormous quantities of the gamma globulin and was looking for ways to "get rid of it". Dr. Rosenthal made a simple request and the Red Cross was more than willing to supply NIH with all the gamma globulin it needed. The scientific group in charge of the burn project at NIH modified the treatment regimen to include gamma globulin i.e. saline solution, saline solution plus plasma, saline solution plus gamma globulin and saline solution combined with plasma and gamma globulin. The gamma globulin solution was to be given in 1 ml per kilogram of body weight intramuscularly on admission and repeated on the third and fifth day. All patients were to receive antibiotics prophylactically.

In 1957, President Eisenhower commissioned me with the rank of Lieutenant in the United States Public Health Service, which was elevated to Lieutenant Commander as soon as I was sent to Lima, Peru. My wife and I were issued special passports, a status between regular and diplomatic passports. We spent a month in Bethesda and I was instructed on the procedures of the research project in Dr. Rosenthal's lab. Dr. Markley, who was working at Dr. Rosenthal's laboratory at the time, was very helpful with information about the project, life in Lima and the Peruvian doctors working on the project, the Director of the Children's Hospital, Dr. Gilberto Morey, and the technical staff. Dr. Morey realized the importance of the project and was very much in favor of providing administrative support. At the end of July 1957, Jane and I arrived in Lima, Peru. The plastic surgeon at the Children's Hospital, Dr. Augusto Bazan and Dr. Manuel Bocanegra, the internist, were there to meet us and take us to our hotel in the center of the city.

The hotel had been only recently renovated and the rooms were freshly painted. The walls of our room were olive green and because of the high humidity we could see droplets of water on the wall. This was wintertime south of the equator and the chill in the air was penetrating.

Later in the afternoon of the day of our arrival, Dr. Bocanegra picked us up and drove us to the Children's Hospital to meet some of the clinical staff, nurses and orderlies, and the physicians in charge of the clinical and microbiology labs. Everyone seemed happy to see us and meet us and wished us a pleasant stay. That same afternoon Dr. Bazan took us to the Surgical Pavilion where 12 beds were exclusively used in one of the rooms for the care of burn patients. All the beds were occupied.

By the second day of our arrival we found a nice one bedroom apartment in San Isidro, one of the most desirable suburbs in Lima, the other being Miraflores. Our household effects were shipped by air and they had arrived before we did and they were put into storage at the Children's Hospital. San Isidro is studded with beautiful villas, with tropical and subtropical trees, gardens full of flowering bushes and well manicured lawns. Our apartment was part of a complex of six apartments arranged around a small courtyard.

Jane and I went out to buy living room and bedroom furniture at a large shopping center called "Todos", built by funds from the Rockefeller Foundation. It had a Sears and Roebuck department store, a large supermarket and a variety of small shops. We furnished our living room with a set of two easy chairs and a sofa from a special boutique called "Oeschle". The upholstery fabric was unique. Sylvia Von Hagen was the designer who used the locally produced linen and designed a unique pattern she called "Cathedral Windows". The colors were striking – blue, black and green on a white background. We created bookcases by separating wooden boards on piles of red bricks. We found attractive oil paintings of bullfights that we used to decorate the walls of the living room. We managed to furnish our apartment in a satisfactory and attractive way.

With time we bought carvings of Indian heads of mahogany and other types of sculpture depicting native designs. A small supermarket and a private grocery store, the bodega, were within a block of our apartment. Until our car arrived from the States, we used public bus transportation or the ever present "collectivos", the old, dilapidated cars that were shared by five passengers.

The research protocol required that when a patient arrived I was to be notified, day or night, so that I could supervise his or her assignment to the proper treatment arm. In addition to myself, the surgeon of the hospital where the patient was taken was also notified to take care of the burn areas. Dr. Manuel Bocanegra, the project physician in charge of all three hospitals and Dr. Pedro Stastny, the biochemist in charge, were also notified. Dr. Jose Arana, the microbiologist in the project was also present to take wound cultures as well as blood, urine and stool cultures. Every admission represented a slice of the social structure of life in Lima. Here was a mother or a father bringing a young child, severely burned, crying in pain, and looking at the nurses and doctors with pleading eyes, the parents surrendering the life of their child to the people who, to them, were "miracle workers". The majority of the children came from shantytown areas that surrounded the northern and eastern parts of Lima. Their homes were no more than one room huts with corrugated tin roofs. The huts served as sleeping quarters, kitchens, places to cook a meal or to heat water for washing and bathing. In these close quarters it was easy for a young child to accidentally fall on an open fire resulting in a serious burn. Another common cause of burn among adults was the fire generated by maids working in a house and trying to melt the wax to polish the wooden floors with a kerosene torch, resulting in severe burns.

Parents brought their severely burned children to the hospital and left them to the mercy of the doctors, without knowing what was to happen to them, without having any idea of the kind of treatment they were about to receive, whether the protective gamma globulin or the saline solution alone which protected against the development of shock but which was ineffective against preventing infection and septicemia. The concept of informed concent was not in existence.

What impressed me most was the absolute faith the parents of the burned children as well as the burned adults had towards the hospital personnel. The other impressive thing was that in the course of the five years since the project was initiated, the professional personnel had developed a perfect routine of handling each patient. If a patient died, it was the result of two main factors: the extent of the surface area burned and whether there was staphylococcus or pseudomonas septicemia. All burned patients, especially young children, had another thing against them, they behaved as individuals with reduced immune defenses, irrespective of their age and the level of gamma globulin in their serum.

Soon after we arrived in Lima, I began to study Spanish by taking private lessons from a local teacher whose English was excellent. I found out that within two months I was able to master the grammar and be able to form sentences with great facility. I, therefore, stopped my formal lessons. A major factor with my success to learn the language quickly was my knowledge of Greek, whose pronunciation of words is, as in Spanish, phonetic and in hearing a word I could immediately form a mental picture of it. My daily contact with the hospital personnel forced me to converse in Spanish and my ability to speak it well resulted in an invitation to give my first lecture to the house staff on the rational use of antibiotics, in Spanish, six months after my arrival. My love for the Spanish language persists until today, and when more than 50 years later I have an opportunity, I make use of it.

Jane joined several women's clubs, including theater, bridge, bowling, painting classes, archeological digging and silver and copper metal work. Mementos of Jane's social and cultural activities that survive today include a sterling silver dish with the inscription from the bowling club, "Most Improved Bowler", several "wacos" (pots uncovered in old Chancay Indian graves), and a child's blanket wrapped around a mummy. She has a memorable collection of silver dishes, ashtrays, iced tea spoons, a large copper plate with a silver Inca symbol for November (the month of our wedding) in the center and a copper wall mask of a Inca Puma cat – all hand-filed and hammered by her over the three years we were in Lima.

During our stay in Peru, we made longstanding friendships with several of the American families living in Lima. With some of them we traveled to the interior of the country and had the opportunity to visit picturesque towns, like Huancayo, Cuzco and the incomparable site of Machu Picchu (which means "Ancient Peak").

*Cold is the heart, fair Greece! that looks on thee,*
*Nor feels as lovers o'er the dust they loved;*
*Dull is the eye that will not weep to see*
*Thy walls defaced, thy mouldering shrines removed*
*By British hands.*

Lord Byron: Childe Harold's Pilgrimage

*Thy Naiad airs have brought me home,*
*To the glory that was Greece*
*And the grandeur that was Rome.*

Edgar Allan Poe: To Helen

## 13. Our trip to Europe - The visit to Greece

### Visiting famous cities

In the spring of 1959, Jane and I took a 45-day summer vacation to Europe, which included visits to England, France, Germany, Greece and Italy. Both of us were yearning for this sojourn for a variety of reasons. It would be an unparalled opportunity to visit Europe for the first time in our lives and for me to visit Greece for the first time in 12 years and for Jane to meet my family. From Lima we traveled to Washington, D.C. where I spent a few days in the laboratory of Dr. Rosenthal discussing the status of the burn project.

From Washington, D.C., we traveled to New York where we spent three days touring the city and enjoying the sights. We boarded a TWA DC-7 at Idlewild International Airport and began our memorable trip to Europe. (Idlewild International Airport was renamed John F. Kennedy International Airport one month after the assassination of President John F. Kennedy in November of 1963).

In London, our first stop, we visited my high school classmate from

223

Thessaloniki, Alekos Andreadis, who was specializing in neurosurgery. The meeting was quite emotional. We both bombarded each other with questions about life in the medical school, in Thessaloniki during the last 12 years and news about the other classmates. We spent the time reminiscing our school years together and our subsequent careers. Although 12 years went by since we saw each other, the topics we talked about were timely as we jumped from the 50's to the 40's and back again.. We agreed to meet the next day where Alekos and his wife invited us to go see a play in London"Irma La Douce", a magnificent romantic comedy that eventually was made into a movie in 1963 with Shirley McLaine, as Irma La Douce.

Our next stop was Paris. The architectural and physical beauty of the city was captivating. We immediately fell in love with it. We loved its beautiful women, walking or sitting at the sidewalk cafes in the boulevards, its long streets with the elegant buildings, the famous squares, the obelisques, the arches, the gardens and most of all its night life. The only high school classmate living in Paris was Jo Saporta, a holocaust survivor. The surprise and enjoyment of Saporta on hearing my voice over the phone were immediately felt.

We got together the next day and we toured a few must areas such as the Louvre, the Grand Magazines, "Galleries Lafayette" and "Printemps" and the specialty boutiques. At night Jo and his brother took us to see the Follies Bergeres. The beautiful girls, the typical dancing and the excitement of the audience made the night a memorable experience.

Jo and his brother reminisced about our past years in high school, the classmates, the teachers, living during the war and the occupation. Jo gave me some details from his experience in the Bergen-Belsen concentration camp during 1944 and 1945. He and his family were being transported to another place in the summer of 1945 as the Russians were closing in on Berlin and the American armies were moving into central Europe. After spending the night in a forest under guard of the German soldiers, they woke up to find out that they were alone. The German soldiers had disappeared abandoning the prisoners. They in turn, began to walk in all directions, since they had no idea where the other prisoners were until they were met by the advancing American soldiers, who took them to a processing center. It was truly a miracle that the whole family survived the holocaust.

Our destination after Paris was Dusseldorf. I am not sure why Dusseldorf was added to the itinerary but it's obvious that the travel agent in Lima had arranged it. The city appeared dreary as we traveled by cab to the hotel. My concern about the attitude of some of the people towards Americans was justified as we approached the registration desk at the hotel. The man behind the counter was a tall, well built man, I would guess in his early 30's. He greeted us politely but his whole demeanor changed when we handed him our "Special Passports". He apparently associated us with some official capacity and the initial smile was immediately wiped off his face and he assumed an almost menacing stance as he processed our room registration. I must confess I felt unsure and almost frightened by the hotel employee's attitude.

Our next stop was Zurich, Switzerland. The city had charm, warmth and was bustling with tourists, many of them Americans. As we began to walk around the center we could see the majestic, snowcapped peaks of the Alps to the south. Lake Zurich on whose northern tip the city is located provided another breathtaking view with its lakeside promenades and the elegant homes. Another notable feature was the cleanliness of the streets with the trams going in different directions. What surprised us again was the large number of people who spoke English and I don't mean the tourists. From the streetcar conductors to the store clerks and grocery vendors, people spoke English. We did some shopping, buying souvenirs for the relatives in Greece and for us. The one thing I thought would be an excellent buy was a self-winding gold Omega watch. It was beautiful and it quickly replaced my first watch that my Aunt Bettie bought me for my first birthday in the USA, in January 1948, a stainless steel Movado.

## The vist to Greece

We left Zurich bound for Athens. The flight was less than three hours long and as the plane approached the western coast of Greece I could sense the excitement of seeing Greece again after 12 years. The voice of the pilot came on to inform us that we would be flying over the city and that the Acropolis could be seen on the left side of the plane. The Acropolis came in plain view with the Parthenon crowning the top of the hill. Jane and I were at awe for the few minutes the plane took to cross over the city of Athens.

It was early afternoon when we arrived at our hotel. We immediately called Uncle Niko Spyrou and Uncle Thanasos who lived in Athens. The next calls were to Thessaloniki to tell my parents and Aunt Helen that we had arrived. The emotional excitement was clearly evident in our voices and the voices of all the people at the other end.

We spent three days touring Athens and visiting with Uncle Spyrou and his wife Margarita and Uncle Thanasos, my mother's brother, Aunt Lesvia and their daughter Nitsa, who was now a grown up lady of 22 and a student at the University of Athens.

In the 15 years since the liberation of Greece, Athens had begun to change. New high rise buildings began to appear, the number of automobiles noticeably increased since my first visit in 1947, a harbinger of the city's becoming in later years one of the most highly polluted cities in Europe.

Our eagerness to visit Thessaloniki was rapidly turning into an ardent desire and we were greatly elated when we began to fly out of Athens. My parents had moved to a new apartment in a high rise near the center of the city. We took the elevator to the sixth floor. The door to the apartment, where they lived, was open and there stood my mother and with arms outstretched she took me in her embrace and kissed me repeatedly. My father, just behind her, was equally moved as he hugged and kissed me. Jane was received with the same excitement and warmth. When we entered the apartment we were greeted by a large contingent of relatives who eagerly embraced and kissed us. Uncle Elias, Aunt Stasa, Aunt Helen, Aunt Anastasia and my cousins Soula and Nikos. My cousins were anxious to hear news about their younger brother Michael who was brought to the United States by Uncle John. Uncle John adopted Michael, changed his name from Kefalides to Nicholson and arranged for him to attend high school and then Northwestern University in Evanston where he received a BA in Civil Engineering.

During the next few days we spent our time visiting the various relatives in their homes where we feasted on the tasty dinners of the Greek cuisine. Aunt Zografia and Uncle Stavros went out of their way to show us their culinary talents. We made almost daily visits to see Aunt Helen, Uncle Minas and above all, my Big Yiayia Evdoxia who at this time was 87 years old. She lived to be 101. Aunt Helen had a beautiful penthouse apartment on the seventh floor of a high-rise building facing east with a fantastic and breathtaking view of the Aegean, the White Tower, the park, the eastern part of the city and the mountain of Hortiatis in the background that treated the viewers to magnificent sunrises and at night the light of the silvery full moon. We spent hours visiting with Aunt Helen and Uncle Minas, sitting on the beautiful veranda drinking coke or orange juice and at times ouzo while feasting on soutjoukakia (oval meat balls) or pizza, watermelon, cherries and peaches. Our conversations invariably gravitated in reminiscing the past, the years of war and occupation, the periods of starvation and persecution, the civil war following the liberation and the friends and relatives that we lost during those years.

The visit to Thessaloniki fulfilled another long held desire, to see my high school classmates. The friends with whom I spent seven years in the same classrooms, the boys with whom I began to interact as an eleven year old boy and grew up with them into my teen-age years, living the carefree prewar period and experiencing together the catastrophic period of German occupation, the starvation, the persecutions, the years we fought in the resistance and the joy and delirium of the days after the liberation.

The time in Thessaloniki was taken up by more visits to some of the suburbs and towns near the city. We visited Edessa, where we met cousins of my mother's and where we admired the now famous waterfalls. We also decided to visit the island of Rhodes with my parents.

We flew to Athens and then took an overnight boat trip to Rhodes. Daybreak came as the boat was entering the harbor of the city of Rhodes. At the entrance, two massive columns, with an elk on top of each, adorned the passage into the harbor. It was there that the Colossus of Rhodes, a gigantic bronze statue, stood as the ancient ships sailed underneath it.

The city of Rhodes with its abundant palm trees, paved streets, buildings of varied architecture and design, emblematic of the various conquerors and their cultures that passed through the island in the course of time. My folks, Jane and I first visited the old city, the most picturesque area of the town, which was surrounded by medieval walls and where seven gates allowed entry into the city. The old city is full of tourist shops, cafes, restaurants and museums. After the ancient Greeks came the Romans who were followed by the Venetians and then the Ottoman Empire. All these conquerors, like the people who came after them, left their mark. The most impressive structures that we admired were the medieval walls and towers that once protected the city under the aegis of the Knights of Rhodes. Walking around on the cobblestone streets we were treated to an endless array of jewelry shops, restaurants, small squares with old fountains and mosques with their minarets. At one end of the town we discovered a very old synagogue and a lady who was looking after it. We were unable to learn if any of the 1,700 deported Jewish people ever returned to Rhodes after the end of World War II but if any survived, the number must have been infinitesimally small. Out of the 44,000 Jewish people deported from Thessaloniki, for instance, only about 1,000 made it back.

The Acropolis at Lindos with its Temple of Athena, is older than the one in Athens but it doesn't exactly match the grandeur of the latter. We went by taxi to the town of Lindos and from there we climbed by foot to the top of the hill, up an ancient stairway called the Helenistic Stairway. On the way up we passed a most attractive relief of an ancient ship carved on the side of the rock. The top of the hill was adorned with columns, remnants of the ancient temple and of other unknown structures.

The following day we treated ourselves to another unexpected surprise. We visited the valley of the butterflies. We were instructed to proceed to a cave, where myriads of the butterflies nested. As we stood inside the cave by the entrance, we could easily observe what appeared to be thousands of little black creatures, with colorful wings, plastered against the walls in layers, one on top of another. We were told that clapping our hands would stir the butterflies and they would begin to fly, and so they did! (Now, clapping is forbidden since this practice disturbs the metabolic balance). They circled inside the cave and large numbers of them rushed out through the cave entrance into the open air. It was a rare and awesome sight. Unfortunately we had no guide and there was no one to ask about the history of this beautiful sanctuary.

On the fifth day of our trip we took the ferryboat to Piraeus and on to Athens where my parents took the plane back to Thessaloniki. The separation was painful. My mother would not stop crying despite the fact that I promised her we would be back soon. This promise turned out to be wishful thinking for circumstances did not permit us to visit Greece again until ten years later when on the way back from a scientific trip to Sweden, I stopped over in Greece and visited Thessaloniki. However, the promise had a reverse fulfillment, for in 1965, when our first-born Alexandra was almost one year old, my folks visited us in Oak Park, a suburb of Chicago. Their visit was short, only 45 days but full of joy and excitement. They got to know their first grandchild, a beautiful, blond, blue- eyed girl.

After my parents left Athens for Thessaloniki, Jane and I traveled to southern Peloponnesos.

Jane's parents came to the USA from a small town on the west coast of Peloponnesos, Filiatra. There, we met her maternal grandmother, her mother's brothers and their wives and her cousins. Twelve years before, Jane visited Filiatra and met all her mother's relatives. This was her second visit and it was a true reunion. We spent our time visiting the homes of each of the relatives and we were treated to a wonderful Greek cuisine. We had an afternoon picnic by the sea and the cousins got together and sang and danced to the tunes of popular Greek songs that one of Jane's cousins, Koulis, played on his guitar.

While in Filiatra Jane and I took a bus trip north to the ancient site of Olympia where the original Olympic games were held. The ruins were sparse; a few columns were standing on the site where the Palestra once stood. There were remnants of the Temple of Zeus and of the Stadium where track and field games were held. The place that was an eye opener was the small museum that housed the sculpture of Hermes of Paxiteles. In the midst of several marble relics from the Olympic site stood the statue of Hermes, with its elegant, beautifully proportioned form, holding the infant Dionysos. Looking at the statue from the right side it appears as if Hermes is smiling, while when observed from the left, he appears to have a sorrowful countenance and when viewed from the front, his face is calm. This was a memorable and unforgettable experience for both of us.

After about five days in Filiatra we returned to Athens to prepare for our return trip to the USA and on to Peru. However, before the long trip back, we visited Rome for a few days. The visit to Rome was unprecedented. We had the good fortune to be hosted by Sister Sophia, a nun of the Carmelite Order and a niece of the Mother Superior of the same order that ran the Children's Hospital in Lima, our project's headquarters. Sister Sophia, who had been informed of our impending arrival, contacted us at the hotel where we were staying. The day after our arrival she came in her chauffeur- driven car and took us around to some of the main sights of the city.

The second day of our visit with Sister Sophia was again full of interesting surprises. We were fortunate to be in the square facing the balcony from which the Pope blesses the crowds. Sister Sophia was visibly excited when the Pope appeared on the balcony and began his blessings. There were several other nuns and priests among the throngs of lay people, many of them tourists like us. Our final visit with Sister Sophia was the Sistine Chapel with its unbelievable and incomparable ceiling. The pictures of the paintings that we had seen in books and brochures were right above us

At the end of the day we bid good-bye to Sister Sophia and we thanked her profusely for giving us such a wonderful time and experience. We spent two more days visiting the sights in the center of Rome, the commercial district, the fountains and the various arcades. On the fifth day after our arrival we took the TWA flight back to Washington, DC and Lima.

On the way back to Lima, we made a two-day stop in Washington, DC. At NIH I had in-depth discussions with Dr. Rosenthal about the project's progress as well as my future plans. We agreed that the research protocol should remain unchanged since we needed more cases and also because we began to notice a positive effect from the addition of Gamma Globulin in children of preschool age with up to 30% body surface area burned. Dr. Rosenthal agreed, based on our earlier discussions, that I could stay for another year as director of the project, if I chose to, even though it meant postponing the start of my residency training for a year.

# Finishing up my part of the burn project in Peru

Our return to Lima from Europe marked the beginning of my third year with the burn project. During our absence additional cases were admitted and were handled ably by the staff. Dr. Augusto Bazan was tirelessly working to find ways for the local treatment of the wounds in the burned children and to create conditions favorable for skin grafting, his specialty skill. His dedication was exemplary and his devotion to the welfare of the patients unparalleled. It was always extremely gratifying to see a child survive his or her burns and hospitalization and return home with the skin grafts in place and only a small degree of disfigurement. Everyone among the medical and technical staff was working diligently, trying their best to make the project a success. Dr. Manuel Bocanegra, the chief clinical doctor, was on call 24 hours a day. He, with the aid of Dr. Napoleon Hinostrosa, would make the initial assessment of the patient's condition and assign him or her to the appropriate treatment regimen. Dr. Jose Antonio Arana, an excellent microbiologist, with the aid of his dedicated assistant, Loli, took cultures of all burn cases on admission, including the blood, skin, urine and stool. Blood cultures were taken also on the second and third day after admission and at daily intervals thereafter, whenever indicated, to establish the earliest time of development of septicemia. There was evidence from our studies that the shock may have been contributed by an early septicemia. Dr. Pedro Stastny carried out all the biochemical analyses on the blood and urine specimens with accuracy and consistency.

As the year progressed, we began to analyze our data in preparation for publication. By the middle of 1960 we had accumulated data from 454 burned patients who were admitted with burns involving 10-90% of body surface area. The mortality from shock in 133 severely burned children treated with saline solution or saline solution in combination with albumin was 15 percent. The addition of albumin did not decrease mortality as compared with saline solution alone.

In burns involving 10 to 30 per cent of body surface area, plasma administered for shock therapy, or large intramuscular doses of gamma globulin, reduced by approximately half the delayed mortality, as compared with alternate groups receiving saline solution alone or saline solution and albumin. This reduction in mortality was observed in children under six; beyond this age the early and late mortality was quite low in all therapy groups. The reduction in delayed mortality from the use of plasma or gamma globulin or both was due primarily to a decrease in the incidence of septicemia caused chiefly by *Pseudomonas aeruginosa*.

The results indicate that saline solution in combination with plasma is the preferred treatment for severe burns in young children. The use of albumin, plasma expanders or saline solutions alone should be restricted to emergency conditions, and should preferably be fortified by large doses of gamma globulin given intramuscularly. Today, pooled human gamma globulin has been replaced by microorganism specific hyper-immune globulin.

A report of these findings was presented at the First International Congress on Burns, Washington, D.C., on September 19, 1960. The complete manuscript with me as the first, and Dr. Rosenthal as the senior author was published as the lead article in the New England Journal of Medicine on August 16, 1962.

These studies clearly demonstrated that in an emergency situation, where plasma is not available or where the number of casualties are so large that supplies of blood or plasma are inadequate, the use of saline solution is warranted to prevent shock from developing. The use of saline replacement therapy was instituted some years after the burn project was terminated, during an epidemic of cholera in Southeast Asia with enormous success. As is well known, patients with cholera develop massive diarrhea causing excessive loss of water and salt, which reduces the circulating vascular blood volume leading to irreversible shock.

As the time was rolling on in the early months of 1960, Jane and I were making plans for our return to Chicago. Dr. Rosenthal decided to come to Lima and assume the directorship of the project, a decision welcomed by the doctors and staff of the project. He was approaching the retirement age of 65 and the two years he intended to spend with Mrs. Rosenthal in Lima would come as a pre-retirement sabbatical. After all, the burn project was his idea. The enormous time and effort he invested in the animal experiments, which led to the clinical trials of the Peru burn project did not receive the appropriate recognition within the scientific community. Dr. Rosenthal deserved a period of work under relaxed conditions in the project he created.

We planed to leave Lima on a 707 jetliner one week before I was to begin my residency at the University of Illinois Research and Educational Hospitals. The farewell scene at the Limatambo airport was emotional; many of the hospital physicians and personnel, including Dr. Rosenthal, came to wish us bon voyage. There were many "fuerte abrazos", strong embraces, and wishes for us to return soon to Lima. Our first trip on a jet plane was an unequaled, almost exhilarating experience. The high speed and the relative quietness gave us a sense of awe.

We arrived at Miami International Airport where we took a connecting flight to Chicago. We proceeded immediately to the Staff Apartments on the University of Illinois Campus, the same building we occupied for almost five years before going to Peru. The next day I contacted the Department of Medicine where I was to begin my residency training in Internal Medicine on July 1, 1960.

# EPILOGUE

The decade of the sixties was one of the most productive and fulfilling periods of my career.

It started on July 1, 1960 with my entering the residency training program in Internal Medicine, which was followed two years later by a fellowship in Infectious Diseases.

As I was beginning my fellowship, Drs. Harry Dowling, Chairman of Medicine, and Mark Lepper, Chairman of Preventive Medicine, informed me that the NIH Training Grant provided funds for an advance degree, in my case a Ph.D.

Having considered the advantages and disadvantages of my pursuing a Ph.D. program at this stage of my career, I decided to accept the challenge. My research adviser was to be Dr. Richard Winzler, Chairman of Biochemistry and my clinical adviser Dr. Mark Lepper. The goal of my research was to identify the antigenic components of glomerular basement membranes. (GBM).

The rationale for the project was based on the observation that several immunohistochemical and ultramicroscopic studies in patients with post-streptococcal glomerulonephritis or nephritic syndrome demonstrated thickening of the kidney GBM, as well as deposits of the patient's immunoglobulins on the membrane.

In the process, I was able to isolate three major components, not only from the GBM but also from the lens capsule of the eye, namely a collagen, which I named Type IV, and two non-collagenous glycoproteins, which subsequently were purified in other laboratories and named "laminin" and "entactin" or "nidogen", respectively.

In June 1965 I received my Ph.D. in Biochemistry and on July 1, of the same year, I was offered a position as Assistant Professor of

Medicine at the University of Chicago School of Medicine. My research progressed in a very successful fashion and in 1969 I was promoted to Associate Professor of Medicine with tenure.

Questions of the biosynthesis of the various protein components, as well as their structural organization remained to be answered. These studies were put on hold until 1970 when I accepted a position at the University of Pennsylvania Department of Medicine. There I joined Dr. Darwin Prockop's group that was working on the biosyntehsis of interstitial collagen (type I). In the two years after arriving in Philadelphia, Dr.Michael Grant, a post-docroral fellow from England, Darwin Prockop and I published three seminal articles. These papers were the first to demonstrate the physical properties of newly synthesized and secreted basement membranre collagen (Type IV). Dr. J.D.Schofield was a coauthor in the third article.

With the collaboration of Dr. Bjorn Olsen, an electron microscopist, Dr. Robert Alper and I prepared undegraded, solubilized lens capsule collagen and subjected it to transmission electron microscopy. We demonstrated the presence of long filamentous structures with a globular end. These structures formed side-to-side aggregates in the presence of ATP with the globular ends occupying one end of the aggregate. This observation led us to suggest that basement membrane collagen (Type IV) was secreted in the form of procollagen, i.e. with its globular end intact and incorporated as such into the basement membrane, in this case the lens capsule of the eye, without further processing. Later studies, using organ cultures of mouse parietal yolk sac, by Drs. Ron Minor and Chris Clark in my laboratory, supported this conclusion.

This decade was full of pleasant surprises. In January 1964, Jane looked up at me from above her coffee mug and said, "I think I am pregnant". On September 24, Alexandra was born. She had the bluest eyes and golden blond, curly hair.

In the summer of 1964, just before Alexandra was born, Aunt Helen, Uncle Minas and their two children, John and Doxa visited us from Greece. We were excited to see them and we showed them around Chicago, although as guests of Uncle John they were assured of visits to many of Chicago's tourist attractions.

In July of 1965, my parents visited us from Greece. They were extremely happy to see and play with young Alexandra who was now 10 months old and began to take her first steps.

My parents' visit to the USA was an added source of excitement and joy for them but especially for my father. He was given the opportunity to see and visit with his older brother George, whom he had not seen since the latter left their home in Turkey in 1919 to immigrate to America. My father was 70 years old and Uncle George 73 when they met at Uncle George's home in Astoria, Long Island. As I have mentioned earlier, Uncle George was married to Aunt Katina and they had a son, a handsome, blue-eyed, blond boy also named Nicholas. My brother Chris, who lived in New York at the time, was helping my folks with their visits to the various sights in and around New York. During the four-day visit, the two brothers caught up on numerous events that they lived through during the last 46 years.

Our second child, a daughter, arrived on January 24, 1966 and our third one, a boy, arrived on September 28,1967. We named the daughter Patricia and the boy Paul. Patricia was a beautiful baby with brown eyes and dark curly hair. Paul also had beautiful features, a round face, sandy hair and brown eyes.

We moved to Philadelphia in late June 1970. The trip to Philadelphia, Pennsylvania took two days as we stopped the first night in Indiana and the second night in Youngstown at the border of Ohio and Pennsylvania. The next day we crossed Pennsylvania and we reached Radnor in the evening, about eight miles outside Philadelphia.

The next morning we drove to our new home, located in Merion Station, a suburb of Philadelphia in the so-called Main Line. Our home is a beautiful southern colonial-style house, with four white columns on the front porch. A smaller side porch with columns on the side of the house and a big fireplace made for a pleasant addition. The house has five bedrooms, three baths, a powder room, a living room, a dining room, a big kitchen, a spacious laundry room and a finished basement.

This has been our home for the last 38 years.

On the first Monday after arriving in Merion Station, I began work at the Philadelphia General Hospital (PGH), where the city's four medical schools had their medical, surgical, pediatric and obstetrical services. The Chief of the University of Pennsylvania Medical Service was Dr. Truman Schnabel, who answered to the moniker "Nipper". He was my superior in my clinical responsibilities. Dr. Schnabel was an excellent clinician with a caring attitude for his patients and his staff. He was always pleasant to talk to and eager to help with whatever needs presented at the time. My responsibilities were divided between my hospital attending rounds and my research studies.

In 1971 we made our first trip to Greece with our children. My parents and all the relatives who congregated in my parent's apartment were very excited to meet the children. They were hugging and kissing them and asking them questions in Greek about their trip, which we had to translate into English. However, after several trips to Greece they became quite conversant. The young children were overwhelmed with the outpouring of love and affection and seemed to enjoy themselves.

We visited Aunt Helen's apartment almost daily and had the opportunity to see and talk to my grandmother, Big Yiayia. She looked much older from the time Jane and I last saw her in 1959, but she was quite alert, smiling and effusive with her expression of love towards her great-grandchildren.

While in Thessaloniki, Uncle Elias and Aunt Stasa asked me to be the best man at the wedding of Kaiti, their adapted daughter, to Salvatore Colucci, a young Italian she met while the two were studying at the University of Bologna. I accepted with pleasure.

The wedding was beautiful, with the bride elegantly dressed and the groom handsomely attired next to her. The three people who stole the show, besides the bride and groom, were Sandy, Patty and Paul. Sandy and Patty were the flower girls and Paul the ring bearer.

Another important event that took place in 1977 was my sabbatical leave to the university of Oxford, England. I received a fellowship from the Guggenheim Foundation, which covered 50 % of my expenses for a 12- month period. The other half came from the university of Pennsylvania.

While at Oxford, I worked in the lab of professor Henry Harris, at the Dunn School of Pathology, where I learned to make cell hybrids using human endothelial cells and mouse fibroblasts. I was trying to identify the chromosome that was responsible for the synthesis of type IV collagen by endothelial cells. The system did not prove very reliable.

However, my experience in the lab of the Dunn School of Pathology was exciting and rewarding.

Jane and the children enjoyed their stay in Oxford immensely. We bought a Fiat and we were able to travel to several places in England. The children enjoyed their experience in the Bishop Kirk public school.

In December 1978 I traveled to Tokyo Japan as a guest of the Japanese Society of Nephrology to attend an international symposium on glomerulonephritis. Dr. Sheishi Shibata, who was my host, took me around to beautiful sights in Tokyo and the historic cities of Kyoto and Nara.

In late July 1978 we returned to the USA. When we arrived at Kennedy Airport we were surprised to find out that all our bags, boxes and paper shopping bags (all 26 of them) came through intact. We subsequently learned that one of the passengers on our plane was the late Princess Grace of Monaco. Two of our colleagues from the lab, Drs. Chris Clark and Ed Macarak, had the good sense to rent a van, with ample space for all our personal effects.

In 1984 I took another sabbatical at the university of Oxford. This time I worked in the lab of Dr. Michael Fenwick, where I studied the effect of Herpes Simplex virus infection on human endothelial cells.

During this decade, our lives were rewarded with several pleasant events but also saddened with two very painful occurrences. In 1987 I was awarded an honorary doctorate degree from the University of Reims Medical School in France. Dr. Jacques P. Borel, who had spent a sabbatical year in my lab from July 1975 to June 1976, sponsored me.

The decade of the 80's will also be remembered by three events that saddened us deeply.. In 1984, Jane's mother died following a stroke. My father died in 1985 from a stroke, at the age of 92 and in 1988 my mother died at the age of 88 from congestive heart failure due to congenital aortic stenosis. Jane and I felt deeply the loss of our parents and our children the loss of their grandparents. We loved them very much for they constantly showed their love and affection to us.

The decade of the 90's began with a cruel, sad and devastating event. In February 1990, Sandy told us that, on a routine medical check-up for health insurance, she was told that her white cell count was greater than 30,000. The diagnosis, after consulting with the hematology division of the University of Pennsylvania, came back "chronic myelogenous leukemia".

We got in touch with the Cancer Institute of the National Institutes of Health and they advised us to try a bone marrow transplant, if we could find a suitable, matching donor.

Jane, Patty, Paul and I were tested for matching histocompatibility antigens with those of Sandy's and the verdict was that Patty was a "perfect match". Weighing all the options, Sandy and the rest of the family decided to go ahead with the bone marrow transplant. We chose the transplant center at the University of Minnesota. Sandy, Jane and I visited the center and after discussing the pros and cons we decided that, despite the rigorous and life threatening preparatory steps, like total body irradiation and chemotherapy, Sandy should go ahead with the transplant. A date was set and in September 1990 the whole family traveled to Minneapolis and rented rooms at a hotel near the University. During the period before and after the transplant Jane lived day and night in the same room as Sandy, taking time off only to go to the hotel to bathe. Jane's care and dedication to Sandy's welfare was unprecedented.

In October 1990, Patty's bone marrow was given to Sandy and within a few days there was evidence that the transplant took. Patty's cells were multiplying and making new blood cells.

Two weeks after the transplant we all returned to Merion Station, our home. Sandy gained some weight and her hair began to grow back. Things were going well and Sandy was being followed at the Hematology-Oncology Division of the University of Pennsylvania. However, by mid-December Sandy developed signs and symptoms consistent with graft versus host disease, better known by its acronym, GVH. The donor's cells were attacking the recipient's tissues. Sandy, Patty and I traveled to Minneapolis where Sandy was hospitalized and given immunosuppressive and anti-inflammatory agents. After her condition stabilized, we returned home.

Gradually, Sandy began to develop jaundice which indicated liver involvement. In the next few months her condition deteriorated until it was necessary to hospitalize her at the Hospital of the University of Pennsylvania in early December. She gradually lapsed into coma and brain MRI's revealed several abscesses. Cultures established the presence of the microorgnism nocardia. On December 24, 1991 Sandy died at the age of 27. The loss of Sandy was an unprecedented event for she was full of vigor, full of life and was giving us so much pleasure to be with her. We miss her terribly and seventeen years after her death remembering her forms part of our daily existence.

Following Sandy's death, our family established "The Alexandra J. Kefalides Memorial Lecture Fund". The fund provides for a lecture to be given every two to three years by a young investigator, selected by an advisory committee, for outstanding work in the field of leukemia. About five years ago the fund has been renamed "The Alexandra J. Kefalides Prize for Leukemia Research".

As Sandy was battling an illness with an inexorable end, Patty and Paul entered medical school at the University of Pennsylvania on September 1991. They both did very well and in June 1995 they graduated. On the day of graduation I was given the opportunity to present the diplomas to both Patty and Paul. Patty pursued pediatrics for a year in Chicago and then switched to pathology. Paul took his internship at the University of Chicago and specialized in gastroenterology.

The same month that Patty graduated she also got married. The groom, Ted Theodosopoulos, is the son of a teenage friend of mine from Thessaloniki, Lakis Theodosopoulos. Lakis and I were part of the same resistance team during the German occupation. Ted attended the Americnan School in Thessaloniki and then entered the Massachusetts Institute of Technology in Boston, where he studied mathematics and received a BA, MS and a Ph.D. in that discipline

In October 1996 Patty gave birth to a beautiful healthy girl that we named Alexandra. Two years later we baptized Alexandra in a Greek church in Thessaloniki. The godmother was Eleni, the daughter of my cousin Doxa, Aunt Helen's daughter.

Another memorable event of this decade was my retiring from the University of Pennsylvania on June 30, 1996 and assuming the title "Professor of Medicine Emeritus". The last 12 years of retirement have been full of intellectual activity. I continued my research until the year 2002 when I closed my lab. However, I kept busy with a variety of University and Medical School committeees. The most demanding and rewarding job was being the executive chair of the Institutional Review Boards of the University. I stayed in this job from 1998 to 2003 and I had the chance to experience a number of interesting but dramatic events. Most notable of them, the death in 1999 of a young man, Jesse Gelsinger, who was a subject in a gene therapy project. This event received local and national attention, since this outcome was the result of an experimental technique. As investigations had shown subsequently, the patient died from an overwhelming inflammatory reaction to the adenovirus, the particle that was attached to the gene responsible for the synthesis of the enzyme that was supposed to correct its deficiency in the young man. The patient suffered from a genetic disorder that prevented the proper processing of ammonia by the liver. The FDA suspended all gene therapy research at the University of Pennsylvania and accused the researchers of not disclosing to the patients the complications they had noted in non-human primates and other human patients who received the enzyme gene-adenovirus complex.

As emeritus professor I was allowed to continue my other activities, such as teaching first year medical students in history taking and writing and in the course that emphasized doctor-patient relationships. Later I was asked to participate in the course of medical bioethics for first year students. The purpose of the course is to introduce students to the ethical issues inherent in the use of humans in clinical studies. Another goal is to instill in them the need to protect the research subjects from the risks of research. I have taught in this course for five years and I am enjoying it very much.

One of my long-term involvements in the university has been with the Admissions Committee of the Medical School. I started in 1982 interviewing applicants and in 1993 I joined the Selections Committee. In 2005 I moved to the Screening Committee where we review the applications and score them in a way that the computer and the administrative office could decide whether a student is qualified for an interview.

Starting in 2001, I became the scientific mentor of the more than 30 biotechnology companies that are housed at the Science Center. In 1998, I initiated a series of monthly scientific seminars to which scientists from the faculties of the universities in the Phildelphia area are invited to speak. I have dubbed the seminar series "Lunch for Hungry Minds". The series has been a tremendous success.

In 2000 Patty had a second child, a girl, which we named Efthemia. Again the baptism took place in Greece and it was a joyous experience. In 2002 a third girl arrived and we named her Eugenia Nicole. In 2004 she was also baptized in Greece and we had a memorable party.

In the past 12 years our grandchildren have given us an enormous amount of unconditional happiness and joy.

Printed in the United States
219118BV00001B/25/P